They Made a
MONI

CW00547738

Out of Me

DAVY JONES

in conversation with

ALAN GREEN

aBM

They Made a Monkee Out of Me
First Edition, January 1987, Dome Press
Second Edition, October 2014, A Book's Mind

ISBN: 978-1-939828-08-8

Library of Congress Control Number: 2014954460

Copyright © 2014 by The Estate of David T. Jones

All rights reserved. Except for use in any review, the reproduction or utilization of this work in whole or in part in any form by any electronic, mechanical or other means, now known or hereafter invented, including xerography, photocopying and recording, or in any information and retrieval system, is forbidden without written permission from the publisher.

Front cover photo courtesy of Tiger Beat
Back cover photo © 1986 Michael G. Bush
All other photos © listed in Photo Credits section
Original cover design by Alan Green and Carla J. Faye
Original book design by Dome Press
Cover recreation by Floyd Orfield, A Book's Mind
Book recreation by A Book's Mind

A Book's Mind
PO BOX 272847
Fort Collins, CO 80527
www.abooksmind.com

—dome press acknowledgements—

Davy has wanted to put this book out for years. But it could never be made the way he wanted it—and still keep the price reasonable enough so that his loyal fans could read, and **see**, the whole story. Dome Press has come into existence to accomplish just that.

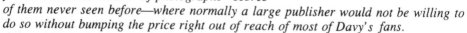

But why form one's own publishing company? Why not go with an already established publishing house? The answer, we feel, is in these pages. By publishing ourselves we have been able to offer you an enormous number of photographs—scores of them never seen before—where normally a large publisher would not be willing to do so without bumping the price right out of reach of most of Davy's fans.

Another advantage is that we have total creative control over every stage of the lengthy process of production. The entire book was typed, edited, laid-out, designed, type-set, proof-read and proof-printed on a personal computer system in my living-room at home. The only stages of publication that needed to be done 'outside' were the resizing and half-toning of the photographs, (Bojalad Printers), the designing of Davy's name and book title on the front cover, (Bojalad and myself), the production of camera-ready boards, (MacTypeNet), and the final printing and binding (Bookcrafters). Everything else, from the choice of typeface, to the graphics, to the final period—was done on an Apple Macintosh™ Plus computer.

Davy and I would like to thank the following companies and individuals who all helped tremendously by giving of their services, advice, and in many cases, donating software and loaning hardware to aid in the production of "They Made A Monkee Out Of Me".

—Alan Green

•Apple Computer, Inc.
(Macintosh™ Plus; ImageWriter™ II; LaserWriter™ Plus; Apple® Personal Modem; Mac-Write & MacPaint.)

•MicroGraphic Images
(Especial thanks to Diane Wessling for the MEGASCREEN™ Can't imagine setting pages without it!)

•MacTypeNet™
(*Especial* thanks to Frank & Suzi for your truly professional services, and the final camera-ready boards. I still can't believe the entire book went over the phone lines to you!)

•R. J. Bojalad Color Corporation
(Thanks to Maggie, Cindy & 'mum' for untiring patience with me while I huffed and puffed.)

•BookCrafters
(Thanks to Kathy King—also for her patience. There was so much to learn doing this.)

•Leasametric, Inc.
(Thanks to Rosemary Pedretti and Ed Elber for the LaserWriter™ Plus & Macintosh™ Plus.)

•Scandinavian Computer Furniture, Inc. ('ScanCoFurn')
(Many thanks to Soren Storm for the wonderful MacTable. A joy to work at!)

•LoDOWN
(LoDOWN 20 SCSI Hard Disk)
•Manhattan Graphics Corporation
(Thanks to Lisa Grey for ReadySetGo! 3® Couldn't have placed all these pics without it!)

•Thunderware® Inc.
(ThunderScan High-Resolution Digitizer for the Macintosh—produced the scanned images.)

•Borland International
(We used SideKick® with PhoneLink™ and Reflex for the Mac™. Thanks to Kim Tarter.)

•Affinity Microsystems, Ltd.
(We used Tempo—and would *still* be working if we hadn't had it.)

•Ann Arbor Softworks, Inc.
(Thanks a lot for FullPaint™. A great leap forward!)

•Miles Computing, Inc.
(Mac the Knife™ clip-art graphic images.)

•T/Maker Company
(Thanks Dean Walker for the ClickArt® graphics.)

•Microsoft®
(Thanks to Jonathan Prusky for the early use of MicroSoft® Word v3.0. Fascinating.)

•DUBL-CLiCK SOFTWARE, INC.
(Thanks to Cliff Joyce for the World-Class Fonts. We used Kawasaki for 'manchester boy'!)

•MindWork Software
(Thanks to Susan Raab for a fabulous new word-processor, MindWrite™.)

•Living VideoText, Inc.
(Thanks to Pat Janning for MORE™. A little late—but we'll use it on the next book!)

•Forethought™
(Thanks to Wendy Meyers for FileMaker™ Plus)

•Aldus Corporation
(Thanks, Carolyn Bachamus for PageMaker®)

•Computer Clinic, Inc.
(Thanks *forever* to Dave Heffner and Mike Adamson for turning me on to computers.)

Also a very special thank-you to Carla J. Faye for mastering all the above programmes, putting up with my utterly unreasonable deadline demands, and for making the whole thing work. You're fired!

Additional thanks go to David, Monica, Serena, Julia & Fran at David Fishof Productions. Also to Diane Umansky at Tiger Beat (D&S) for all your help and for rooting out the cover photo. We also acknowledge Glenn A. Baker for much bibliographical information. And a special appreciation to Eric and Mattie Staniek for making *many* things possible. And Mum—thanks for **everything**.

Although every effort has been made to give credit where due, and to verify all information contained herein as factual, it's almost inevitable that certain details may be found to be unintentionally inaccurate. Anyone having information leading to the arrest of these inaccuracies is encouraged to contact the authors so that we may correct the mistake in future printings.

Look out for our next publication,
"The Monkees Evolution"
—the picture story of our
1986, 20th Anniversary Tour.

—steppin' stones—

r

lovingly
dedicated to
my mother and father
my sisters
my beautiful wife, anita
my three lovely daughters,
talia,
sarah lee
and
jessica

and
to all my loyal fans

with a special thank-you
to auntie jessie,
my first agent

Good evening ladies and gentlemen, boys and girls, fellow fanatics. And welcome to yet another showbiz, 'This is My Life'.

Okay, I admit it. . . I've finally caught the entertainers' epidemic—the dreaded, **'let'sputitinabookandseeifwecangetit*right*thistime-itis'**. As if living it once was not enough!

But the funny thing is—reliving it over and over again to get it all down on paper has given me a whole new perspective. Frankly, I had no *idea* I'd had such a good time.

Writing it is something I've been wanting to do for ages, but I could never find a pen. Then about six years ago, along comes this Alan Green bloke. Plays piano for me on a couple of tours. We'd only been working together a week when he turns up on stage one night wearing a scuba-diving outfit—oxygen tank, flippers, the whole bit. I think— this is interesting—I mean, I like him, even though he *is* trying to upstage me all the time. We start trying to outdo each other—and now the tour is really looking like it could be fun.

So we're at this club and I'm in the back kitchen doing a live phone interview with a local DJ—and he asks me if we're enjoying the tour. Well, just at that moment Alan comes in, dressed in his tux, goes over to the stove and pours a saucepan of water over his head. So I start a running commentary to the DJ. I still have a tape of it. . .

"Well, yes as a matter of fact, we are," I say. "My musical director is standing in front of me—we're due on in half an hour—and his show clothes are soaking wet. Wait a minute—he's just broken two eggs on his head. Uh-oh—now he's into the refrigerator and he's got some fruit salad and. . . I don't believe this—he's pouring it *inside* his dress shirt and patting it down. There goes a pint of yoghurt down his trousers and. . . oh, nice—strawberries in his ears."

The DJ doesn't know *what* to make of this interview.

"You'd love this, all you people out there in Toledo, I'm telling you—he's giving himself a butter masque. . . and now he's putting rashers of bacon in each pocket and fill- ing them up with milk. . . Oh, what's this? He's found his mouth! At *last*, ladies and gentlemen, he's actually *drinking* the orange juice. . . well, some of it. The rest he's rubbing into his armpits. . . "

Round about here the rest of the band are clutching their sides, Alan is an absolute mess—and the radio is silent. The DJ's probably sorry he asked. I decide there and then—this guy, looking like the leftovers from a walking 'All-you-can-eat Buffet', is the one who should write my book with me. *He* understands. So I tell him the stories and he writes them down. And when I don't feel like it he keeps on at me—making me talk, making me remember—bringing it all back and making me laugh about it.

Alright—so we go back to England. More touring, more work on the book. One night he introduces me to Anita—(I'll never forgive you for that, Alan!)—and while I'm shaking hands with her. . . he's taking notes. On our first date. . . he's there sharpening pencils. On our *honeymoon*, Anita and I keep saying, "Don't you have a home to go to?" I mean—this guy's relentless.

Anyway, we finally get most of it down—after seven years, on and off—talking, fighting, laughing. Up 'til dawn sessions. It's not all in the right order, I know. It's not all in, period. You try putting *your* life into a couple of hundred pages and see how far you get. Sometimes the best bits can't be spoken. I mean. . . there are people in my life who aren't in the book. And verse vicer. But if you're one of them please don't be offended, okay? (Or relieved, as the case may be.) I'll get you next book.

One word of warning—the story you are about to read is true. . . only the names have been changed to protect the guilty.

10/23/86 New Orleans
David Jones

(Not yet by appointment to
Her Majesty the Queen.)

4

One of my favourite movies is, 'My Favorite Year', in which the real-life, magical, Peter O'Toole plays the fictional, magical, Alan Swann—who is based on the real-life, magical, Errol Flynn. The last line in that film is, "It's like Alfie says— with Swann, you forgive a lot, y'know?"

Well, there's a real-life, magical, David Jones who plays the fictional, magical, Davy Jones—who is based, loosely, on the real-life, magical, Davy Jones. But to be frank—not to burst any bubbles here or anything—the real-life David Jones is not always all that magical—like all of us, he has his off days. Many times, since we started putting this book together seven years ago, I've wanted to throw in the pen. Too much frustration—too many misunderstandings—too much aggro. You can lose a friend that way. Yet, inevitably—just when it feels like it's simply not worth the trouble—that magic happens. Every time. And it's such a bright, clear magic that it totally eclipses any burning gripes I may have been harbouring. With David, you forgive a lot.

I've seen it. Again and again, I've seen that magic sneak in. Sometimes it's so subtle you don't know it's happening until it's been and gone. Other times it's about as subtle as a flying breeze-block—slapstick all the way. I like both kinds.

The latter magic can happen during a phone conversation, or an afternoon spent, supposedly, working on the book—and you end up doing only one thing. . . laughing. Laughing 'til you hurt. Laughing until you know you can't laugh anymore. . And he'll ease up for just a beat. . . until you think it's safe to look at him. . . and you risk it. And it starts all over again.

When I first joined Davy's band in '79, being an entertainer myself, and somewhat insecure, I would try hard to cut him—to be funnier than the Monkee, you see. And there were times, I think he'd agree, when we both wanted to laugh like crazy at the other's antics—and we'd hold back a bit. Just a bit. I think we've grown a lot since then. For my part it just feels so good to take a back seat when he's around, and have that luxury of bathing in the man's brilliance. I let him do all the work. All I need be is the laugher. All he needs be is the funniest person I know.

The former magic is the kind that the universe seems to bestow on only a few, blessed individuals. It happens around Davy all the time and, more often than not, he himself is utterly unaware that it's even working. He appears to me like the figure-

head on the bow of a ship—propelled by some inner force that he need not know too much about just now because he's way up front anyway—he's where it's all happening. And the magic that he causes, almost incidentally, is in the wake—

I bring Davy to my home one day—the steaming metropolis of Beavertown, PA.—population: about twelve. We arrive five minutes after the city's late-night hot spot, the Quik-Mart, has closed. I need some groceries and Amy, the store's very pregnant cashier, won't let me in—so I drag Davy out of the car ("I need your face— you're famous.") and we plead, on our hands and knees, outside the locked doors. Amy, recognizing one of us (and it isn't me—she only **knows** me) screams out loud, nearly goes into labour, and—jabbering incoherently—lets us in.

Davy asks to use the bathroom whilst Amy calls up Beavertown—and before he's flushed, a car pulls up almost **inside** the store, losing a months'-worth of tire rubber in the process, and the Clarke family piles out with cameras and pens at the ready. Davy signs an autograph for twelve-year old, Wendy Clarke, poses for the obligatory pictures, and casually remarks that should she want to come to the concert at Hershey Park Arena he can probably swing some tickets. Simple. No big deal. . .

. . . except to Wendy.

She'd had a rough few months, you might say. Normally full of energy, and a bright spark at school—she'd become withdrawn after a personal, family difficulty nearly ended in tragedy. Attempts by her family and friends to bring her back to her old self, plus weeks of counselling, had all failed. She had crawled into a world of make-believe and the only time she smiled during those months was for half an hour each day, when 'The Monkees' was on the Nickleodeon channel.

She worked odd jobs to buy their albums and once she watched twenty-one straight hours of MTV's Monkees Marathon. But she didn't want to know the outside world anymore; she felt happy and safe only in her dreams.

Then she heard that the Monkees were coming to Hershey on their 20th Anniversary Tour of America. She sent away for tickets and brightened daily as the date approached. The family all hoped that this was going to do the trick. But on the Tuesday before the Friday concert, her mother called the box office to ask why they hadn't received their tickets yet. There had been a mix-up. The order was lost and it was now too late—the show was already sold out. All the box office could do was send back their check. The real world came crashing in for Wendy again, but this time with an unforgivable vengeance; it wouldn't even spare her dreams.

Now here's the magic that chooses Davy Jones to do its tricks. After all she'd just gone through, how could this girl dare dream that on the Wednesday she'd meet her idol (in Beavertown, of all places); that on Friday she and her family would see the show; and that later that night she and her cousin would be in Davy's hotel room receiving gifts and personal tour photographs from him? Surely, this is some kind of magic. . . dreams do come true!

I'd gone to America in 1961 to play the Artful Dodger in Lionel Bart's musical, 'Oliver!'. I thought it was going to be just another gig—maybe last a few weeks. But it stretched into months, then years. After that came 'Pickwick'. . . Hollywood. . . and then all that crazy Monkees stuff. And always in the back of my mind was the idea of going back to my old job in the stables at New-market—ride some winners.

I'd come a long way. I didn't have any set ideas about where I was going—just bob-bing along with the tide. But all of a sudden it was 1966 and I realized I'd got a whole new lifestyle. Something they wouldn't be able to imagine back home in Manchester. I was living in a big house with a swimming pool. . . free cars, free motorbikes, free corn-flakes—everything we promoted, we got to keep!

Except ourselves.

It was a far cry from growing up in Manchester, England. . .

manchester boy

i'm a manchester boy,
me mum's pride and joy
a chip off the old block, me dad
i can dance, i can sing,
i can do anything
there's nothing too hard if i try
when the going gets rough i can
brave it
if i set myself straight from
the start
i'm a manchester boy,
me mum's pride and joy
a chip off the old block,
me dad

When i was fourteen i decided to leave
and me dad came to wave me goodbye
i got on the train, it started to rain
and me dad, well, he started to cry
as the train pulled away from the
station
i shouted, "i'll be home soon!"
y'see, i'm a manchester boy,
me mum's pride and joy
a chip off the old block, me dad

i've travelled the world,
i've found me a girl
i come home once in a while
relations to meet me,
my friends they all greet me
we laugh, we talk about old times
nothing has changed much around here
'cept me mum and me dad's passed away
but i'm still a manchester boy,
me mum's pride and joy
a chip off the old block, me dad

david thomas ___ jones

12

that was then. . .

Factories. Rain. "What about the workers!" Shades of grey. My dad. He'd give advice like a sweet-tasting pill. None of your cod-liver oil about 'Arry Jones. Just a feeling of strength and security.

I remember as a kid, holding his big hand and being carried by him. Mine are as big now and I've carried my own children so I know—he liked it. Own up—how many of you can remember conking out so that you got carried? First you fake tiredness—drop back a few times and get shouted at—then you get carried. I'd start just around Peter Pan Park and by the railway bridge, near the reservoir, I'd be faking it—just to get that feeling of being carried.

My dad wasn't a tall man. He wasn't short. He was about this big. What he actually did at British Railways, ('the tank', as he called it), was always a mystery. All we knew was he went and he came back.

He seemed to paint the kitchen for most of my childhood. Twice a year, regular as Cup Final and Christmas, until I was about eleven. Then he let me help. 'British Railways Cream' was the colour. He never changed it.

"What colour are we having it this time, dad?"

"British Railways Cream."

"Ooh, that'll be nice." We'd all snicker.

Mother always stayed out of the way for this event. She'd suffered badly with her lungs—emphysema—for as long as I could remember. The paint smell made it worse. On the other hand she was strong-willed and—emphysema or no, she'd make her point. . .

My father smoked and mother disapproved. Strongly. So much so, that one day, tired of him ignoring her asking him to stop, she bought a pack for herself, sat down in front of the whole family, and lit one up. Five mouths gaped open. This was unthinkable! Besides her illness, she was just too refined a lady to be a smoker. I don't think she'd ever been that near to a cigarette in her life—she held it all wrong. Soon she was coughing and spluttering. My dad ignored the hint so she lit a second. This was too much. Dad protested—

NO SMOKING

"Don't be silly, Doris—you'll kill yourself."

When she started coughing on the second one he couldn't take it anymore. He got up, snatched the pack away from her, and started wrestling her for the cigarette.

"No!" she said curtly. And tried to turn her head to take another puff.

He picked her up and they started larking around in the middle of the room. Still holding the cigarette she fainted right out in my father's arms like a rag doll. He lay her gently on the settee. She was deathly white and my dad kept saying, "Doris. . . Doris. . . Doris, love." He must have said her name a hundred times.

Looking at the photographs of their courtship days I notice they were always smartly dressed up for each other. My mother never left the house without a hat and fresh lipstick—always a subtle pink—and usually wearing one of the dresses she'd made herself. She'd made lots of my sisters' dresses too—about the only articles of clothing that didn't get handed down to me. I was the only boy in school whose raincoat buttoned on the girls' side.

During the war my father had been in the Home Guard—a sort of army reserve but not exactly equipped to defend King *or* Country in the event of attack. Adolf would have had a field day if he'd known.

For most Home Guardians, the nearest they ever got to a weapon was a photograph of a gun that the government issued them. Black and white, regulation Kodak. Officers got an additional wallet-size picture of three rounds of ammunition. My father's unit was, by comparison, a crack troop. They had an actual rifle. *And* two bullets. . . their pride and joy—until dad fired one of them by mistake. He told us—

"They put me in the brig and fined me two shillings and fourpence." His war stories were great. But my mother was the real hero. I'll never forget her telling the story of dad's unit practicing manœuvres. A right circus.

What they had to do was make their way around the houses and get from 'A' to 'B' on this course without getting 'shot'. They had people hidden with bags of flour—they were the enemy. If they managed to put a dab of flour on your uniform you were shot, see?

Well, my father always prided himself on being neat and tidy and he was no different as far as his uniform was concerned. No way was he planning on even getting wounded— not General Jones.

So he was doing great, well ahead of the others, and 'B' was close to our house anyway, so he figured he'd pop in for a quick cup of tea before finishing the course. He had his tea and was just nipping out the front door, straightening his cap, all proud of his spotless uniform, when Mother opened the upstairs bedroom window and emptied a whole bag of flour over him. The lot!

Of course, my father still had to report to 'B', right?

"What happened to you, Jones?"

"A bloody land-mine, sir."

The Jones's were a typical, north-of-England, working-class family. Davy and his three sisters, Hazel, Beryl and Lynda, lived with their parents in a crowded, two-up two-down, terraced house at 20 Leamington Street, Openshaw, Manchester. The four children shared a bedroom; a double bed for the girls and a single bed behind a partition for Davy.

Davy's talent for entertaining was always apparent. Beryl recalls that he brought the house down in his earliest school play, 'Tom Sawyer'. He and another child were supposed to have died and had to lie still under a table for about twenty minutes. This, of course, was far too long for young Davy to be out of the limelight. So a very serious scene became transformed as Davy's hand reached up and took a water jug, then a cup, off the table—and poured a posthumous drink. The audience was laughing so much they were in tears.

He also had an eye for the ladies even then. One time, during the Lees Street Congregational Church School play, Davy was in the wings chatting up some future starlet (aged seven) and was so engrossed in the impression he was making that he missed his cue. He was playing,
'Abdullah the Turkish Magician' and was supposed to fly in on his magic carpet.

"Look! Here comes Abdullah now!" rang out for the third time, louder than ever.

Suddenly aware of the situation, Davy raced onto the stage, panting, and delivered an ad-lib that any pro would have been proud of. . .

"Sorry I'm late—got me carpet stuck on Hugan's chimney!"

Someone once said that men are born from the womb and spend the rest of their lives trying to get back in. Actually, the womb business was a bit before my time but I do remember sucking on my mother's breast, and I've certainly spent quite a bit of time and energy trying to recapture *that* feeling.

From about that same time I recall my first mate, Harry Hoskinson. I can vividly remember sitting in my pram, looking across at him in his pram, looking across at me—while our mums nattered away about the price of tea, probably.

Other bits of mental film from that magical time include that north-country ritual, 'the stand-up wash'. Standing in two inches of water in the kitchen sink, being rubbed down with a soapy flannel. One day a neighbour walked in, in the middle of my rub-down. I was ten and it was the first time I was embarrassed in the presence of a woman. The second time hasn't happened yet, but then I don't have stand-up washes in the kitchen sink anymore.

A bath was something to look forward to. Once a week my dad used to fill up the tin bath and there I'd be, in front of the fire, having my back scrubbed and looking forward to the story I always used to get afterwards. My father would do the honours. Usually it was from the comic strips—the 'Beano' or 'Dandy'—none of your posh, 'Heidi' stuff around our house!

My dad had a real down-to-earth, northern sense of humour. I remember us watching University Challenge every week. It was a ridiculously high-IQ television quiz show but we'd always tune in just to hear the host, Bamber Gascoigne, introduce the week's team members:

"Rodney Plumbersbreath-Smythe, King's College, Cambridge—reading Psychology."

"Good evening." (Rodney's big moment.)

"Sybil Fondlemebum, Oxford University—reading Greek mythology."

"Hellewe."

Then from his armchair my dad would announce himself—

"'Arry Jones, 'igher Openshaw Secondary Modern, reading gas meters!" Every show without fail. We all waited for it. Fell about.

Whenever my father took me to have my hair cut, he'd tell the barber,

"Cut it t' th' wood, Charlie!" And they'd share a grown-up sort of chuckle.

I never understood that chuckle. I'd been going to Charlie's for six or seven years on my own, and each time I'd tell him, "Cut it t' th' wood, please," without thinking. It was just one of those things you say like, "Turned out nice again, hasn't it?" Then one day, fourteen years old, I suddenly heard myself say it. Oh, very funny, I thought. *Now* I get it.

I suppose my father was looked upon as a sort of street healer. I don't mean he performed miracles (other than bringing us all up) but everyone used to come to him for help or advice. If there was a sick budgie* or a family squabble—"Go an' get 'Arry!" was the cry.

There were fourteen families on our street—two or three kids in each. Every Guy Fawkes night, November 5th, they all waited for dad to light the big bonfire. Couldn't start without Harry. He'd always arrive early in the evening with a lorry-load of wood that he and his mates from the tank had got—to add to what us kids had been collecting for weeks.

The bonfire would always be on the land at the back of our house. 'Jones's Back' it was called. Maybe because mum and dad did so much to help the festivities. My mother would do baked potatoes, toffee apples, treacle toffee and lemonade for everyone. Only charged tuppence a head.

I remember one year, me and a couple of local terrors had been out collecting old boxes, branches—anything that would burn. For most of the day we'd been dragging a disused railway sleeper (the huge wooden block that sits under the track) for about two miles. Seemed like ten. With home in sight the heavens opened, as they do quite frequently in Manchester, and my two mates abandoned the sleeper in spite of my cries.

"Please don't leave it!" I shouted. "Someone will nick it!"

Nick it? It weighed a ton! But they left and the rain bucketed down. It was the Great Flood all over again and I practically had to row the thing back the last couple of hundred yards to 'Jones's Back'—proud of my spoils.

I walked in, soaked to the skin, expecting a good telling off. But mother had a hot bath tub waiting for me and I got my back scrubbed and ended up falling asleep with a fish sandwich in my hand. What a life!

*short for budgerigar—English word for a parrakeet.

16

Funny thing about Manchester and rain. Like bed and breakfast. . . fish and chips. Uncle George used to say that it was the only place in the world where sparrows have webbed feet. And I believed him. Used to try to catch them to have a look. I even managed it once when a bunch of us kids were playing cricket in the street.

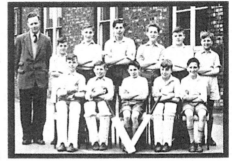

I'm at mid-off position at the corner of Leamington Street when Ronnie Whitfield hits a powerful drive straight at me. The ball's really moving—skidding low—and on its last bounce before reaching me, it scatters a bunch of sparrows having dinner in the Chorlton Street gutter. I take a flying leap to my right. A perfect catch—no problem.

But something's definitely wrong. You know when you think there's one more stair to go, and there isn't? Well—that kind of feeling. It turns out that what I think is the ball—isn't. It's a sparrow!—which turns out to be webless—which turns out to be four runs for Ronny Whitfield, who still ends up thrown out 'cos he can't resist coming over to check out my catch. Harry Hoskinson cries, "Howzat!", the sparrow makes its getaway, Ronny threatens Harry with the bat, and I'm called in for tea.

"Eee—our David can't 'arf spin 'em." The usual reaction to my stories. Like when I saved a girl from drowning at Whitworth Baths swimming pool.

"But it's true! Honest!"

"Aye—and I'm a monkey's uncle!"

Very frustrating. I found out the important thing to remember whenever you're going to do something brave—or just simply amazing—is to make sure somebody sees it.

My dad thought so too. He liked his little flutter on the horses. Never spent all the housekeeping money or anything like that but he had his regular little trips to the bookie's shop. Or sometimes he'd send me so that mum didn't know.

One night she'd been shouting at him about his gambling and the next day he came in all chuffed—but mischievous. Mother was out and he turned to my sister, Beryl, all proud.

"Look at this, our Beryl. Didn't cost me five shillings to win all this." He had a fistful of pound notes. It seemed a fortune.

He knew that mum would come in by the back gate so he went out and made a path of pound notes all the way to the kitchen door, and then inside. Then he sat down with his paper, pleased as Punch with himself.

Sure enough, she opened the back gate. Everyone was trying to act perfectly normal but secretly we were watching her. She took one look, thrust her nose in the air, walked *on* the money all the way to the kitchen door, then slammed it shut.

"You bloody gambling sod!" she said to the air. Didn't even look at him.

"Son. . . stay a bloody bachelor," said dad, from behind his newspaper. "And always bring yer kids up th' same way."

north, south, east, west

My first day at school—Varna Street Infants—we played with blocks and had a bottle of milk which I couldn't finish. Who would have thought that by next year I'd be wanting another? (Even in those days I was on doubles. That's when I started drinking.)

I started out bright. . . David Jones, Class 1a. From there on it was downhill— 2b. . . 3c. . . Then the 'eleven plus'. To put you in the picture—the eleven plus was the modern-day version of the 'rack', from the Middle Ages. The system was that you left Primary school when you were eleven and moved on to Secondary school where you stayed and finished out your sentence. That would be 'til you were 17 or 18 if you were smart and knew what was good for you—or 15 if you just *thought* you were smart—like me.

Depending on your examination result there were two sorts of Secondary schools. Winners and losers. The winners, like my sisters, went to Technical Fairfield High or Spurley Hey Grammar. I got Varna Street Secondary Modern. They called the losers' schools 'Modern' as a sort of consolation prize—but I knew better.

The news of my failing the eleven plus was a surprise to my teachers and the end of the world for me. I didn't want to go out or talk or anything. Except maybe stow away on a slow boat to China. China seemed like the only place to go—nobody there would know I hadn't passed.

"Jones!"

"Yes, sir."

"Tomorrow you're going to Manchester with some other children. Report to me at the start of school."

What's all this, then? They're sending me away for not passing? The Army, maybe.

Next day, me and a couple of other kids get put on a bus. We pick up some other losers from a couple of nearby schools, then head into Manchester. They haven't told us anything yet. They're ashamed of us. I try to figure out an escape, but no luck. We're ushered into an old building with the biggest echoes I've ever heard. My grisly imagination is working overtime. If I'd known they would go this far I'd have tried harder. They sit us down in a room with no windows and they tell us to relax and not to worry— they're just going to ask us one or two questions.

First off, a bloke wearing somebody else's false teeth reads us a story and then asks us questions about what he's just read. The usual stuff. "Why didn't Janet invite John to her party?" ("'Cos she's a stuck-up cow?") I didn't say it but I'm really tempted, y'know? Then I realize no-one knows where we are—they could bump us off like *that* and nobody would be any the wiser. Better behave.

Joker # 2 comes in and asks me to point to north, south, east and west. Is he serious? They've driven us halfway across town— we're in a building we've never seen before. This is a trick question, right? Apparently not. He's staring at me, very serious. I'd better think. If I fail this as well, China will probably hear about it. I mentally struggle to think the bus journey backwards to school. It's impossible.

"North, south, east, west, sir?" A wild guess—pointing half-heartedly.

"Are you s-u-r-e?" he asks, scribbling my death sentence on his stupid notepad.

"No. . . err, not really," I say.

"Very well. Just a few more questions." Who cares? I just want to go home.

They pile us back on the bus. A typical, grey, Manchester day—pouring down. Just how I felt. We never heard any more about the inquisition.

I don't really remember too much about my twelfth year—the new school. The shock of the eleven plus set me back a bit. I remember holding a spear for Gentle Jesus in the nativity play, and fancying everything in a skirt. Ah, yes— girls. I remember during P.T., standing next to Moira, who was the only one in class with more than little pimples under her vest, and having a quick honk-honk. . . showing off for the lads. Well—it *was* Physical Training.

My mind was on girls so much I started getting everything wrong. In metal-work my doughnut maker would only make the hole. As a punishment they put me into cookery classes.

"Oh no, sir—please sir, no! Don't put me in there with all those silly *girls*, sir!"

About the only things I enjoyed at school were acting in the plays, being funny in class, and chatting up the girls—and I'm not too sure about that order. The teachers probably thought—well, he's no good at the doughnut-makers. . . obviously he'll end up in the theatre. Poor little bugger.

"Why are you late for geography, Jones?"

"I'm not very good at geography, sir. Couldn't find the classroom!" Everyone thought I was funny.

"Bend over, Jones." Out came the slipper.

"How did you like that, Jones?"

"Not bad, sir. I liked the fifth one, that was alright." Over again.

Mr. Withington used to hit me with the slipper all the time. Discrimination because I took such a lot of time off school to do the plays and readings. Whenever I was bored I'd say, "Can I be excused, sir? I've got to learn me lines." It used to really get to him.

"You'll never amount to anything will you, Jones?"

"Shouldn't think so, sir." Slipper again.

Outside of school I enjoyed music and chatting up more girls. My sisters and I went to music lessons at the weekends—all four of us, back to back. Mum played piano for the local amateur dramatics group when her health would permit and I got to play cornet in dad's 'British Railways Brass Band'.

The damp, foggy, Manchester air only served to aggravate Doris's emphysema. There was always an oxygen cylinder by the side of her bed, even during her 'healthy' periods, when spring and summer brought some slight relief, and she was in and out of convalescent homes throughout Davy's childhood. He always knew that when the cold, damp months returned she would be bed-ridden most of the time, unable to breathe properly. Then everyone would rally round and do their extra share of housework and caring for her.

She had one collapsed lung and the other was ailing. When she was in her early forties she was one of two people in Britain to undergo a new, experimental operation which involved sticking the collapsed lung to the chest cavity wall. (The other, a man, did not survive.) The doctor said at the time that she had a tremendous will to live.

But her health started to get noticeably worse, and at the same time, hardly co-incidentally, Davy's talent for diversion improved in leaps and bounds—whilst his school work suffered in like proportion. His abilities on stage however, could hardly go unnoticed by the school teachers and staff. So much so that they even started to choose the plays especially with Davy in mind. Coming home from one of his dramatic successes Beryl rushed upstairs to Doris, whose poor health had prevented her from seeing her son's performance, and enthused,

"They all loved him, Mum. He's good enough for television—he really is." To which Doris just nodded knowingly and whispered,

"He will, he will."

She knew inwardly that she would never see the fulfillment of her prophecy. The next night, on Beryl's twentieth birthday, Doris died in bed. Harry came into the children's room, tried to smile, but his anguish overtook him as he told them all,

"She's left us." They all broke down in tears.

The day before she died she had told Beryl, three or four times, not to forget to pay the electricity bill. "It's in the top drawer of the cupboard—don't forget it."

"I couldn't understand why she was being so insistent," recalls Beryl. "She was always very methodical and it wasn't due for about ten days."

Not until two days after her death did Beryl remember her mother's reminder about the electricity bill. She went to the drawer and found the bill, with the exact money: eleven shillings and sixpence. Beside it lay a magazine cutting—a poem by Patience Strong.

— Love Still Abides —

She has passed on beyond the range of sight
Into the glory of the morning light
Out of the reach of sorrow and despair
Safe in the shelter of the Father's care.

Weep not for her, say not she is dead
She has gone on a few short steps ahead
Faith looks beyond this time of grief and pain
Love still abides, and we shall meet again.

— Patience Strong —

Later on, our family doctor told dad that she'd held on a good six years longer than he felt humanly possible. I'm sure it was because she loved us so much. Looking back, I suppose from the time she married, at twenty-eight, until she died, at fifty-one, her body was just barely able to cope with the child-bearing and the strain of living in a foggy, cold climate—six people in a two-bedroom house. She'd fought for so long to live, for us—but finally her energy had just given out.

I hadn't seen much outward affection between them, but the grief her death brought my father was all too plain. I was fourteen when she went. For a year before I left home I watched him struggle, alone with his pain. He continued to work at the tank. I took school dinners and saw him in the evening when I came home—no longer in overalls, always a suit. I could have made a three-piece suit out of the turn-ups on his trousers. At times I'd come in and see him, head in hands, sobbing like a baby.

"I can't go on," he'd say. "I feel as though my arms have been cut off."

Many times, later on, my sisters had tried to get him to come to America to see me in 'Oliver!'—but his health was always dodgy, and he wouldn't make the trip. So once, just before The Monkees started, I managed to get him away for a holiday. He fought against going, but I was determined. The plan was to go to Marjorca—Beryl, Hazel and her husband, me and dad.

"I've got the flights booked. The hotel reservations are made. You're coming."

"I'm bloody not."

"Hey, you know how warm it is there? Great for your health." Finally he agrees.

So he's packing his case. Long-sleeved shirts, pullovers, cardigans. Beryl says, "Here, dad—this is more like what you'll need there." She'd bought him a couple of short-sleeved shirts.

"Well, you can take those back for a start. I'm not wearing *them*."

He's finally on the plane—the first time—he's never been any further than Blackpool. He's wearing a shirt, tie, waist-coat, jacket and overcoat—and a scarf!

"Undo your seat-belt, dad. Get comfortable."

"Not bloody likely!"

Getting off in Marjorca—he's still got his overcoat on—we get down the steps and he says, "By 'eck, that engine's 'ot, isn't it?" It's something like a hundred and two in the shade, y'know—but he's never experienced anything like it.

So, we're in the car on the way to the hotel, and he's sweating like a pig. He turns to Beryl, "You'd no right to take them short-sleeved shirts back. I'll need 'em 'ere."

Beryl winks at me—she's got them in her case. All he wore that whole trip were those two shirts and a pair of huge moccasins that he bought over there, and later denied ever even seeing—even though I have a home movie of him coming over a bridge. All you can see is these huge white things followed by my dad, grinning ear to ear. But no, he says—"You must be joking. You'd never get me up in a pair of those. Take 'em away!" A funny man, my dad.

I remember vividly that first summer after mother's death. The whole family went to the seaside. We needed to—nobody had laughed in a long while.

They had a talent competition on at the pier, and Beryl entered me for it. So we're all sitting there—you know the sort of thing. . .

"And now, mermaids and sailors, we have a whistling tap-dancer for you—all the way from Wigan."

When my turn comes I give Beryl a shove for her to go up and play for me. I've

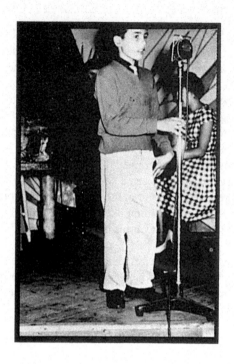

seen the pianist they've got—she's a hundred and nine! But Beryl won't have it.

"I'm not going up there," she hisses.

So I go up and whisper to the MC.

"Oooh—this one's got his own pianist. Aren't *we* professional!" The mermaids and sailors are in an uproar.

"Is *Beryl* here?" he says, all smarmy.

Now she's got to come up. She flashes me an evil look and starts to play, all embarrassed. We do 'Donna'.

"*I had a girl, Donna was her name. . .*"

My dad used to say, "Be like Elvis, son—*swing* it!" It worked. Brought the house down and won a fiver.

I could see this showbusiness lark might be okay. My father's sister, Aunt Jessie, was always encouraging me to go further with it. It was she who had answered an ad in the 'Manchester Evening News' that got me started:

WANTED:
SCHOOL BOYS
TO AUDITION FOR
RADIO PLAY

She wrote to them—
"You must audition my nephew, David. He's very good. He played Abdullah, the Turkish Magician. . . "

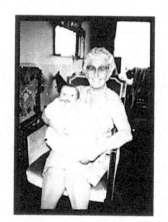

North Regional Head Office: Broadcasting House, Piccadilly, Manchester 1

Broadcasting House, Woodhouse Lane, Leeds 2

TELEPHONE AND TELEGRAMS: LEEDS 31516 & 7

Dear David,

12th December 1960.

I am very pleased that you can take part in "There is a Happy Land" which will be rehearsed and recorded in Leeds on the 6th, 7th and 8th January.

It would be a good idea if you could come to Leeds on the evening of the 5th and stay over until the Sunday evening. I think it would be best if you stayed at the Barrington Court Hotel, which is very close to Broadcasting House in Leeds, and I would like to make reservations as quickly as possible. Will you please drop me a line on the enclosed card saying whether you would like a room booked for you. The BBC will of course pay an allowance to cover your stay at the hotel. It is important that I should know this as soon as possible as reservations over the Christmas period are not always easy to obtain. I have arranged for somebody to look after you during your stay.

I will let you have the script in a few days and look forward to seeing you.

All good wishes,

Yours sincerely,

(signature)

(Alfred Bradley)
Drama/Features Producer
North Region

Mr. David Jones,
20 Leamington Street,
Higher Openshaw,
Manchester 11.

Evening Chronicle

1st July, 1960

Mr. and Mrs. Jones,

Today I have been talking to Mr. Vivian A. Daniels, the producer of the BBC TV play "June Evening". He tells me that of the youngsters he has taking part in this drama he has a very high regard for the performance of your son David.

I would like to know a little more about him before writing up the play next week. Do you think it possible you could either phone me here or send a few details about his school etc.? Mr. Daniels tells me he plays the trumpet in the play, and that suggest he may have a musical background at home.

Best wishes,

Yours sincerely,

(signature)

Malcolm Moss
TV Correspondent

So I went along to the Piccadilly office in Manchester, but I wasn't right for the part. It called for an older voice and a Bolton accent. But I was put in touch with another producer and from that I was asked to read the 'Morning Story' a few times on the radio.

Shortly afterwards, through another recommendation, I did my first TV part in 'June Evening' by Bill Naughton, of 'Alfie' fame. The producer, Vivian Daniels, passed my name on to another B.B.C. producer from Leeds, Alfred Bradley. He called me to Leeds for an audition, and I stayed on to do a part in a B.B.C. Radio Play by Keith Waterhouse called, 'There is a Happy Land'. At the time it was supposed to be the longest part ever written for a teenager in a B.B.C. play.

Jennifer Moss had been in the production of 'June Evening', and subsequently helped me to get the part of Ena Sharples' grandson on 'Coronation Street'—Britain's longest-running soap opera. And that was the sum total of my professional training. . . Instead of going to the Royal Academy, I played a little kid who wouldn't eat his strawberries. Mary Quinn, who played my mum in 'June Evening', has written to me a couple of times saying, ". . . by the way, why wouldn't you eat your strawberries?".

At home we discussed my future.

"Well, what are you going to do, our David?"

"I'm going to give this acting a go."

I'd been earning £11 for a 'Morning Story', £17 for a play, £22 for a TV show. Pretty good—but I still didn't actually *want* to be an actor. Partly because that's what everyone expected me to be, especially my teachers at school. So—speaking of horses. . .

My dad was mad on them and thought I could be a jockey 'cos of my size. So I thought, "Yeah, fool everybody. *Don't* be an actor. Confuse the bastards."

My Dad wrote to a sports writer for a Manchester paper saying, "My son is interested in racing. . . "—bump di bump di bum. They gave him the name of a stable owner, Basil Foster, in Newmarket.

We went along and Mr. Foster thought I'd be perfect—I wasn't going to grow. (I was fourteen and still only four foot five.) So he offered to let me try it for a while.

I worked there for six weeks during my summer holidays and really got to like it. So at the end of 1960 I said goodbye to school and started working at Basil's— 'Holland House'—as a stable boy. I was

"Son, you're the paperweight champion of the world. Ride 'em, cowboy!"

—Harry Jones—

there until May the following year, taking every other weekend off for radio plays and TV work. By now I was really hooked on horses and I felt I'd like to be a jockey—though I'd never ridden in a race at that point. But no luck at Basil's—I was employed mucking out stables, grooming—general dirty work. It was an apprenticeship that served to whet my appetite for the racing life, but at the same time fate was pulling me very strongly in the opposite direction.

Basil, it turned out, was a true ally of fate and always encouraged my theatrical pursuits. Maybe he could see that was where my true destiny lay—or perhaps he just couldn't risk having me around too close to the business phone. . .

I happened to be in the office one day when the phone rang. I answered it and very nearly ruined Basil's relationship with one of the most valuable riders in racing history, Lester Piggot.

"Hello. Basil Foster's stables."

HOLLAND HOUSE
THE LEYS
NEWMARKET
SUFFOLK.

Dear Mr. Jones,

Thank you for your letter. Sorry to hear that you missed me at the races. I would liked to have had a talk with you regarding David.

It will be O.K. for him to come anytime he wishes after Christmas, if you would let me know a week before he intends to come. I will fix him up for accomodations.

"Could I thpeak to Bathil, pleathe?" lisped Lester. (I should explain that Lester was often seen, but seldom heard.)

"Thertainly." I said. "Who'th thpeaking, pleathe?"

"Lethter Piggot!" he barked—a bit indignant, but rightly so, I suppose. So, shouting past the mouth-piece, I promptly added salt to the wound—

"Bathil. Bathil!" (It was nothing personal, y'know—I just thought I was being a funny bastard.)

Basil put his head round the door, a bit bewildered.

"It'th thomebody called Lethter, thir!"

Basil went crimson. He lurched across the desk to wrench the receiver out of my hands before I could do any more damage. After the call he gave me a clout round the ear 'ole. I thought I'd never live that down.

Basil already knows I meant no harm, but Lester, if you're reading this—I'm thorry.

Basil knew lots of showbusiness people—all track fanatics—so he used his 'pull' on my behalf. Colonel 'A', the owner of a theatrical agency, had some horses at the stables so, through Basil's recommendation, I earned some extra money beating the ground for the Colonel's party when they went grouse-shooting. (It's a wonder I'm alive today—agents are *terrible* shots!)

Anyway, Basil talked the Colonel into taking me to London to audition for a part in a new musical, 'Oliver!', at the New Theatre. (It's now the Albery.) I didn't know it at the time, but this trip was to steer my life in a whole new direction. And very quickly too.

The part I went up for was 'The Artful Dodger'. I remember singing 'Consider Yourself' and complaining to Beryl about the key. I walked out on stage, not fully realizing what a big deal it was to actually get a chance to audition. There were lots of kids in London who could do the part. But I sang out loud and felt good. It was a great treat to be in a theatre like that, but I honestly didn't want the part. Certainly didn't expect to *get* it.

I did the song in cockney, but words like *book, look,* and *cook* came out all Manchester.

"Why are you talking Manchester and singing cockney?"

"I give up," I shrugged.

They laughed at me. I checked my fly.

Back to the agents and the verdict. They said if I could get my cockney better I had the part.

"So back to Newmarket?" I asked Colonel 'A'.

"Not yet," he said. "We have another part to see about."

Off we went to the Scala Theatre for 'Peter Pan' auditions. John Gregson, Anne Heywood and Jane Asher were the stars. I was up for the part of Michael, the youngest of the Darling's children.

Here we go again. I watched as boy after boy came on stage. Fat ones, thin ones, short, tall—what is this? The line they were all saying was, "Father is a cowardy, cowardy custard." The director kept saying, "Next!"

The key word was 'custard'. I sat there—"Custard, coostard, castard"—I'm making my mouth go into all these strange shapes, trying to be posh, English upper-class. Book, look, cook. . . pit, pat, buk, luk, cuk, castard. . . carstarrd.

"Next!"

I walk on. I'm standing with five boys. Here we go again. . . north, south, east, west.

"How old are you?" he says to the first one.

"Thirteen."

"You?"

"Fourteen."

"And you?"

"Carstard." More laughs.

"Yes, very good but. . . how *old* are you?"

"Err, I mean—nearly sixteen, sir." (I was fifteen and five months.)

That's probably why I got the part. . . didn't need a chaperone.

Next thing I knew I was eating in cafes—had my own room—bump di bum. Great. I enjoyed the lie-ins in the mornings but I wasn't used to it—the first couple of weeks my body was in shock. I wrote cards home to my dad, uncle George, the stable lads, Basil—everybody.

Seeing my name in a real programme for the first time was fantastic. I'd seen it flash by on 'Coronation Street' and other TV shows, but now—on posters outside the theatre, it felt different. I was impressed.

My part was not much, actually. In fact it was so slow I fell asleep once—during the show. I had to go to bed, on stage, see? So Jane Asher's nudging me 'cos I've missed my cue. Under her breath she's going, "David. Daavvid!" I wake up.

"What? What's up?" It's the strangest feeling. . . waking up and seeing eight hundred people looking at you.

After a short tour of England my cockney was sharp. I stayed in London's Holland Park with Mr. and Mrs. Mills—John and Kaye. They had a daughter, Maureen, who worked at International Artists, my theatrical agency. Family life again. Food and laundry. 'Mrs', as I called Kaye, did the same for me as a mum would.

I landed the part of the Dodger, second time around.

Enjoyed living in London—great city. I used to walk a lot and see movies during the afternoon, until one day I sat down and the guy next to me put his hand on my leg. I froze—then gave him an Artful Dodger—

"Leave orf, mate!"

I guess all boys and girls go through fiddling about times with friends, but this was a bit different. (I remember when I was about six or seven standing Amanda Lee on the outside toilet seat and prodding her privates. She stayed late after our puppet show that we held in the back yard. Charged a penny for that. They had a go on my stilts and looked at my budgie, all inclusive.) Well, anyway—this fella wasn't going to get a look at *my* budgie. I scarpered. Left out going to the pictures after that.

I'd been in the show for four months. The American producer, David Merrick, had started taking British shows over to the States and touring them for five or six months in major cities before bringing them into New York. With overheads already covered, if they made it on Broadway—bonus time.

It was a Saturday night, and the murmurs started. "Merrick is in." "Merrick is in." I had no idea—I thought they were saying, "Maverick is in." So after the show, he comes backstage.

"Howdy, pardner," I drawled in my best western twang—make him feel at home, I thought. How the hell was I supposed to know he was big time?

29th March, 1962.

Harry Jones Esq.,
20, Leamington Street,
High Openshaw,
MANCHESTER, 11

Dear Mr. Jones,

I don't know whether David has written to you, but he went for an audition last Friday for the part of the 'Artful Dodger' in the very successful musical "Oliver".

The Management liked him, with reservations. As you know, he had rehearsed the song from the show, and at the audition sang this with a cockney accent very well, but when it came to the reading his native Lancashire was very prominent. However, they are prepared to give him a trial and if all goes well they would like him to rehearse and open in the part on the 7th May, 1962.

You will realise that this is a replacement, as the original boy has grown up and got too big. I might add that this is a wonderful chance for a boy who was not even in the profession as shorter while ago as Christmas, and no doubt you will be very proud of him.

I hope to see you down here on the 7th May.

Kindest regards,

Yours sincerely,

REG CAMPBELL
for International Artistes Representation

David Jones Esq.,
c/o Mrs. Shortland,
35, Bowness Crescent,
Kingston Vale,
LONDON.

3rd April, 1962.

In consideration of your having negotiated the undermentioned engagement :

To appear for Donmar Productions Limited in "Oliver", the part of 'The Artful Dodger' as from the week commencing 7th May, 1962 for a salary of fifteen pounds per week. (£15. 0. 0d).

I hereby agree to pay you a commission of **10%** on the weekly earnings accruing to me from this engagement and on any prolongation thereof and a like commission on the next two engagements with the said management.

For and on behalf of
INTERNATIONAL ARTISTES
REPRESENTATION

Signed:
Date: 6/4/62.

"I want you to come over to America and play the Artful Dodger."

"Thanks very much," I said. Kind of casual.

Then I started thinking—wait a minute—this is all a bit too quick. I'd have to leave my dad, the horses—fish 'n' chips!

"I'm not goin'," I told Maverick.

"Why not?" he asked, a bit taken aback.

I told him I had to think about it. (Talk about Mr. Cool.) But seriously I just really had to think about it. I hadn't planned this at all.

I talked to Basil and he said I must go.

"I don't want to, guv'nor." (I was all cockney by now.)

"You *must*," he said. "Then come back and *own* horses—there's still plenty of time for all that. But take this opportunity now." (As it turned out, years later I did buy a couple of horses, 'Chicamono' and 'Pearl Locker', and stabled them with Basil.)

But right now, I had no idea all that craziness was in store for me. All I knew was I was going west. . . I think.

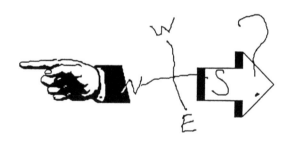

a dickens of a time

> *"After tonight, this
> city is yours."*
> —Judy Garland—

It was one month before my sixteenth birthday when I left for America. Can't remember much before going. Goodbyes at the theatre. "Goodbye, Mrs. Mills." "So long, dad." On the plane going over, the stewardess asked Larry Oaks, the assistant director, what he was drinking. And then—

"What about your son? Milk?" Very funny. Beer was my drink now.

That's when I started drinking.

So we landed in Toronto, Canada. I was checked into the Royal York Hotel, plush red carpets everywhere. Men in uniforms were rushing to pick up my Woolworth's cardboard suitcase. I had my own room which I stayed in alone for a whole week while Larry was busy working on the show. He called me a few times each day to check that I was alright.

Alright? I was in heaven. Remote control TV—twelve channels—Room Service! My first experience of a *real* hotel. It was a different planet. I didn't see any of Canada, apart from the ride from the airport. Very cold—brass monkeys—didn't even leave my room. The Guinness Book of Records should've had a section on the most hours a fifteen year old has watched TV with the least amount of sleep. I'd have clinched it, hands down.

But after a week of this record-breaking stint, I was getting antsy. And just a little homesick, too. The novelty of hotel life was wearing off. I decided I didn't like Canada anymore.

"Larry, I'm getting fed up. I want to do the show, or go home."

He assured me it would open soon. Equity was wanting more Americans in the cast, so Merrick was slipping me in through Canada to conform to the rules. The kid lined up for the part of Oliver was a child actor from a long-running American soap opera, 'As The World Turns'—so, no problem. But the Dodger was snuck in for the Toronto show at the O'Keefe Centre—a 3,000 seater. The whole thing looked so big after the New Theatre in London, which held 800.

The cast were not too pleased with my being there at first, but Michael Goodman, their Dodger at the time, was *too* cockney. His trouble was, he was a natural cockney. Mine was something I had to work on. I spoke slow, so the audience could understand me

33

better. There was also the fact that fourteen-year olds start growing fast, and Oliver and Dodger were getting too big, too fast. Georgia Brown was short and Clive Reville, who had taken over from Ron Moody, was also quite small. The Dodger and Oliver should be child-like. (Actually, the Dodger, as far as Dickens wrote, was an undersized eight-year old.)

So anyway, the cast were all saying things like,

"You're not a *real* cockney, are you?"

"No, I'm an actor." Pretty cheeky but I had to hold my own, d'in oi?

Georgia warmed up first, and then, gradually, they all came around. After only a week the show came to America. Broadway!

On arriving in New York City, I jumped for joy—it could've been Mars—it was so different from anything I'd imagined. I'd seen Superman fly over some pretend city on Saturday mornings, down at the Rex Cinema on Ashton Old Road, Manchester—but this was
for real. There were a hundred people at every corner waiting for the light to change to 'Walk-Walk-Walk'. That's what I did mostly. Walk-Walk-Walk. Run-Run-Run. From the 40's to the 80's—from the West side to the East—what a place! Nothing under twenty stories for miles.

The people were so friendly to me. I didn't even have to open my mouth. I'd be standing there, in a lift or on a street corner somewhere, and I'd get—

"What a smart young man." "Hi, cutie!" Thick New York accent.

Really, it was amazing—people used to talk to me all the time. I guess I looked sort of different, being so short, and obviously, when I spoke I had 'em hooked with the old Dodger accent. I really put it on. People would invite me home for tea—I loved New York City!

I was in the States on a temporary work permit and had to have a chaperone. I thought that meant I had to live with someone but it didn't work out that way. They found me a chaperone alright—at least, the woman signed the papers. I never actually had to live with her. Maybe she thought she was signing a drinks tab or something. Anyway I was left pretty much to my own devices. It was great.

I moved into New York's famous old theatrical digs, The Whitby Apartments. High ceilings, tiled bathrooms. I stayed there with Bruce Prochnick, (who played Oliver), and his mother, Wanda, a good-looking lady from Watford.

Bruce Prochnick—

"The entire situation was terribly tense. Michael Goodman, the original Artful Dodger, had just been told that he was out and Davy Jones (whoever he was) was in. I was livid. I couldn't wait to meet this Davy Jones and his phoney cockney accent.

I shall always remember entering our dressing-room. There he was, standing in front of his mirror, flexing his muscles. He seemed quite aloof and indifferent to everything that was happening around him.

There we stood, two teenage English boys all alone, 3,000 miles from home and neither one of us could think of a decent way to start a conversation.

I wondered whether he was any good or just a lot of hot air.

I found out pretty quickly. Once Davy hit the stage for the first time, it was obvious that this kid had everything. I still don't believe how well the show went that night. Davy was simply smashing and the audience gave him a standing ovation. He responded by giving them one in return. It was love at first sight."

It was an exciting time. Nothing can compare with the magic of an opening night on Broadway. Incredible. I was not quite sixteen years old—still had the smell of horses in my clothes—and there I was looking down into the front row seats at Judy Garland and Sammy Davis Jr.. And that was just one seat!

My heart started to pound faster and I swaggered and swayed more than usual. It worked. Lots of smiles and applause. A standing ovation at the finish. What a feeling.

There were no reviews to wait for 'cos the papers were on strike—but we knew the show was a smash, so it was going to be a carefree, fun night. We all went out to celebrate. What a blast! Flowers on the tables, the lights of the city all around, a band playing—all sparkling dresses and dinner suits! (My Burton's brown only just made it past the doorman.)

"I was still only a little fish in a big pond. But I was a different little fish."

After a meal we went up onto one of those huge skyscraper buildings—the Time and Life Building, I think. As we were looking out over the city lights, Judy Garland put her arm around me and whispered, "After tonight—this city is yours." I'll never forget that. Didn't think much of it at the time—it sounded so corny. But I must admit I like it now. And of course she was right. 'Oliver!' was a box-office smash. For a whole year or more, tickets were like gold-dust.

After about six months at the Whitby I had to find another place. Bruce was replaced because he had grown too big. As it was, I had cuban heels on—Beatle boots. The 'Oliver!' boys were the pre-Beatle moptops.

I moved in for a time with a lady and her daughter. Strange times. I wasn't sure if she wanted me to be with her fourteen-year old, her, or both of them. I was a bit slow there. She flashed herself a few times and I fancied them both actually—Willie could have gained some useful experience. (I was pretty sure there was more to it than standing the girl on the loo seat and prodding her privates.) Anyway, come visa time we parted company—got the old cardboard suitcase out again.

The management recommended another house: Mrs. Ester Votos and her son, Chris, who was one of the boys in the show. They had quite a posh apartment on 70th and West

End Ave, overlooking the river. And some weekends we used to go to their summer house on Long Island. Ester used to take my rent every week but I remember when I finally left she gave most of it back to me.

There was a big to-do about my card-playing. I'd only played pontoon and brag before arriving in America, but I wanted to learn poker. I used to watch the cast and crew playing under the stage during shows and finally I sat in on a few hands. Black Maria, seven and five-card poker, high, low—the lot. Lost a bit, won a bit.

One day there was this guy I hadn't seen before, Mitch Maran, who became a great friend of mine over the years. I sat down and got my hand. There was never much time— I'd be running on stage seconds after playing a hand, money dropping as I ran. Anyway, this particular time I squeezed three Queens and two Aces out of my hand. A full house. The pot was getting pretty big—about $30—and finally only this Mitch guy and I were left in.

We bet back and forth for ages, me with one ear on the show going on above us. The pot was well worthwhile now but I was almost due on stage so I made my last raise and asked to see his hand.

"Two pair. . . " he said, still holding his cards close to his chest.

I thought this guy must be mad—all that money and only two pair.

"Full 'ouse!" I shouted as I went for the pot. It was just like in the westerns—he stopped my hand in mid-air—

". . . of Kings." Meaning four of a kind.

"What are you, mate? Some kind of comedian?" I exclaimed, in my best Dodger cockney. Every time we meet he reminds me of the way I said that.

After that first encounter whenever he'd win he'd slip out into the audience, grab the nearest available seat to the stage, if there was one, (rare)—or stand at the side—and count his winnings, with a Fagin smile on his face. Cracked me up.

I was finally banned from the game for being under age. But that wasn't the end of our games together. Mitch was dating a girl from the show, Mary Ann. And I was involved with a young lady named Sally. Often the four of us would go to the Loews Midtown Hotel together. We'd swim in the pool and eat the greatest hamburgers, right off the grill.

Sally was my first *actual* sexual encounter. I'd fiddled around plenty of times but this was for real. I was living with Miriam and Herb Neal in Forest Hills at the time, and one afternoon, Sally and I found ourselves alone. Remembering the Boy Scouts' motto— 'Be Prepared'—I'd equipped myself with a condom. Mind you, I'd been prepared for about eighteen months at this point—I couldn't believe I was actually going to take it out of the wrapper. I wondered whether it'd gone off yet.

'I went into the bathroom to put the rubber on, but Willie wouldn't respond. He thought he was going to be put away for good. This condom thing—I'd never seen anything like it. I knew everything was supposed to be bigger in America, but this was ridiculous. It looked like one of my socks!

A little deflated but undeterred, I made my way to her bed. Her little eyes peered over the covers, I snuck in next to her, and we cuddled. Little Willie woke up, I put the bag over his head, and everything was fine. Our first time. Sweet.

When I figured it was all over I withdrew and Willie hit the air—without his raincoat. I looked down and there it was—like a cat's tail in a door. Sally and I burst into hysterics. Still giggling, we embraced and felt very secure. She was warm and her little smile never changed all the time I knew her. Ah, Sally—remember those days?

At that time, Broadway was literally full of shows with English casts. 'Chips with Everything' had Michael Standing and George Layton (an old friend of Davy's from his days doing the B.B.C. plays); 'Luther' had Albert Finney; 'Becket'—Richard Burton; 'Beyond the Fringe'—Dudley Moore and Peter Cook; 'The Rehearsal'— Adrienne Corri; and 'Stop the World I Want To Get Off' featured the multi-talented genius, Tony Newley. Also playing within a two-hundred yard stretch of West 45th Street were, 'The Irregular Verb,"To Love"' and 'The Private Ear and The Public Eye.'

It was like I'd never left the West End. All of us Britishers used to meet at Downey's Steak House. The best spare ribs in town. (Those were my red meat-eating days. I'm a vegetarian now.) The proprietor was Jim Downey, an Irishman who had made his way to New York soon after the war. His restaurant was great. In one of the rooms there were three walls lined with Tote betting slips. He used to tell everyone he'd bought every single one of them himself.

"A hundred thousand dollar wall that, son!" he'd say, with his arm around my shoulder. Expensive wallpaper.

Another room had the walls covered with pictures of celebrities. All signed, "To Jim—you're the greatest" or some such thing. He *was* the greatest—he always made you feel at home when you came in.

He took a special liking to me, being a horse man himself. Many a night we'd sit drinking 'til four or five in the morning. I seldom got to bed before six. But then, New York's an ideal place to spend the day in bed—summertime it's too hot, and wintertime too cold. Jim used to take me to the track and we'd watch his horse do its morning workout. He became my substitute father—eyeing the same starters as me. And his restaurant was the start of many an intriguing encounter.

It was there that I first met the Baker twins, Jenny and Suzy. They were both in 'Stop the World'. Jim had a crush on their mother, and I was sort of fancying Jenny—although you really couldn't tell her and Suzy apart. Not in the dark, anyway.

So Jenny and I would often meet at Downey's for drinks. She was the first woman-looking woman I was ever with. She bounced along with confidence and fun—until one night the fun stopped. My fault.

I was snuggling with sister Suzy at the Whitby, and in burst Jenny. I jumped up—

"I thought she was *you*!" (What else could I say?)

Jenny wasn't impressed with my witty ad lib. She decked me. (Packed a good wallop for a lady!)

So I stopped off at the flower shop a couple of blocks from the theatre. Not for flowers though—I should apologize for a simple case of mistaken identity? No—into the back for a quick couple of hands of rummy with a bunch of grownup Fagin boys. I'd be there every week. It was a knock-three-times gambling den. By the time Thursday night came around I'd have just enough left for corned-beef hash, egg and chips. . . 78¢. On Broadway and broke!

But help was on the way. A guy called Ward Sylvester, a Screen Gems executive, had come to see 'Oliver!' After the show he came backstage and said he'd like me to come to Hollywood and do some tests—was I interested?

Was I *interested*? I got on the plane (my second flight ever—this was in '63) and within minutes my cheeks were aching from being pinched, and the old, "Aren't you cute!" routine. Stewardesses this time. There's nothing worse than fancying some beautiful air hostess—figuring out what line you're going to give 'er—and she comes over, pinches your cheek, and says, "I have a little boy *just* like you!"

You can forget, "Okay, darlin'—you an' me for the old 'Mile High Club' then?" That one's *right* out!

So we touched down in L.A.. Very flat—spread out. In the early sixties it didn't have anything like the smog it's got now. Very much the City of Angels. It seemed like all the buildings were white or pink. . . all palm trees and sunshine. I didn't get to see much of it, mind you—just a day to do my Columbia studios chores—screen tests and meeting people. Ward was trying me out for 'Wackiest Ship in the Army' and 'Hogan's Heroes'.

I saw the Osmonds rehearsing for the Andy Williams Show. Donny was about eight then, I think. Sat in on a conversation with two Indians, a cowboy, Dracula and assorted Monsters from the Deep. And that was just at a hamburger stand on Sunset Boulevard!

"How!" Thought I'd try the old Indian conversation starter.

."Watcha, mate!" he replied. (One of the Indians was from London. Small world.)

I chatted up a Shirley Temple lookalike and that was about it. No time for the Good Ship Lollipop—had to fly back. Pity though—I always fancied Shirley. Just my size.

Meeting Ward and doing those screen tests was the beginning of the ideas and connections that led to 'The Monkees'—though no-one knew it then. For me it was just a nice diversion and then back to work. But my life has constantly been full of little surprises—and the next bit of sparkle was not far away. . . the Tony Awards.

Georgia and Clive were up for Best Actress and Actor, and me for Best Supporting Actor. Looking back I didn't really understand what an honour that was—I was still only sixteen. I was in a group with all the other Best Supporting Actors, and they read out the winner—

"David. . . " I really did expect to hear "Jones" next. But no.

". . . Burns." (From 'How To Succeed in Business Without Really Trying'.)

I was pretty disappointed. I'd rented a tux and everything. Turned out Georgia and Clive lost, too—so none of us got to say our carefully prepared acceptance speeches. We're leaving and Georgia says to me,

"I'll tell you mine, if you'll tell me yours."

Georgia became like a sister to me. We were on the Ed Sullivan Show together the day The Beatles were on but I wasn't really into pop music at that time. (I'd signed with Colpix records in '63, and had a couple of releases—but it was more like 'show-tune' kind of stuff.) The closest I'd got to the 'pop' world was I'd bought 'Poetry In Motion'—and I'd gone to a Dave Clark Five concert at Carnegie Hall. All the girls mobbed me—they thought I was Dave's brother.

"Hey, he talks just like them. He must *be* one. Let's GET him!"

I never understood all that. We always got stage-door people after a show—but nothing like the hysteria that was going on when The Beatles arrived. One of our stage-door regulars was Liza Minelli. She wasn't really *in* show business at the time, but all the stage-school kids hung out with all the 'Oliver!' kids.

When I was seventeen I got my own place—425 West 46th Street—'Hell's Kitchen.' Scenes straight out of 'West Side Story' enacted every night. The street had a dip in it and at the height of summer they used to block off the drains and flood it. You'd see people just hanging out. There'd be swimming, boxing matches, knife-fighting—a real family show. If you're ever in the city check it out.

The house I lived in used to belong to the Governor of New York. A big iron gate led into a courtyard. The story was that this courtyard was used for hangings and there were rumours of an underground tunnel to the church across the street. I never found the tunnel, but the hangings were Mondays, Wednesdays and Fridays.

The place was all red brick and had a lampost and a balcony around the courtyard— very early something or other. I bought some cheapo furniture from a famous New York furniture house. It looked more like garden furniture, but it was *my* place. I took the apartment over from Elizabeth Ashley, so she'll tell you—it's all true about the swimming and fighting. Honest.

Well, the show finally closed on Broadway. The touring road company took off, with American actors replacing most of the other British members of the cast. But I hung in there.

One city we played—I can't remember where—I lived in another of the New York Whitby-types of hotel. It was hot and clean. I like that—the clean towelling and sheets all the time. I love staying in hotels. Or maybe it's just that I hate doing sheets.

One night there was a knock on my door. I don't really know how it all came about—I guess you could call it rape. Sheila was much older than me—I was just eighteen. My heart started beating faster and faster and I couldn't swallow or talk. She was the first woman that had approached me—actually made the first move. (I guess I must have looked so young to everyone. Lots of girls I fancied didn't take me seriously—sort of like, "Come back when you're taller.") But she obviously knew what she'd come for and went straight after it. She kissed me as I leaned on the door and my heart felt like it was going to explode. She undid my pants—kissed my stomach—and walked me over to the bed. It was her show entirely. For once I didn't mind being upstaged.

'Oliver!' made it to Chicago in early 1965. The windy city was right. No matter where you were going you started off the other way. I met the tallest man in the world there—Don Koehler, 8'2". We ate together at the Blackhalk Restaurant—me in the cellar and him on the first and second floors. Our picture was on the buses. I guess it was a promotion thing for the show and for the restaurant—"No order too tall for us"—something like that. Big time—got a free pork chop for that, every week.

Chicago also marked the end of my 'Oliver!' run. It was a very sad time. I felt as though I'd abandoned the assault—like it was the military and I was retreating, or going AWOL. But, onward and upward—

Maverick called. . .

'Pickwick' was opening. Another Dickens show—starring the great Harry Secombe. (English cast again—including Anton Rodgers, who's been my good friend ever since.) Merrick offered the same money I was making in 'Oliver', which by then was $450 road money, salary and subsistence. I asked for $550 and finally got it.

There was a catch though. It was only for three months. Harry Secombe had promised the part to the wonderful Roy Castle, since he had played 'Sam Weller' in the London production. I hesitated at first. You get so attached to everyone doing theatre—I thought it would be difficult to only do the three months and then leave. But I'd been trying, for the last four years, to make it to Hollywood—and 'Pickwick' was playing Los Angeles and San Francisco. So I joined up.

Gillian Lyn was the choreographer. We worked out for about three weeks at the Music Centre, Los Angeles. I had to dance more in this show—I liked that. There was Anton Rodgers, Oscar Quitak, the late Julian Orchard—and Ian Fraser, the musical director. Ian would have fun giving me the wrong bell-note at the beginning of a song. He had asked me during rehearsals if I needed him to cue me with the note, see? "Narr—no problem!"—real cocky, I was. So from then on, any time I missed my note, he'd start me off the next night, *miles* away from the actual note. I'd have to sort of fake my way into it by talking the first line or so. Fun times.

There was a dancer in the show who tickled my fancy, so to speak. Jinny—a different kind of woman. . . bouncy, thin, very athletic. Turned me on just watching her during the show—couldn't wait to see her after. Squiggly, wiggly, Jinny was a teacher. (I never enjoyed my homework quite so much—"Do it again—until you get it right!") We had some exciting nights in the Montecito Apartments—L.A.'s 'Whitby'.

I had been in company with one other lady in 'Pickwick', a singer who could really hit the high notes. Looking back, it was a set-up. I liked her—I also liked Jinny. She liked me—*she* also liked Jinny. Mmm. . . interesting. So one night we all got together for wine and kisses, and upon reaching the Montecito the girls popped an amyl-nitrite under my nose, and took advantage of me. (To those of you who are unfamiliar with these funny little capsules—they're called 'poppers'—and no *way* you can be held responsible for your actions once you get near one of them. They're not supposed to be used other than under medical supervision—they're for getting the heart going again with heart-attack victims. They certainly do their job, no problem! They're lethal.) Anyway we all rolled around like kids. I remember it well 'cos it was the only time I've ever been to bed with two females. We were all sort of giggly for days. Ah!—corrupted at last.

I also fell very much in love at that time, with a special lady, Eileen. She worked front of house as an usherette. Dark, with long black hair that she wore tied back—she was the most beautiful girl I'd ever seen. Time and again I asked to see her after the show but she wouldn't. I never gave up though, and eventually she warmed up. I was asked home for dinner and met Rose and Charles, her mum and dad.

Hollywood, to most people, means only movie stars and glamour. But this family was one like you'd find in any town, anywhere. Charles played golf, father of two girls, very straightforward—Rose loved me very much and was very kind. Eileen and I saw a lot of each other whilst the show was in Los Angeles.

'Pickwick' turned out to be just what Davy had hoped it would be—a perfect vehicle for showcasing his talents to the L.A. set. Agents, writers, TV people—all came to see the show, and all were impressed by his 'Sam Weller'. His potential was apparent to everyone, but the credit for pinpointing just where and how this new, young talent should be directed, must go to two young Screen Gems staff-writers, Paul Mazursky and Larry Tucker, who came along at the behest of Ward Sylvester (then acting as Davy's manager). They felt they had an idea for which Davy would be perfect. Right there and then they promised Ward and Davy a script to look over. All they had to do was go home and write it.

Meanwhile, 'Pickwick' went on to San Francisco.

FORM 11-3 20 RMS. 8-65

INTER-OFFICE COLUMBIA COMMUNICATION

From __Bruce Cohn Curtis__

By _____

Date __June 22, 1965__

To __Mr. M. J. Frankovich__

Attention of _____

In Regard to __NEW TALENT PROGRAM__

Last night I went to the Music Center to see the new musical comedy, PICKWICK.

I went to the play mainly to see DAVID JONES. I need not repeat what we all know -- that he is a great talent. In my opinion he steals the show from HARRY SECOMBE, who plays Pickwick. This is no easy feat as Mr. Secombe is an entertainer in the most encompassing sense of the word. I also want to add that David Jones was the only person who I could hear clearly and distinctly when he spoke and sang, without benefit of a mike. The rest of the company's diction was slurred and most of their lyrics were hardly understood, even with the use of mikes.

Dear Ward:

I can't thank you enough for your hospitality last night. We all certainly enjoyed "Pickwick". It's a delightful show, and I was pleased to see David Jones is everything you said he is.

Thank you again for your warm hospitality.

Sincerely,

DC/cpb

CC: Mr. Lester Sill
    Miss Rosalind Ross

DICK CLARK
DICK CLARK PRODUCTIONS

It was great fun working with Secombe. He joked all the time, blowing raspberries whenever he got me laughing, just to make it worse. In the ice-skating scene, my legs had to support the two of us, and while I'd be struggling to keep my feet on the ice, he would press his mouth to my ear and spray a raspberry all over my face. He'd still be laughing, in his high tenor burst, as we wobbled our way off-stage. On my last night, in Cincinatti, I decided I was going to beat Harry at his own game. . .

The scene is the debtors' prison. And how it usually goes is—Harry's there ('Pickwick') with his partners in crime—and I show up with a basket of goodies for them.

"'Allo, Mr. Pickwick."

"Sam! Sam Weller. It's good to see you lad."

"I brought some food for ya, Guv'ner." General jubilation amongst Pickwick and his cronies.

"I got some apples. I got some oranges. And I got some chicken sandwiches for ya."

"Chicken sandwiches?" They can't believe it. Harry puts his arm around me and starts singing 'If I Ruled The World'.

Well, it's the last night, so—

"'Allo, Mr. Pickwick."

"Sam! Sam Weller. It's good to see you, lad."

"I brought some food for ya, Guv'ner." General jubilation, etc..

"I got some apples. I got some oranges. But all the bakeries are on strike and I couldn't get no bread."

"You couldn't get no bread, aye? Well, never mind. . . "

"I'm really sorry, Guv'ner. I did try, honest. I went everywhere I could to get some bread for yer sandwiches, but. . . "

"WELL—never mind, Sam," interrupts Harry—suspicious of where I'm going with this.

"But I didn't let ya down alltergevver. I got ya chicken." Cheers (and relief) all 'round.

So I open up my basket. Out come the apples. Out come the oranges. And out comes a live chicken. Harry can't believe his eyes. He starts laughing uncontrollably.

Now—if you've ever heard Harry once he starts laughing—infectious would be an understatement. The whole cast are in stitches. Helpless. They can't do a *thing*. Every time they start to ease off, they spot the chicken again. . . cluck, cluck, clucking around the stage. For ten minutes the show stops. The audience are laughing hysterically. The cast are paralyzed—tears rolling down their cheeks—and the chicken's still cluck, clucking around the stage.

Well, eventually it calms down and we're just about to start again. Harry puts his arm around me, takes a breath—"If I ruled. . . "—and the chicken spreads its wings and flies right across the stage and up into the flys. Harry blows one of his famous raspberries while trying to stop himself from laughing again—and everyone loses it all over again.

Finally, some sort of order is restored.

"That was a foul trick!" says Harry. (He still got the last laugh.)

He gave me a beautiful silver cigarette case when I left, engraved, "Thanks for all the laughs and wonderful co-operation. Affectionately, Harry." I enjoyed private times with him and his family. He's a wonderful, warm person. And a great farter. He'd always drop one on stage and look at me accusingly. I had the hardest time I've *ever* had, trying to keep a straight face with Harry. I really respect his work. And his farts.

The show was received well and Ward Sylvester played an active part in drumming up a lot of interest at Screen Gems/Columbia Pictures. Most of the executives came to see me in it—all full of agent smiles, and very excited about *their* boy. A party was given at the Beverly Hills Hotel—lots of debs and celebrities. A signing—the launching of an artist. Things were on the move.

... here I am

here we come. . .

Colpix Records, Columbia Pictures Inc., Screen Gems Music Publishing—all different departments of a whole multi-million dollar organization—were all convinced that their new acquisition, this bright-eyed Britisher who had wooed everybody with his performances, was definitely going places.

They were looking for a film for him to star in, or the right song for him to record, or the next smash Broadway show. But somehow they couldn't come up with the right combination. Paul Mazursky and Larry Tucker's brainchild however, was just that. It called for all of Davy's talents—singing, acting, comedy—to be channelled into one zany television show that simply cried out to be made.

The Beatles were riding a wave at that time that was far ahead of anything or anybody else and it was inevitable that someone would try to emulate their successful brand of comedy in the same way that many were already copying their musical style. Mazursky and Tucker were perhaps not the first to come up with the idea, but theirs was the one that clicked.

Certainly later successes such as, 'I Love you, Alice B. Toklas', 'Bob and Carol and Ted and Alice', 'Blume in Love' and Mazursky's solo efforts with, 'An Unmarried Woman' and 'Willie and Phil', have shown that they had truly original talent as screenwriters, which would have surfaced anyway, with or without the success of The Monkees. It may be however, that the show gave them a well-deserved, though short-lived, boost. They wrote the first episode but were soon phased out as the show gained a foothold on the ratings ladder.

Some of the other key people who did get to stick around for the lion's share were:

Bert Schneider—

The son of Abe Schneider, President of Columbia Pictures, Bert began his career as a production assistant for Columbia Pictures, Screen Gems' parent company. In 1954 he moved over to Screen Gems as production assistant in the commercial division, later was named Assistant Treasurer and eventually served the company as Vice-President and Treasurer until 1965, when he moved to Hollywood to enter the field of motion picture and TV production.

In association with Bob Rafelson, he formed Raybert Productions, one of the first independent companies to take offices on the Columbia lot in L.A.. The Monkees was their first venture.

Bob Rafelson—

Co-producer of The Monkees. A native of New York City, he had a degree in philosophy from Dartmouth College and a Master's degree in Theatre Arts from Columbia University. He played drums with a jazz group in Mexico and did a two-year stint in Japan as radio news editor for the Far East Network, at which time he started writing and producing documentaries.

Back in the U.S. he was writer/associate producer on 'The DuPont Show of the Month', and later worked as associate producer of 'Channing' for Revue in Hollywood, and as producer, for Desilu, of 'The Greatest Show on Earth'. At Screen Gems Rafelson co-produced, with Danny Arnold, the pilot episode of 'The Wackiest Ship In The Army', prior to teaming with Bert Schneider in Raybert Productions.

Don Kirshner—

Head of Screen Gems Publishing in New York. His own independent publishing company, Aldon Music, had access to the cream of the day's pop writers, including Carole King, Gerry Goffin, Neil Diamond, Barry Mann, Toni Wine, Bobby Darin and Neil Sedaka—**plus** the team initially responsible for the Monkees' unmistakable sound, Tommy Boyce and Bobby Hart. (They wrote 'The Monkees Theme', 'Last Train to Clarksville', 'I'm Not Your Stepping Stone', 'Valleri', 'I Wanna Be Free', 'She', and many others.)

It was Kirshner who was primarily responsible for choosing which songs the Monkees would record and release, although after the first two albums he was relieved of this responsibility.

Jim Frawley—

A 28-year old dramatic actor who had never directed a TV show when Schneider and Rafelson signed him for their series. With a distinguished acting background on Broadway and in Hollywood, Frawley had spent several years experimenting on film. With his own money, he wrote and produced 'J-24', a thirteen-minute art piece which won an award at the San Fransisco Film Festival. Jim heard about certain 'creative' aspects of the Bert Schneider/Bob Rafelson project and asked to see The Monkees pilot. He liked it. . . screened 'J-24' for Bob and Bert. . . they liked it. And Jim Frawley became a director.

Ward Sylvester—

Employed by Screen Gems in New York, he was sent out to L.A., it seemed, as a sort of 'hatchet man', to fire most of the executives at Colpix Records. Also he was Davy's manager from his Broadway period until the beginning of The Monkees, when he became associate producer for the show.

48

Steve Blauner—

Vice-President of Columbia Pictures in New York. Blauner (who was Bobby Darin's manager in his early days) was perhaps the only one in the Columbia camp who did not believe their bright hope, Davy Jones, was going to make it. "He's too short," he insisted.

Lester Sill—

Vice-President of Screen Gems Publishing. He was put in charge whilst Colpix was being changed to Colgems, the Monkees' label.

There were more, of course—but these guys are the main cast of the story that follows. Stay tuned. . . and if you lose track, don't worry—it's very simple. Basically, the deal is—everybody sues everybody else.

INTER-OFFICE COMMUNICATION

AIR-MAIL

To _____
Attention of ___NORMAN MAURER___
In Regard to _____

From ___Ward Sylvester___
By _____
Date ___February 16th, 1965___

Dear Norman:

Roz Ross asked me to confirm by memo that David Jones will be available for a suitable role in the feature.

Roz and Dick are both aware of the boy's acting credits, and I am enclosing some promotional material the record company has developed. David is now featured in "Oliver" in Chicago.

Since I am feebly trying to coordinate a schedule between television, record and movies; early word as to when and how long you require his services would be appreciated.

Regards,

Howard C. Sylvester, Jr.

HCS:bj
enclosure.

CC: <u>Columbia Pictures</u>

Mike Frankovich
Arthur Kramer
Stanley Schneider
Jonie Taps

<u>Screen Gems</u>

Bert Schneider
Steve Blauner

<u>Publishing</u>

Don Kirshner
Lester Sill

<u>Colpix Records</u>

Bob Yorke
Ben Hurwitz
Orrin Keepnews

<u>Dick Clark Productions</u>

Dick Clark
Roslyn Ross

I left 'Pickwick' in Cincinatti and returned to Hollywood. Ward Sylvester and I rented a house on Ivar Avenue. I'd had a single out on Colpix Records, called 'Dream Girl', which was doing alright. It wasn't a spectacular hit or anything, but it did get me on various bop and pop shows like 'Shindig' and 'American Bandstand'. The songs I was recording in those days were from Don Kirshner's stable of writers. These people would often produce my records as well—usually just on their own particular song.

David Gates produced a couple of things for me around that time and I was very happy for him that he later made it big with his group, 'Bread'. Songs like 'If', and 'I Wanna Make It With You'—they're standards.

But at that time I still didn't have such a song. Ward started spending a lot of time over at Screen Gems. His old friends from New York were there now—Steve Blauner, Bert Schneider, Bob Rafelson. It seemed that everybody was moving out west—the whole business was shifting from New York to L.A. and it was a very productive time to be in California.

Mazursky and Tucker were true to their word and came up with this idea for a show. It was based on The Beatles' 'A Hard Day's Night'—four rock 'n' roll musicians trying to make it—living together in a house on Malibu Beach—sea, sand, surfboards. Replace the Pierre Cardin suits with bathing costumes. . . the two-up, two-down terraced houses of Liverpool with a rambling, California beach house. . . well, maybe it was *nothing* like 'A Hard Day's Night'. Four guys in matching suits, I'll give you that.

The real idea of the show was a band trying to make the big time—their trials on the way up—all the crazy situations that they could possibly get into. The songs were to be happy, fun songs—family viewing, right?

Rafelson and Schneider loved the idea and gave Ward Sylvester the job of scouring L.A.'s music and theatre scene, to try to come up with the other three guys. Meanwhile, they worked on convincing Columbia and Screen Gems.

So Ward and I started going around the clubs. We saw so many groups—didn't know what we were looking for, really. All I knew was that they shouldn't be too good-looking—I didn't want too much competition. I remember we saw Micky Dolenz in a club on Sunset Strip, owned by this guy—Tony, I think his name was. Looked like your typical movie caricature of a gangster—cauliflower-ear, bent nose, spaghetti hanging off his cigar. Everyone kept saying, "Hey, To-o-o-ny!" (If you're reading this, Tony—loved your place. *Loved* it.)

Anyway, Micky was the DJ and he kept coming out with stuff like, "and 'round about now, we're gonna take a pause for the cause—but we'll be back in five for more jive!" I'm thinking, jeez. . . pause for the cause? "Ward, get me outta this place! Hey T-o-o-o-ny—see you!" But Ward sees something in him and wants to stick around.

"Him? You must be joking!"

Suddenly though, Dolenz turns sideways, and I see he's got no profile. ('Skillet Face' we named him later on.) "Okay," I'm thinking. "There's *one* I don't have to worry about. He's in."

So we arrange for Micky Braddock (as he was called) to come along and audition. He had actually been a child-star back in the fifties with a TV show, 'Circus Boy'. Looking at him I could see the connection. But he was an experienced actor and that was good.

We got tó see some interesting groups doing the rounds. One night we saw The Byrds. Then Sonny and Cher doing their thing, in those sheepskin waistcoats they used to wear. Paul and Larry were with us and we got talking about those sheepskin things, and gimmicks in general.

"That's what *we* need. Some sort of gimmick."

Well, the name hadn't been thought of yet. There was The Beatles, The Animals, The Byrds, The Turtles—so we started thinking of animal names. Somebody came up with The Parrots.

"Yeah, that's it—you can all have parrots on your shoulders!"

"Not me, man," I protested. "I ain't having no parrot on me. . . shit all over my clothes!" Good job, too. Can you imagine?—"Hey, hey—we're the Parrots!" No way.

"I know—we'll get a monkey—sort of a mascot for the group." Suddenly, we knew we had it. 'The Monkees'—spelt rong, like Beatles, Byrds. Everybody was excited about it.

Well, we'd eventually exhausted the clubs and come up with Micky, Chip Douglas (a Paul McCartney lookalike who later produced 'Daydream Believer' for us), Jerry Yester (from the Modern Folk Quartet) and Bill Chadwick (who looked a bit like Micky).

Meanwhile, Raybert had convinced the powers-that-were at Columbia, that this show was going to be the next really hot thing. So much so, that Jackie Cooper, Screen Gems TV President, allocated $225,000 for the pilot show. They put the word out to casting agents as far away as Chicago, New York, and even London. The now famous ad, asking for four 'Ben Franks types', went into 'The Hollywood Reporter'.

About five hundred hopefuls showed up at Colpix for some of the strangest auditions ever held. The applicants were insulted, ignored, asked irrelevant or impertinent questions. ("Hey, where'd you get those awful shoes?") A whole arsenal of strange tactics were employed to see how they would react to the unexpected.

At Micky's first meeting with Bert and Bob, so the story goes, Rafelson ignored him completely whilst Schneider was engrossed in balancing paper cups in pyramid formation on his desk. After a minute or two, Micky had the presence of mind to grab a spare cup and slam it down in front of Schneider. . .

"Checkmate!" Apparently it was or we'd never have seen old Skillet Face on our screens.

Peter Tork was a folk musician, jamming with various bands in New York, including The Mugwumps (later to become The Mamas & Papas) and The Lovin' Spoonful. He was friends with Stephen Stills at the time the ad came out. Stills had auditioned but was turned down. (Supposedly he failed because of his crooked teeth.) But he encouraged Peter to try and, as we all know, fate favoured Thorkelson.

Then there was Mike Nesmith. . .

Lester Sill, Ward and I were down at the old Colpix Records offices one morning, to see a certain Michael Blessing. Eleven a.m., on the dot, in walks this guy with his jeans tucked into his high cowboy boots, a green wool-hat on his head, and a pillowcase full of laundry over his shoulder.

"Howdy. Ar'm Michael Blessing. Ar hope this ain't gonna take too long—got ma laundry t'do."

I didn't like the looks of this at all. He was slim, dark-haired *and* good-looking! After a flurry of questions and sharp, witty answers, Mr. Blessing left to do his laundry.

So it came down to a short list of about eight. I was always in because I was already signed to Columbia/Colpix—it was a question of finding the other three. But when it was all decided, I felt like *I* was the odd one out. I went to see Bob and Bert.

Dear Dave:

This memo will confirm our conversation with reference to the arrangement concluded with Michael Blessing regarding his writing contract with the Music Publishing Company.

As I was advised, it will be necessary to put up $5,000.00 to buy Michael out of his existing contract with Randy Sparks. Of this sum, 50 percent will be underwritten by the Music Publishing Company Screen Gems will agree to advance this sum of money.

Please be advised that Raybert Productions has expended $2,000.00 to free Michael Blessing from his personal management contract.

I have been advised that 50 percent ($1,000.00) will be underwritte by the Music Publishing Company, and the other 50 percent by Rayber Productions in line with the formula outlined in my memo of May 27, 1966.

It is understood that twelve songs which will be released Sparks will become the property of Screen Gems Music.

As indicated above, any amounts unrecouped from this advance will be chargeable against the negative cost of the MONKEES series.

Dear Don:

Regarding music for the TV pilot "THE MONKEYS," and talking to Burt Schneider (at Columbia) he has requested two songs be written for the above mentioned pilot. The theme song to be entitled "The Monkeys."

Don, if you feel the title limits the writters lyrically we have the flexibility to chang the title of the theme song if we feel it is necessary. The second song is to be entitled "The Chase." This particular song is to be written around and about the last few scenes of the pilot script.

You suggested Roger Atkins for this particular script and I am in complete accord with your thinking.

I must have Demos and leads on both songs by the 11th of October.

"Look, I feel weird. This is not 'The Beatles Mk. II'—this is three six-footers and a short kid!"

Their answer was that the Monkees should be four guys who are so different from each other, that if you stuck their heads in the sand with their arses sticking up, you'd know who was who. So that's exactly what they did to us for three years. We were perfect—Mike the Texan, Peter from Connecticut, the Skillet from California, and me from Manchester. Four arses!

The pilot was a simple story about a girl who wanted this new group (us, of course) to play at her graduation party. But her father wanted 'Sven Helstrum And The Rhythm Kings'.

It was shot at this private club on some huge estate. We copied the romp scene straight out of 'A Hard Day's Night'— all sped-up stuff with us falling down, doing handstands, bumping into each other. Real corny—but it worked. I suppose it was the first time it'd been done on television.

What is not generally known is that around this time, (the beginning of '66), several other groups, including The Beach Boys, and Jan and Dean, were involved in making TV pilots on a similar theme—but the networks didn't bite, not even for The Monkees at first. After finishing the pilot, they each went back to their own things. It was six months before anything happened.

I kept saying to Ward—
"Don't they like the pilot?"
"What's happening?"
"I'm hungry."
"When do these handcuffs come off?"
Rafelson and Schneider were getting uptight as well. They went home one night, got drunk, cut all the film up, thought better of it—and stuck it back together again in any old order. Worked perfectly! And *that's* how The Monkees style was born. At least, that's their story.

As soon as a commitment had been made by the network, everything started to move fast. Too fast, really. I mean, we'd been thrown together—
"You, you, you and you. You're Monkees. Learn to play instruments."
Mike and Peter were already pretty good musicians. Micky could play guitar and

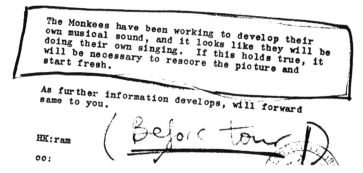

The Monkees have been working to develop their own musical sound, and it looks like they will be doing their own singing. If this holds true, it will be necessary to rescore the picture and start fresh.

As further information develops, will forward same to you.

HK:ram

oo:

Before tou

53

sing but he ended up drumming, simply because, when they asked who wanted to be the drummer, Mike, Peter and I took one step backwards, and there was Skillet Face, volunteering. I was given a tambourine. (People don't realize what a tricky instrument that is. I still can't play it!)

We spent four hours a day, cooped up with each other, trying to be a band—and another four or six hours each day with Jim Frawley, who directed many of the first episodes, doing improvisation work with him, learning how to bounce off each other. For six weeks we did—

"Okay. Be a tree."

"I'm not being a tree, Nesmith wants to be a dog!"

"Okay. Be a gangster. Shoot the dog." So Dolenz would do,

"You dirty rat—you're the one who gave it to my brother." He would always do Cagney in the show. All that sort of stuff. Whatever we each were naturally good at, really.

One day we're all pretty tired—Frawley had been working us hard, and we decide we're taking off. Nesmith jumps in the driver's seat and somebody suggests we get out of Hollywood—we really need a break from the place. I get cosy in the back, Nesmith gets onto the Santa Monica Freeway—and for the first time since I'd arrived there, I'm seeing the L.A. freeway system by day, and it looks great.

Everything's bright and white, and the new gig is starting and we're gonna get something to eat and. . . all these thoughts are dashing around, y'know? This is the first time that the four of us have done anything together. Socially, I mean. I'm looking forward to it.

After a while of just dreaming, I see hundreds and hundreds of ships' masts over to the right. We're coming into Marina del Rey, and from the looks of it, half the population is living in the water. But, more to the point, the water's population is readily available on dry land—the streets are alive with sea-food restaurants. Great—this is just what I fancy.

"Pull up, my woollen-headed chauffeur. Anywhere—there's hundreds of 'em."

Oh, boy. In my mind I'm already tasting lobster drenched in butter. Micky suddenly shouts, "Here. Here!" And Mike promptly pulls into the only *Crummies* for mile around.

'Crummies' is not the real name, of course—I'd get sued, sure as eggs are powder. But it's one of those mass-franchised cheapo family restaurants that America is famous for. The country is inundated with these places from coast to coast—sort of like a certain chain of holiday hotels, only without the bedrooms. The food and furnishings are just as awful whether you're in New Jersey or New Mexico. You always know what you're in for, though—I'll give 'em that.

Suffice to say, my dreams of Sea Food Heaven are severely dashed, and I make a mental note to keep this group idea strictly business.

Once inside, my worst suspicions are confirmed. And not just about the food. Micky Dolenz, it turns out, has the *worst* table manners—atrocious. Probably still has. Fame has no reputation for changing anybody for the better. But to be fair—I admit I'm not prepared to risk finding out. I think I've eaten with him a total of three times since we met—and that's two times too many.

They give us four plates of wilt, called *'Pacific Paradise Salad. . . exotically different'*. There's even a photograph of the original one. I'm sort of playing with my lettuce, trying to find a piece that might put up a fight—still dreaming of hot, succulent, lobster—dripping with garlic butter. . . just like the ones they're serving up the road, down the road and *across* the road. I'm not very happy.

Slowly, I become aware of this banging noise coming from across the table. I look up and there's Dolenz, his fork in a sort of cave-man grip, stabbing repeatedly at his plate. It looks like he's stamping passports. On a busy day. Everytime he spears something, there's half a beat pause while he disposes of it—the salt and pepper pots settle—and then. . . stab, stab, stab again. Really loud. I mean—the whole restaurant's looking at this guy like, "Who's *that?*" And this is just a *Crummies,* y'know? Murderers eat at these places!

Dolenz is oblivious. Stab, stab, stab. Bits of plate and pieces of Paradise flying everywhere. He doesn't care. He just isn't conscious of anything other than getting this garbage down. He's *enjoying* himself. I can't stand any more. I put my knife and fork down and I just stare at him. Stab, stab, stab.

Slowly, Mike and Peter stop talking. Then they stop eating. And now they're just staring at me, staring at him. STAB. STAB. STAB. His eyes catch mine for maybe one stab. Shovelling another mouthload, but without chewing, he glances at Peter, Mike, and then me. Then—chew, stab. . . *stab.* . . STAB.

That's it. I've had enough. I speak up, very deliberately—very slowly.

"Your. . . table manners. . . stink. My dog eats better than you!"

Deathly silence.

"That is the *worst* thing I've ever seen at a table. Anywhere."

Micky really has no idea what I'm talking about. He looks around like, "What'd I do?"

"You're just disgusting, Dolenz. That's all. *Disgusting!"*

Nobody dares speak. I pick up my knife and fork and begin to cut my salad, like a surgeon. I've got them right where I want 'em. Carefully, I place my knife and fork down at the side of my plate—pick up the oil and vinegar dressing, and apply liberally—but very neatly. I replace the bottles in their filthy *Crummies* rack, smile politely at the three stooges—then pick up the entire salad in my bare hands and rub the whole lot in my face. Then my hair, neck, armpits—everywhere. I've got bits of tomato in my ear, oil and vinegar all over my clothes.

"Mmmm. . . exotically different."

The ice is cracked. Pandemonium. You should have seen their faces. Now nobody wants to eat with *me* ever again. Which is just fine by me.

Back to work.

Just before the show first went on the air in America, a promotion guy in a three-piece suit comes up to me and sticks a clip-board under my nose.

"Now then, Mr. Jones. Whose son do *you* want to be?" he asks.

This is in the middle of shooting. I'm just having a quick touch-up with the make-up lady, Cyril—and some flash menial from the network is asking me nonsense questions. It's north, south, east, west—*again.*

"Well?" he asks. "A doctor's son? A lawyer's? What sort of background shall we give you? English gentry? Country estate and all that?"

"What the hell are you talking about?" I say.

"Maybe something more simple might suit you," he drones on. "How about "A country boy at heart"? Yes, that's it! "He grew up on a rambling farm in the Scottish highlands." . . . "

"Just *wait* a minute! Okay?" I stand up and wrench my make-up napkin off. Cyril is tut-tutting. . .

"Thit down, darling—I'm not finished with you *yet*."

I sit. Good dog. More of the powder puff.

"Well, it's just for the promotion, you understand."

"Oh, is it? Well, why didn't you *say* so?" Now I'm up again, strutting around the set—gesturing broadly with my arms, like I'm doing 'Hamlet' or something. The pouf with the puff is trotting after me—he's doing 'Swan Lake'. The suit and clip-board is stumbling over cables. *He's* doing Tom, from Beavertown.

"Well, in that case," I continue, "why don't we say I'm actually the Duke of Openshaw, seventy-third in line to the English throne? My mother was Lady Penelope and father retired from the bar years ago. He's now. . . a *smoking jacket*."

I sit down again. Cyril tries once more. Clearly the three-piece suit is bewildered. Oh well, he's only doing his job, so I decide to put him out of his misery.

"Alright. Just for the promotion, you understand? Me dad's a railwayman. Harry Jones—fitter/engineer. We lived all our life in a two-up, two-down, damp, terraced house with an outdoor toilet—and I'm proud of it!"

I gave him my old home address and all the details of my family life and childhood. The whole story. The promotion people were doing a compilation biography of the four of us. Baby pictures, family snap-shots, the lot. It went to every newspaper, magazine and radio station in the country. They probably even had it up in the post offices. It was hard on my father. Before long, his life wasn't his own anymore.

On Monday, September 12th, 1966, at 7:30 p.m., the first episode of 'The Monkees' was aired in America. NBC had fired the first salvo of their assault on the hearts of young Americans. Even the normally aloof New York Times had some encouraging remarks about the unorthodox production style: "Progress can turn up in the strangest places," they said. And although the initial Neilson ratings placed the show only at number 70 in the TV popularity chart, it nevertheless quickly moved up to the Top 20, and, by mid-season, had an estimated ten million kids glued to their sets every Monday evening.

By October of that year, the group's first single, 'Last Train to Clarksville', was #1 on the American singles chart, selling in excess of 400,000 copies in only three weeks. A month later, their debut album, 'The Monkees', also went to #1, and stayed there for fifteen consecutive weeks, eventually selling over 3,000,000 units, (more than any Beatles album at that particular time). The only record able to knock it from the top spot was their own follow-up album, 'More of The Monkees', which zoomed from nowhere to #1 within a week of its release, greatly helped by advance sales of a million and a half—also more than any Elvis Presley or Beatles album up to that time.

Paul Mazursky and Larry Tucker had written the first episode, but Bob Rafelson and Bert Schneider (Raybert) then assumed complete control. Mazursky and Tucker retaliated by filing suit, claiming they were integral to the whole conception of the show. Schneider retorted by claiming he had been working on the idea himself, since 1962. Eventually it was settled out of court and nobody but the parties concerned knows how much Mazursky and Tucker got. But they were never again seen in connection with The Monkees.

created & produced by
robert rafelson
and
bert schneider

NOVEMBER 5, 1966

Cash Box
November 5, 1966

Billboard

1 LAST TRAIN TO CLARKSVILLE 10/29 10/22
   MONKEES-Colgems-1001   2

This Week
Last Week

THE MONKEES
Colgems COM 101 (M); 102 (S)   7
TITLE—Artist, Label & No. (ABP News & Steve No.)

"The Monkees...the most original situation comedy swinger of this or any other recent season."
—Dwight Newton, S.F. Examiner

"The Monkees...A delectable treat."
—Bob Williams, New York Post

"Beatlemania has been exchanged for Monkeeshines: every Monday night"
—Newsweek

"...frantic fun"
—Variety

"...different but with class and imagination...they threw away the rule book for T.V. comedy."
—Ernest Kreiling, Valley Tribune

"...one of the pleasant surprises of the new season."
—Terrance O'Flaherty, San Francisco Chronicle

"...moments of wonderful wild humor"
—Harriet Van Horne, World Journal Tribune

"...could be the first evening comedy hit of the new season."
—Jack Gould, New York Times

"...completely irreverent, cliche cracking half hour...to see them is to disbelieve."
—Bob Hull, L.A. Herald-Examiner

"Whacky charm"
—Bettelou Peterson, Detroit Free Press

"The Monkees, wild and wooly and full of ginger."
—Daily News

Nielsen #1

Reaching more teenagers than any show on television*

* October 1-November 1, 1966
Nielsen Television index audience composition

Raybert represented the New School of radical thought in American television production at that time. They were responsible for the many zany, way-out, visual stunts and camera pyrotechnics used in the show.

No two episodes had precisely the same ingredients. Raybert tried out new directors from week to week. Film was used, instead of videotape, which gave greater flexibility—allowing new artistic ground to be broken almost every show. Cameras were sometimes hand-held; film was under-exposed, over-exposed, turned upside down, even run backwards; freshly shot material was intercut with archive footage—all of which made for a fast, hitherto unexplored style of television.

Most days there'd be as many as ninety set-ups, compared with an average of twenty-five for conventional shows. And the degree of excitement and camaraderie that was being generated by everyone on the set, was unique in post-unionized filming. Often there'd be conversation back and forth between actors and technicians that would end up on the screen; cameramen would do cameo appearances; the superstars would carry cables—and nobody downed tools. Something special had to be happening for that degree of exhilaration to prevail, week after week. It must, very simply, have been fun—for everyone involved. And that exhilaration communicated itself past the screen and was felt by millions of viewers the world over.

Don Kirshner, President of Screen Gems/ Columbia Music, was the other side of the golden coin; the Old School of established record industry know-how. It was Kirshner who masterminded the musical side of the operation with flawless, commercially-aimed, insight. He had wisely decided, from the outset, not to use Columbia's dying record label, Colpix. Instead he conceived a whole new company, Colgems, and arranged a worldwide distribution deal with the then highly efficient and healthy RCA Company.

Now they had an army big enough, and experienced enough, to explode a phenomenon. With the calculated precision of a Presidential Election, with only one candidate, the advance publicity machine went into overdrive, spearheading a campaign whose intention it was to launch The Monkees as America's answer to The Beatles.

Across the country, thousands of DJ's were given preview records. Radio stations, record stores, the music press—all were inundated with bio-kits, T-shirts and bumper-stickers proclaiming, "Everybody's Going Ape For The Monkees". Weeks before the first Monkee smile was glimpsed on television, franchises were being sold that would soon spawn dozens of Monkee products, such as chewing-gum, green wool-hats and electronic dolls that precociously reproduced each Monkee voice!

By the end of 1966, fan mail was averaging 65,000 letters a week, and foreign TV stations were eagerly bidding for rights to show The Monkees in their territory. The series would eventually be sold to thirty-eight countries, and still today is seen by a whole new generation of Monkees fans, all over the world.

Even for America—this was a **big** one.

"I remember
the first time I heard
'Last Train To Clarksville'
on the radio. . .

Micky and I were
in a car—we
screamed out
with joy and hugged
each other.

Hearing our own records

has never
been quite
the same
as at that
moment."

—Davy—

land of hype and gaudy

*"We just had to show up
and not be drunk."*
—Mike Nesmith—

To the guys behind the scenes it was like a military operation. They planned it that
way, and once we started, it was like *being* in the military—everything was clockwork
precision. It wasn't speculation. It wasn't a gamble. The Monkees were *going* to happen.
The only question was not—would we make it big? But—how big?

We did twenty-six weeks of shooting in that first year. We'd get to bed at four or
five in the morning, and have to be up again at seven for make-up. It was ridiculous. I'd
have to call Ward, my manager, for a diet pill to get me going—then a beer at noon to
give the pill a kick. Not that we were into speed or anything like that—but just to keep
going—to stay awake and get the shows filmed.

I was late one day—three hours sleep—came screeching up to the barrier in my car.
"May I see your pass, sir?"
"Haven't got it, sorry. I was a bit pushed this morning, okay?"
"Can't let you in without a pass, sir. It's The Monkees—we have to have very tight
controls." Some guys just take their jobs too seriously, y'know what I mean? I stick my
head out and I say,
"See this face? I'm *in* The Monkees and I'm late—would you mind lifting the barri-
er?"
"Can't help that, sir. Everybody is issued with. . . "
BANG!—screech—splintered wood—great! Just like the movies. I got famous all
over again for that. Signed what was left of the barrier and had it put up on my wall. Old
Jackie Cooper, the head of Screen Gems TV, called me up to his office for that. Didn't go
though. Went for a beer instead.

We were always pulling stuff like that. I guess we felt we had to be *on* most of the
time. Particularly at the beginning, when it genuinely was fun. I remember when we were
recording the first album, Don Kirshner came in from New York to oversee the sessions.
He was responsible for the selection of the songs and he knew he had hits on the album—
a couple of Gerry Goffin/Carole King tunes—four or five Tommy Boyce/Bobby Hart
numbers. He *knew*. The whole thing was sewn up.

But we were just playing—having a good time. We all thought we were *so* funny, y'know? Dolenz didn't even know who Kirshner was—all he knew was this guy came in and was sitting there saying what a smash hit this album was going to be—a lot of jive about how we were all going to be millionaires. So Micky's going over the top, as usual, and Kirshner says,

"I'll tell you what, boy. I'll give you $50,000 right now in exchange for your first royalty cheque."

Micky just pours a glass of water over Don's head and says, "Yeah, sure."

We had no idea just how big it was going to get. To me it was just another show, another cast. I never thought of it as an ongoing thing.

Not expecting The Monkees to be the phenomenon it was—that's one thing. But it seems as though success has followed you all through your career. Have you ever, in any of your ventures, thought of failure?

I had never had to deal with failure, because I had never failed. Well, there was the eleven plus, yes—and I'd certainly been second in a running race, or lost as part of a team in school soccer, y'know. But in my theatrical experiences—school and church drama groups—it was never a question of win or lose. I never thought about the numbers of people watching 'Coronation Street'—or the audiences in the West End theatre or on Broadway. Same thing with The Monkees. Success breeds succes. I never worried about it—other people were responsible for that department. . . getting the people in. . . advertising and promotion. . . bump di bump di bum.

Now that I think about it though, that is a fear—butterflies—will the people come? But failure just wasn't happening somehow—I mean, the success of The Monkees was only too clear. Lobbies of hotels were always jammed, impossible to move through—a barrage of flash cameras whenever you stepped out of an elevator. All of a sudden people knew my every move. It was as if they'd all received a copy of my schedule. They probably *had*, come to think of it—all part of the plan. The producers were always very careful to make sure there was a commotion—a phenomenon happening. They'd tell the press where we were going to be. It's the whole name of the game—publicity. But I felt as though I were being held hostage. You *must* do this—you *have* to be there—*wear* this—but *don't* say that, whatever you do.

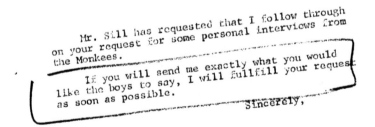

Mr. Sill has requested that I follow through on your request for some personal interviews from the Monkees.

If you will send me exactly what you would like the boys to say, I will fullfill your request as soon as possible.

Sincerely,

Marilyn Schlossberg

MS:hk
cc: Lester Sill
blind cc: Bert Schneider
         Ward Sylvester

They had us walking around wearing these matching grey suits all the time—another Beatles sort of thing, except that each one was diferent in a particular way.

Micky had a one-button jacket—in case he didn't make it, he was going to be a waiter. Mine was double-breasted—quite fashionable. (England was leading the fashion world in those days. Carnaby Street and all that.) Peter had, err—I don't think Peter had a suit, come to think of it. I think he gave his away. Peter gave everything away. Most of the time he was into Hare Krishna, brown rice, waterbeds—that sort of thing. He even gave the hole away where the button was supposed to go. Nesmith's had a sort of Western back—his country image, y'know. He'd tuck his jeans into his cowboy boots and suddenly, all you could see was Texas oil.

Speaking of boots. . . for some reason, just as The Monkees was taking off big, I developed a complex about my height. I don't know what it was—maybe because of working so close to three six-footers. I mean, on Broadway, Oliver was taller than me. I had an extra heel on my shoes—and a double inner-sole—but it never used to bother me. The Beatles arrived and Cuban heels became the fashion anyway.

But now all of a sudden it was different. We'd be filming and they'd need to do a four-shot—tight close-up in one frame—the cry would go out,

Before manmaker

"Man-maker for Davy!"

They'd bring a box for me to stand on. It felt very weird—especially if there was a guest on the set. Usually it was a closed set—Stage 7—the heavy security bit. But occasionally someone's friend was allowed in—and it was always some great-looking lady that someone wanted to impress, y'know. I'd arrive for work—oh no, a *girl!*

"Err—no four-shots this morning, okay fellas? I don't feel up to it."

After manmaker

So they'd start with a barage of four-shots, just to get me. Everybody shouting for man-makers. Just the word made me feel like if I was on a sinking ship I'd be with the women and children.

I thought, "Why now?" I'd never felt short before. Well, shorter than most, but it never bothered me. Now all of a sudden I had this great big thing about it.

On tour people would come up to me and say, "You're so short. I had no idea!" Fourteen and fifteen year old girls would say, "That's okay, I'm into little men."

So I had lifts put in all my shoes. With two-inch lifts and a high heel, I was 5'8". It was great—I was taller than some girls. I could dance with them and check out the other talent at the same time. But it only created more problems. I got so used to them that I felt naked without them. At home it got so bad that if there was a knock on the door—on would go the shoes. Sometimes I couldn't answer the phone without them. It was ridiculous. I even had my bed raised.

"Son. . . your arse is too close to the ground. You've got duck's disease."

—Harry Jones—

I had a list of things I wanted to do someday. Win the Grand National was always at the top. But that got replaced with—give up my lifts! I guess like an alcoholic dreams of quitting. It was really hard. But I did it. One day I just decided—no more. I kicked the habit and haven't looked down since.

Davy in Marlboro Country

It was around the beginning of 1967 that the music press, the national press, and to a certain extent, their peer performers, all started to come down on the Monkees like the proverbial ton of bricks. Their common gripe was that they were musically inept and didn't play on their own records.

The Monkees—and a spoof that paid off

A DISGRACE TO THE POP WORLD

THE MONKEES—from left: Peter Tork, Mike Nesmith, Davy Jones, Micky Dolenz.

THIS idiotic Monkee business—was ever a bigger spoof pulled on the pop world?

Today the Monkees' single disc I'm A Believer, has reached No. 1 in the British charts supplied exclusively to the Sunday Mirror by the

New Musical Express. Next week their LP, which sold 3½ million in the U.S., is to be issued in Britain.

THEIR disc?

The truth is that on their TV show, seen on BBC on Saturdays, the group—three Americans plus Davy Jones from Britain—rarely play their instruments. Most of the time they just sing and appear to

pluck their guitar strings while professional musicians discreetly hidden in the studio provide the real beat.

Their musical fame is the result of a gigantic Hollywood TV publicity campaign. The Americans never forgave the Beatles for not being born there, so they decided to create their own. Even the Monkees' TV show is a prolonged imitation of Beatles films.

The fact that the big spoof came off, making the Monkees No. 1 on both sides of the Atlantic, is a downright disgrace an insult to pop fans, a threat to the pop business as a whole and a deterrent to any youngster who has a musical future in mind.

Musicians like myself spent years of hard practice before being able to earn a living then comparable to a grocery assistant's.

Talent

Even the lowliest pop group in Britain can't get a job in a local pub without *some* hard work. Have you ever tried learning the simplest of instruments—the guitar?

To play a few simple chords in tune is no easy matter. Yet here is a bunch of kids trading on other people's talent and cashing in on millions.

Musically, comparing the Monkees with the Beatles is like comparing a milk float with a Mercedes.

The astounding thing about their second-hand fame is that they found it on records before they first exploded on America's TV screens.

Their first disc, Last Train to

Charlesville, sold half a million copies. Another half million were snapped up after the group's first TV performance.

Although the Monkees do play guitars after a fashion, the same musicians who played out of camera range for the TV shows also helped the group make the first million-seller disc.

It took a lot of careful handling when the studio gently broke the news to American fans that the Monkees did not actually provide their own music for TV.

Now their press agent says the Monkees have started playing on TV "whenever time permits."

He adds: "Everything was so hectic and filmed in advance that there wasn't time for them to play their own music at first."

The Monkees have no immediate plans for a British visit, but are booked for a tour across America and tickets have already been sold out in most major cities. Their agent promises that there will be no studio musicians backing them up on this trip.

"It was like the press suddenly getting very angry that Raymond Burr was not really a practicing lawyer, or that Ben Casey wasn't making house-calls. We were actors in a TV show. Period."
—Mike Nesmith—

TOP POPS

Last Week's ratings in brackets

1 (9) I'm A Believer—Monkees
2 (1) Green Green Grass Of Home—Tom Jones
3 (4) Happy Jack—Who
4 (2) Morningtown Ride—Seekers
5 (3) Save Me—Dave, Dee, Dozy, Beaky, Mick and Tich
6 (5) Sunshine Superman—Donovan
7 (6) Any Way That You Want Me—Troggs
8 (12) Sitting In The Park—Georgie Fame
9 (7) In The Country—Cliff Richard
10 (—) Standing In The Shadows Of Love—Four Tops

Compiled by New Musical Express

Of course we didn't play on the backing tracks of those early records. Mike and Peter were competent enough, but as a group we weren't anywhere near capable yet, and the studio couldn't afford to wait around while we got it together. They had to get albums out—now. They had shows to film—*now*. We had promotional visits to fulfill. There weren't enough hours in our day as it was.

And the thing is, it wasn't unusual—loads of groups had session musicians playing on their records, including The Beatles, The Beach Boys, The Byrds. . . At least we owned up. We never tried to hide the fact that we mimed the instruments on the TV show.

The pressure, to refute their critics by performing live, was growing daily. When the day's filming was over they'd then rehearse at night to perfect a live show. Soon, on December 3rd, 1966, they were to play their debut concert at the Miss Teenage Hawaii Pageant. The reaction was genuine, full-blooded hysteria (described by Billboard as "a violent riot with 50 club-wielding cops wailing into the hysterical crowd.")

Things are certainly happening very fast and although the guys are here and others, I'm afraid. It's only going to be a few more hours before we see or should I say meet face to face with 10,000 screaming teenagers. I know I'm going to smile maybe even go close to them, close enough to feel the heat from their bodies. I don't really know them—come to think of it they don't know me either, only from the T.V. They see me once a week so they will recognize me right off. I hope I'm what they expected me to be like. I hope I don't disappoint them. We have about 4 hours to go and now I've got my fears off my chest I feel a little better.

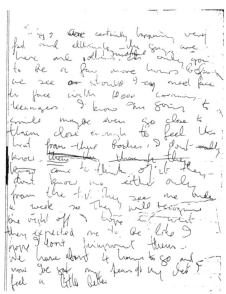

The TV show had only just aired about a month over there, but they had ploughed bags of money into promoting the concert. We only did four or five numbers, and you couldn't hear us for the screaming—we were a big hit.

A reception party was given for us the next day at a private home on the beach. Lots of island people. It was great looking out the bay-windowed living room onto a quiet stretch of beach. Music playing, girls everywhere—I was in my element. Then suddenly—

"Hello. My name is Linda Haines."

Hello, hello, *hello*. A beautiful girl—long brown hair and legs to match. I was in love. Unfortunately, so was my aide and bodyguard, David Pearl. Casual talk—bump di bump di bum. And then she was gone.

It's corny I know, but it really was love at first sight. Later on that night she turned up at the hotel. My heart started again. Somehow, we all got together for cocktails in Bert and Judy Schneider's suite. Pearl talked more than I did and she ended up in his room. I thought about it for a minute or two and then she became just another pretty girl I had fallen for that day. Except that I awoke still thinking about her—her face, her form, her manner—everything. I couldn't get her out of my mind.

Pearl and I had adjoining rooms and the next morning I opened my door and there she was, coming out of his bathroom. I tried to think of something casual to say as I wandered in, but nothing would come out.

"I didn't sleep with him," she whispered as we passed.

"I thought you weren't going to stay," I said.

"I didn't sleep with him," she repeated.

I left. A funny way to start a marriage.

Hawaii had certainly had an effect on me. I'd met two people who, for vastly different reasons, I couldn't seem to get out of my mind. Linda was one. The other was the Russian poet and defector, Yevgeny Yevtushenko. I don't know why I kept thinking about him—or her, really. I'll never understand either of them.

Columbia sent me to London just after the Hawaii concert to do a couple of weeks of interviews and promotion for the show. The record company and the BBC had already had a campaign going over there for weeks. *The Monkees Is Coming,* was the slogan. They had ads all over the place and on television all the time. Just—*The Monkees Is Coming, The Monkees Is Coming.* That's all.

So when I got to Heathrow there was a Rolls to meet me, record company photographers, etc.. I'm in my toy suit—and there's these girls posing with me. Dolly model-types, y'know—miniskirts, the whole bit. Only these girls are *hired*—they don't know what's going on. They're standing there, draped all over me, probably thinking, "Who's this little shit?" It felt really weird.

Anyway, I eventually get up to Manchester and knock on the door. My dad's pretending he won't let me in. He gets ten shillings out of his pocket and says,

"Go an' get yer 'air cut. . . an' tell 'im to cut it t' th' wood!"

"Aw, c'mon, dad—Charlie's is closed today, it's Wednesday." He lets me in.

"You look a right mess, son."

"Thanks, dad. Hey, listen—you're not going to believe it—they're going mad back in the States. I can't walk down the streets."

"I don't care what's 'appening in bloody America," he says. "Don't come 'ome with a big 'ead, son!"

"Yes, dad."

There's a long pause.

"I hope it doesn't get too much for you," I say.

"Gerraway with yer!" he says—and gives me a look like— "I've lived through more than *you'll* ever know."

But in a couple of weeks it was already starting.

I returned to the States and celebrated my birthday on the plane over. December 30th, 1966—twenty-one today! I'm real tired and I need a drink, so I ask the stewardess to give me a beer. She decides the only thing she's going to give me is a hard time.

"I'm afraid I can't serve you alcohol. You're under age."

Aha—got her! I take out my driver's license.

"Have a look at *that*, sweetheart," I taunt. "Today's my birthday. I'll have three beers, please!"

"What *time* were you born?" This girl's a real smart arse—I'm starting to fancy her.

"Very funny," I say. "Opening time!" (I fancy her even more after the beers.)

That's when I started drinking.

January 4, 1967

Mr. Bert Schneider
Raybert Productions
1334 North Beechwood Drive
Hollywood, California

Dear Bert:

This is to confirm our phone conversation of last evening regarding activity on The Monkees' record internationally:

First, some really wonderful news which I received this morning from England; the new single, I'M A BELIEVER has sold 230,000 in five days - one of the fastest takeoffs for a record in that market in years. This is even before the show has had impact, since the first screening was Saturday night - so, I think we can look towards a strong establishment of the act in the English market.

Much credit here must be given to the combination of factors, namely, a great record; the introduction of the show with tremendous advance publicity on the part of RCA and the BBC as well as the local Screen Gems people plus - finally - the intangible extra that Davy Jones' personal appearance in England for some thirty six hours of interviews, etc. gave.

As I mentioned on the phone, the top fifteen international record markets for the industry are as follows:

England	$ 130 million
Japan	80 "
Germany	70 "

the fans

*"Son, it's lovely to
see you—but bugger
off!"*   —Harry Jones—

*After that first visit home to promote The Monkees in Britain, Davy never
again saw his father under comfortable conditions.*

*The first show aired in Britain on New Year's Eve, 1966. That same week their
second single, 'I'm a Believer', was number one worldwide. It sold 400,000 in England alone during the first week of release, eventually reaching two and a half million sales. Monkeemania had hit Great Britain.*

*Scenes rivalling the heady days of Beatlemania were now commonplace
wherever the Monkees went, whether as a group or individually.*

*Davy's sister, Beryl, could probably see the effects of this sudden adulation
more clearly than could Davy himself—at least inasmuch as it affected the Jones
Family. It eventually became impossible, even undesirable, for Davy to stay at the
house he'd recently bought for his father. Every visit caused pandemonium, and even
when in he was in America, a hardcore nucleus of fans held vigil outside the house.*

Beryl—
"It's very strange what fans will do—what they want of a
person. One time, when they knew Davy was in Manchester,
the whole street was packed. It was like a football crowd. The
police tried to cordon off the road, but fans just came inbetween the houses. There were literally hundreds of girls screaming, "Davy, Davy, we love you!" Funny way of showing it. The
garden was trampled. They were all pushed up against the
front door, which had a central glass panel.

Davy didn't come that day. Well, he did, but seeing it was
impossible to get through in the police van—the fans were almost pushing it over, rocking it from side to side—they sped
off again. But the girls never gave up. Some of them were
sleeping in the park shelters; others just stayed outside all
night.

About two in the morning I heard that glass door panel
break. I thought, "Oh, God, they're comin' in!" I went to get a
brush to clear up the pieces, but there were none left. They'd
taken it all. They took broken bricks from the garden wall, too.

And all the flowers.

Newspaper reporters used to offer money to the people across the street to let them use a room overlooking our house—just so they could sit and wait for Davy and catch him. But Davy was too clever for them.

One morning I was in the living room and saw this girl clambering over our back fence, breaking it in the process. She came running up to the window, knocking and shouting.

"Bloody go away!" I yelled. Then she took this turban thing off her head and I saw that it was Davy. In a dress and all made up! It was the only way he could get in past the fans—by pretending to be one of them.

It was like Starsky and Hutch around here that day. The house was swarming with police—all drinking dad's whisky. Davy had brought him a crate of the most expensive stuff from America, and I can remember dad looking at the empty bottles, "Look at that. Four pound three and bloody fourpence a bottle—gone! *My* whisky!"

It was just sad, really. Davy wanted to stay, but he couldn't. Not with all the commotion it was causing. Dad was very ill with emphysema, and it was all too unsettling for him.

To get Davy away the police drove a decoy van up to the house and some coppers—all huddled together—scrambled in and took off as fast as they could—with most of the mob screaming and chasing after them. Then another van came the other way and Davy was able to make a dash for it and get away unmolested. I felt ever so sorry for him."

"The cops who drank the whisky."

He wrote me a letter a few days after that saying, "Nice to see you. Thanks for the whisky. And by the way, you owe me £9.12s. 6d for the fence."

The fans can murder you. They love you but like Beryl says—they've got funny ways of showing it sometimes—in numbers, at any rate. Individually they're fine. I'm asked for autographs all the time and though you hope they never stop asking altogether, it's also a pain sometimes. Like when you're at an airport say, and you've suddenly got to find a toilet, bad. You don't want to appear rude but you've got no choice and you *do* appear rude. I mean, you either ignore them, which is wrong, or you tell the truth.

"Hi, I'm Debbie. I've got all your records and I go to all your concerts. I think you're fantastic. Would you mind if my friend took a picture of the two of us together?"

"Sorry, Debbie—got to take a pee."

It kind of blows the image.

I overheard a guy talking to his friend once, in Vegas. He was telling him how he'd just seen his favourite entertainer in the hotel lobby, and had gone up to him, saying he'd been an admirer for twenty years and how he'd flown all the way from New York just to see his show—thought he was terrific and just wanted him to know that. That's all.

And this 'entertainer' just said, "So what?"

72

The fellow was stupefied—said he felt like going home and breaking every one of his records. I felt like asking the guy who it was so that next time *I* saw him I could punch him in the nose. I mean, you can't ever forget your responsibility to your fans. That's the theory, anyway. Ninety-eight per cent of the time I like to think I manage it.

Alright, you have to balance it. If you try too hard to please you can overdo that, too. Like Micky when we were doing the Wembley gigs.

We're staying at the Royal Garden Hotel, Kensington, and there we all are, drunk and who knows what else, and we stay up all night partying, y'know? Then around eight in the morning, Dolenz is higher than the Post Office Tower and he announces he's going out to talk to the kids. There are like hundreds and hundreds of kids down in Hyde Park, right? Princess Margaret sent a letter of complaint about the noise. So did I.

"Yeah, great Micky. You go talk to 'em—cheer 'em up."

So he's in these long, black robes—some sort of dressing gown—and he goes down there and gets on some bandstand or something, and he starts preaching about love and understanding—giving—caring—sharing. Anyway, he's going on and on down by the pond there. Glorious summer's morning—the kids are on their way to school—birds singing—he's playing Jesus. They're flocking from all directions. The sermon on the mound. Three thousand kids are being told about love by a crazed guy, half out of his brains with no sleep.

The bodyguards are thinking they need more artillery—it's getting dangerous. Of course, I'm on the tenth floor with binoculars so I don't care, I'm safe. I think the whole thing's hysterical.

Now he starts singing. Everybody joins in. Very emotional. No seriously, it really was a beautiful thing. Have you ever heard Micky sing? Moves you to tears. He can make a wall cry. Anyway, the police are pleading—

"You've got to go, Mr. Dolenz—*please.*"

Well, the song's over—and Micky's run out of biblical quotes, so he just very calmly says, "I'm very tired now. I need rest. I have a show to do later. You must make way for me."

Right. Tell 'em, Micky. He takes about three steps and the whole three thousand jump on him—rip his robes to shreds. Well—he sobered up *real* quick I can tell you.

Later I'm saying to him—c'mon Skillet Face, let's go out, man.

"Are you crazy? You saw what happened out there!"

"Look," I say. "It's not that bad. You can go out if you dress normal—forget the flowing robes and the sermons bit—the camera crew—the lights—of course you'll get clobbered. But if you can just, well. . . wear a suit, order a guinness and talk about the price of eggs, you'll be okay. Okay?"

"We can't. We can't!"

"For Chrissake's, Micky, c'mon. . . we're just ordinary guys. We'll put on a suit—preferably two—go down Kensington High Street, into Biba's—check out the girls. No problem."

So Micky puts some real clothes on and we go out the service entrance. We're out on the side street. We take four steps and there's half a dozen kids coming at us. Ten steps—twenty kids. We can't go back through the service door, it's locked—so we have to go round the front.

Well, there are hundreds of kids, screaming and running. It looks like a scene from 'Jaws'—and Micky and I are the bit of beach they're trying to get to! Panic. This is the

first time either of us has been on a street in a year. We don't know what to do. "Where's the limo?"

We nip into a pub. More pandemonium. We get out through a side door and start sprinting for the hotel—pursued by this mad crowd. We're laughing, but deep down we're really frightened. We run up the hotel ramp and into a side entrance, only to come face to face with two plate-glass doors—locked. Hundreds of screamers coming at us.

Now this just shows you the power of adrenalin—what you can do when you're scared shitless. We pull at the doors—two great big eight foot by four foot panels of thick glass, mind you—and the whole lot shatters! We're not even grazed. We're just standing there with two door handles in our hands. Sheer terror did that!

We dash through and make it safely back to our rooms.

"Hello, room service? Err. . . two doors, please."

While we were at the hotel, our names would ring out for hours on end down in the street. . . "Day-vee! Day-vee!" "Mickee! Mic-kee!" I developed agoraphobia for a while. At least, I think it was agoraphobia. Which one's that—crowds or open spaces? Well, I had it anyway. I had them all. We used to 'wall-crawl' around the hotels—sliding around from room to room so nobody saw us. It got to be a game, actually 'cos we always had the whole floor anyway—with a platoon of armed riot police guarding the elevators and stairs. Only a highly-trained guerilla terrorist troupe could have got to us. Usually.

In Japan, however—we were there during the '68 student riots—our lives had been threatened. The police were using night sticks to hit the fans, our limo was literally brushing people aside. I couldn't watch. We couldn't get out or we'd be crushed. The kids were jumping all over the car. Terrifying.

One night I got back to my room after the show—police outside my door, as usual. I'm just dropping off to sleep, when all of a sudden I hear this noise. I begin to panic, remembering the death threats. Then I hear voices. Oh, no. I lie there, not knowing what to do. I decide to go for it—jump up and switch on the light. I got such a shock—four little girls—couldn't have been more than fourteen years old. How they'd managed to get by the police and into my room, I'll never know.

"Please, Daby. . . we have your autoglaph?"

People always ask me what it was like being a *pop idol*— did I get all the girls? Oh, sure—can you imagine?

"Come up to my room, darling. It'll just be you and me—and the vice squad."

They could be real helpful, the cops—saved our lives many times. But they could also be a pain in the arse.

Once, in Texas somewhere, we'd done the gig and we had a day off. We were supposed to go to the local radio station but the other guys didn't feel like it, so I went alone. Did the interview—"Yeah, everything's going great. . . " bump di bump di bum. "We may be coming to your town so—see you next time!"

Left the station in the cop car. The guy's telling me all about his wife and his two kids who *love* The Monkees, y'know. I'm looking about and I see, 'Dallas—44 miles'.

"Err, excuse me. Aren't we going the wrong way?"

"No, don't you worry, boy—ar'm just droppin' off home to see ma wife for a minute."

Sixty-eight miles later. . . we've gone past Dallas—forget Dallas! We're in some tiny hick town with one dog in it. He pulls up to his iddy biddy house with his siren blasting out so the three neighbours can see he's caught himself a Monkee.

The kids are all shy and his wife's sort of embarrassed, but she's obviously used to this. They had Elvis over for tea last week.

"Want some coffee?. . . cake?"

"Err, no thanks—I'd better be going actually."

"Oh, nonsense!"

Nonsense? What does he mean, *nonsense*?!

Well, what he means is he's going to keep me there. I mean—to all intents and purposes I'm under arrest on suspicion of being Davy Jones.

"How do you plead?"

"Guilty, your Honour."

"In that case, I have no alternative but to sentence you to play with the officer's spoilt kids and eat his wife's appalling cake. Court dismissed."

Got back four hours later.

"Where've you been?"

"Been home with a policeman eating cake, what d'you think?"

I got a call from a doctor in a hospital in Phoenix, Arizona, one time. How he found me—I don't know, but here he was on the other end of the line telling me about two little girls who were crossing the road with their Monkees albums, which they'd just been out to buy, and they'd got run over. One of them had very bad leg damage and the other had been unconscious for six weeks.

Well, now she's come around and they're playing her Monkees records in the hospital, and the doctor calls to say it would just be the greatest thing for them both if Davy Jones were to visit them out of the blue.

Well, you get a lot of this sort of thing, and it's really hard sometimes. But this guy is really genuine, I can tell—so I say I'll come if he'll promise not to let the press know. Right! Boy, is he excited! We have a deal.

I get on a plane to Phoenix, and I go to the hospital. I must admit I'm pretty excited myself, just thinking how excited these girls are going to be. You should have seen their faces. Now I know how Santa Claus feels. You can't measure moments like that. If I'd had to fly twice around the world, it would've been worth it.

So we have a little group picture taken, and I meet their families. Both girls live on the same little street in Phoenix—real homey. It's all very moving. Felt nice.

Then a couple of months later I get invited back to this little girl's house for dinner, (the one who'd been in a coma), and I think—yeah, that'd be nice—go and have dinner and see how they're doing. So there I am—and at dinner there's this sixty-year old guy, Tif, and his wife, Clara. He's thin as can be—he's got emphysema, just like my dad and mum died of. They both live out in the desert.

Now, I don't know why, (well, maybe I do if I think about it)—but I found myself on a plane to Phoenix a couple of times. I wanted to see the kids, sure—but I really wanted to see Tif and Clara in their tiny little house on the edge of the desert. . .

I heard you were given the Keys to the City for that incident with the girls?

Yeah, well. . . the deal is, they give you the Keys to the City in a lot of places. It's when you come back, you find they've changed the locks. Hollywood, y'know—they give you an image and then if you don't live up to it. . .

I was in this supermarket once—just stepped out to get a loaf of bread, basically. It's about 1:00 a.m. and I'm checking out the counters—six-pack of beer, okay—don't forget the bread—ooh, those tomatoes look nice. I'm just sort of enjoying the late hour, y'know. Shopping's great for me at that time of night—no lines and usually nobody hassles me.

Wrong. All of a sudden I'm attacked by four or five guys and a girl, right in the middle of the frozen vegetables.

"Hey! You're Davy Jones, right?"

"No."

"Hey, c'mon man—we *know* you are."

"I used to be."

"Listen—this is incredible—this'll blow you away, Davy—you've just *got* to help us, man."

"I've *got* to?"

"Please, man—it'll be far out."

Well, they explain to me that they were at this party, see? And for a forfeit in some stupid game they were playing, they had to go out and bring back a movie star. If they didn't bring one back, they were out of the game. So this is serious, right? Who wants to be out of the game?

I'm sort of eyeing them whilst I shop. I don't recognize Manson amongst them—should I? Brocolli—that'll be good. . . sprouts—I love sprouts. Will I be front-page news tomorrow morning? —'The frozen vegetable murders!'

I switch aisles. Ah, millet. . . somebody I know will love that.

"So how far is this party anyway?" I sort of fancy the girl.

"Not far, man. Aw, c'mon, Davy—we'll get ya high for this, man!" Everything's man with these guys.

"What d'ya drink, man?"

"Everything."

So they take me in their car—into Hollywood somewhere. We pull up at this middle-class, real suburban-type house—front lawn up to the street—kiddies' tricycle left out on the sidewalk. The party's going full swing, but not real loud or anything—they're not junkies, these people. . . just your average, middle-income kidnappers.

Well, we have to do this right—right? So they chair me on their shoulders like I'm their trophy, and they stumble in, shouting and cheering themselves all the way. Looks like the rest of the party gave up this silly game hours ago—they're into crawling all over each other by now—it's got *much* more promise. The only thing this movie star game's any good for, is getting rid of four or five creeps who you didn't want at your party in the first place.

They let me down in the middle of the room—somebody turns the stereo off—all eyes are riveted on me. . .

"Ladies and Gentlemen. . . " my captors proudly announce. "Davy Jones!"

There's a moment's silence. Then, from somewhere in the back—

"Naaarr. . . we said *movie* star, Kirby. He's TV."

That's when I started drinking. Hung out for a while, man.

5 25 66

SCREEN GEMS
COLUMBIA MUSIC INC.
7033 SUNSET BLVD.   SUITE 318
HOLLYWOOD, CALIF.   90028

THE Hollywood REPORTER

Price 10 Cents

Hollywood, California, Thursday, March 16, 1967

Vol. CXCV, No. 1

$35½ Mil Suit Over Kirshner Discharge

New York. — Don Kirshner, former creative head of the Colgems Record Division of Columbia Pictures and Screen Gems, filed a $35,500,000 suit in Federal Court yesterday against the film company, Screen Gems, Columbia-SG president Abe Schneider, SG executive v-p Jerome S. Hyams, Burton Schneider, son of Abe Schneider and president of Rayburt Productions. Latter produces "The Monkees." The suit charges breach of contract and alleged conspiracy leading to Kirshner's discharge from the disc unit Feb. 27.

One of the plaintiff's attorneys, Jerome Stein, told The Hollywood Reporter that Kirshner is still president of Columbia Pictures-Screen Gems Television Music Inc., publishing company, and has nine years to go under this contract, which provides for a profit participation. Stein said that Kirshner also had been president of Colgems until the termination of that pact.

In the complaint, Kirshner claims he was hired as creative head of Colgems for five years, starting last August at $35,000 a year or 15% of the profits from Colgems, whichever was greater. He alleges that Colgems made a profit of $1,450,000 on two albums and two single records by "The Monkees." Notwithstanding, he said he was discharged.

He claims breach of contract for which he demands $17,000,000 in damages. A second cause of action charges an alleged conspiracy among the individual defendants and Rayburt This, Kirshner asserts, resulted in termination of his contract although his efforts in behalf of Colgems had been successful. On this cause, he asked $17,000,000 in compensatory damages; $500,000 for inconvenience, embarrassment and injury to reputation and $1,000,000 in punitive damages.

*sue you. . . sue me**

"Throw your arms around, son—they'll think you've got money."
—Harry Jones—

" What's THIS?" Jackie Cooper had called me up to his office again. This time to wave a newspaper at me.

"Irish raincoat?. . . I give up." (North, south, east, west.)

"It's disgusting, that's what it is! You're bad-mouthing the studio, David. We can't tolerate that sort of thing."

Well, apparently I'd mouthed off to the press again—complaining about the spons-ors or something—and they had said, well. . . didn't the Monkees get given four cars by Pontiac for their *personal* use? Like—did I complain when they gave me a car? And I'd said something like—

"No, but that doesn't mean they own us—for a lousy car. And in any case the studio got forty-one cars, six African elephants, two Boeing 747's and an Apollo spacecraft!"

It was childish, but they were treating us like children. I shouldn't have got upset about it, I suppose. I mean—it's nice, people *giving* you things, isn't it? But then if they turn around and say you *owe* them for it—that's different. It's manipulation.

That's the difference between the fans' giving, and the sponsors' or the network's giving. I mean—I once told a magazine that I liked cuff-links—it was one of those stupid questions they ask, y'know—"What's your favourite article of clothing?"—something like that. And I couldn't say what I wanted to say, which was "a bra", or "suspenders", because with Columbia it was worse than having your parents around all the time. We could be funny, so much the better—but not the wrong kind of funny. So I said I liked cuff-links. Without thinking. It was safe. Stupid really, because I *don't* like cuff-links—never have.

Well, over the next few weeks I got hundreds of cuff-links—actually, well over a thousand pairs. Some gold, some with valuable stones. . . it was very touching. A bit over the top—but then, it happened all the time. We were always receiving sackloads of gifts and letters in the mail. Even now I get hundreds of letters and little packets of choco-late and stuff, from all over the world. The TV show is on every day *somewhere*, I guess. How d'you think I'm surviving? I live on chocolate.

But back then it was a shame really—so much *good* stuff happening to us all—and I

*Used without permission. But Lionel—you're not going to sue *us*, are you?

mean us *all*. . . the network, the label, the writers, producers—hey, it was a nice thing that was happening for everybody. It was fun—and should have stayed that way. Why not? Why can't it stay that way? Whenever there gets to be millions flying around—instead of everyone enjoying it, they all start sueing each other. There was so much strain coming into the whole thing. Lawsuits all over the place. Just a load of greedy kids with every toy in the store—yelling for more. It was really starting to piss me off.

Kirshner was sueing Screen Gems for about thirty-five million, I think it was—something reasonable like that. Mazursky and Tucker were sueing Raybert. Producers of a show called 'Liverpool U.S.A.' were sueing Columbia for supposedly stealing *their* idea—when it was all inspired by The Beatles, anyway. Everybody screwing everybody else as soon as they got half a chance. Nobody seemed to care.

In all this time, the most I'd sent my dad was £7.50 a week—(about $10.00). It was all he'd accept. So at the end of February '67, after we'd done the first six months of The Monkees, I had some time off and I told Ward Sylvester that I wanted to go home to England—supposedly to take a holiday—but really I wanted to buy some gifts for my family and deliver them personally.

So Ward went and spoke to Columbia and we ended up discovering something pretty incredible. I wasn't under contract! At least not securely, as far as Columbia was concerned—I was still on my old Colpix recording deal, but that was running out soon.

Well, I didn't want to hold them to ransom or anything—but I mean, we could've come away with a good deal right then and there—one that would've been fair to *both* sides. But Ward was associate producer of the show now—so, he wasn't about to rock the boat, y'know? I think you'd call it a conflict of interests—trying to represent me and them at the same time.

What happened was Columbia gave me $25,000 to go home with—as an advance against royalties. Well, I was young and pretty inexperienced in these matters. All I'd done before was stage acting—a little recording on Colpix, but no hits. This was BIG time—I should've got some heavy representation 'cos there was *millions* at stake and I knew nothing about publishing rights, royalties, residuals, merchandising, etc.. Twenty-five grand *sounded* like a million to me right then—I was impatient—I just wanted to get home and throw my arms around.

So I signed a deal—a whole load of new contracts giving them my exclusive services and making me a contracted member of The Monkees on a basic salary of $450 a week, period. Probably I wouldn't have if I'd known how to handle myself. But I was rushed and I'd got the impression that if I didn't sign I couldn't get my share of the royalties off the first two albums. Not true but—what did *I* know? I thought I was being taken care of.

Well that $450 a week covered all the concerts, live appearances—everything. We were on salary—no percentage of the gate like groups get these days. On the very last tour we did—Japan and Australia—I personally saw $90,000, and then on another night, $60,000, being counted out in our hotel room. And that was the *last* time I saw it!

But anyway, for the time being I'd got my twenty-five grand and I went home. Threw my arms around that time, alright. Bought my dad a house—my three sisters a present each. I purchased two race-horses, 'Chicamomo' and 'Pearl Locker', to stable with Basil Foster—and I was broke again. Just like blowing your Friday night's pay at the pub. But that's alright—I'd done just what I'd wanted to do—bought my round. No problem.

It was just such a relief to be out of all that madness for a while. It wasn't gone—there were still the fans to contend with, and the press wherever I went—but at least I could breathe.

I went to Basil's stables, rode a bit, put my two horses into a couple of races—didn't do too well—one of them hasn't finished yet. I just generally hung out with the stable lads and the horses for three months. It seemed like I'd left that behind so long ago—I needed to feel it again for a while. Not that I thought I wouldn't go back to The Monkees, but it'd all got a little out of hand and I'd had enough for right then. It doesn't hurt to take a giant step back occasionally—you can see more clearly where you've been. Plus I was missing Linda—couldn't get her off my mind, even though I knew she was going with David Pearl.

Anyway, as usual the press wanted to make headlines of something—anything. This time it was me being in England for so long. They wondered if The Monkees was over. Reporters would ask, "You mean you're going back to horses now?" They always seem to have such a narrow outlook—you're either doing this or you're doing that—you can't do both.

So they made a big thing out of it and two or three days later I'd be thinking—yeah, I'm with the horses again—feels good. All that Hollywood stuff seemed a million years ago. And yet, three months later, I was back with The Monkees at Wembley Stadium and it was like I'd never been away. Hysteria again. Helps cover up a multitude of pains.

It was July 1st, 1967. And it was hot.

London's Empire Pool, Wembley, was jam-packed with ten thousand hysterical teenagers—just as it had been the previous night, and would be for another three shows—all sold out.

The Monkees were playing five concerts in three days and by the time the riotous scenes had died down, 50,000 screaming fans had turned out to cheer on their 'home' boy, David Jones.

Monkeemania had hit England.

Backstage, Davy had asked for a telephone to be installed as close as possible to the stage. His father hadn't been able to come to the concert because of ill-health. But Davy's sisters and all their friends (practically the whole street) had come down from Manchester that morning, in a chartered coach, and were staying in a London hotel for the weekend. This was a special occasion. . . Davy's triumphant return home.

"Okay, me ol' mate—this is it!" he shouted down the line, laying the receiver on a table facing the stage. The Monkees then went out to be greeted by a roar—an almost solid screaming sound—that must have been a strangely unsettling, yet exhilar-

ating kind of music to their ears.

An hour or so later, in spite of the persistent demand for yet another encore, the show finally ended and the boys came off stage for the last time. Harry Jones had been on the other end of the line all of that time and Davy grabbed the phone, eager to get his Dad's verdict.

"What the bloody 'ell was all that about?" said Harry. "What a bloody row! You mean to say you came all the way from America to do that? You must be bloody joking!"

Pause.

"That Lulu was good, though. I'll tell you one thing, son—she can't 'arf put a song over." Davy laughed. He should have known better.

"Well, as soon as I've done another three of these 'bloody rows' I'll be up to see you," he said.

Despite this outward show of indifference however, Davy's father was actually fiercely proud of his only son.

"If you see them bloody Bee Gees, ask 'em if they got my letter, will yer?"

He'd read an article where various music business people were knocking the Monkees, saying that they didn't sing on their own records, etc., and apparently the Bee Gees had said some not too complimentary things about them. So Harry sent the brothers Gibb a nasty letter: "You don't know what you're talking about," he wrote. "You're all on bloody drugs!"

Peter Noone, ('Herman' of Herman's Hermits)—
"I'm a Manchester lad myself and I was at my favourite pub, having just returned home from tremendous success in the States. It happened to be Davy's father's 'local' also, and I went up to Harry at the bar and offered to buy him a drink.

" Who are you?" he said.

"I'm a friend of Davy's," I replied. "I'm in a group, too."

"Oh, aye? Well, our Davy's in America, y'know."

"Yeah, I was just in America."

"Oh, aye? Well, our Davy's had hit records."

"Yes, I know. I've had some hit records me'self, too."

"Aye—but our Davy's had three number ones in a *row,* y'know" He's getting all smarmy now.

"Me, too. We had "Mrs. Brown You've Got A Love. . . "

"YES, yes. . . but our Davy *writes* 'is songs. . . 'imself!"

"Well. . . so do I." I was getting a bit defensive, y'know?

"But of course, he's an *actor* really. . . not just a flash in the pan pop star," says Harry, bating me now.

"Well, I'm an actor first and foremost, actually. I was on Coronation Street once. I played Len Fairclough's son." (In the north of England, 'Coronation Street' is like a religion. I've got 'im now, I thought.)

"Oh, aye? So was our Davy. *He* played Ena Sharples' grandson. . . *twice.*"

I couldn't top that. I just sort of trailed off.

"I'll 'ave that beer now," said Harry."

I guess Linda and David Pearl dated for about a year, I don't know exactly. I kind of stayed out of the way although I'd always see her around when I was back in L.A.. I covered up my feelings but it's like Micky said to me—

"Don't you know what it's like to be a good loser?"

"Yes, Micky," I said. "It makes me sick to my stomach."

She was *mine*, and I didn't know how to tell her, him or *me* that.

Linda Haines Jones—

"When David Pearl came back from The Monkees' European Tour, he and I dated for about eight months, so I was always over at Davy's house at 8571 Franklin. What usually happened was that I, and Davy's date for the night, watched TV—and Davy and David would play pool.

After a while I sort of fell out of sync with all the latest this and that people and didn't go over there so much. And anyway, David Pearl was starting to drop me so I started dating other guys. I'd never intended to stay in L.A.—I was supposed to be going to Aspen to meet up with a girlfriend and then on to Europe. But somehow fate wanted me to stick around and I found myself in a job at Pappagallo's, a fancy shoe store in Beverly Hills.

I hadn't been over to Franklin for ages when, out of the blue, Susan Haffey, whom I'd met at Peter Tork's house one time, came into the store and we got chatting. She said she was working for Davy now, cooking at his house, and why didn't I come over some time. So I did.

As it turned out, Davy came home early from the studio that day and was very surprised to see me there when he walked in. I was embarrassed by his surprise so I offered to go But he insisted that I stay. . . and then he promptly took a nap!

It was really a fateful night because David Pearl and some friends turned up unexpectedly too, and there we all were around the dinner table. I'm sure Davy relished the situation and probably used it to spite David Pearl. But whatever the reason, I too relished it when, in a loud voice, in front of everyone, Davy asked me if I would like to go to a movie. Pearl said he'd been thinking of seeing something too, but Davy made it clear he meant just the two of us. Talk about an atmosphere!

We left the party and went to see 'Bonnie and Clyde'. Then after the movie we went to see John Lee Hooker at the Ash Grove (an old jazz/R&B hangout—now the Improvisation Club). When we got there Davy found he had no money to get us in and I had to scramble around for quarters.

We went back to his place and watched TV for a while and then I asked him to take me home. He was very gallant— we kissed a little and then said goodnight. I didn't expect to hear from him again but a week later he asked me to a party that someone was throwing for Donovan. And two weeks after that we were living together."

Well, how good is it supposed to feel anyway? And what did I do to make things work? To be honest, I wasn't really looking to *make* things work—things always worked *for* me—they seemed to fall into place. I'd always been taken care of. People would say, "Come to me. Come to me. I'll handle your business, your career, your life." Always someone else there—like a foreman in a factory, except that a foreman doesn't go home with you—in show business he does. He's always calling you up at home. He's your manager/agent/producer/director—whatever he is, it doesn't stop, it's with you all the time. It's never like doing a regular job—there's always someone there, a second opinion, someone to do the doing.

So when all of a sudden the thought of marriage pops up—there was nobody to tell me what to do. I was still leaving the decisions to everyone else. So I treated Linda like I treated everyone else—didn't make her important enough, touch her, disclose to the world that she was mine and I was hers. She and I had so much time to develop a relationship that we didn't develop one at all. We didn't know how to.

It wasn't easy for her, let's face it. Nobody was supposed to know we were together. Whenever she flew with me she'd have to have a different seat—or preferably a different plane! Later, even *after* we were married, she couldn't put 'Linda Jones' on her luggage tags in case someone found out and leaked the news. I mean, it was tough. And looking back, I don't know *why* it was that way—just me letting *them* make the decisions as usual—not asserting my own wishes. I didn't want responsibility. I couldn't deal with it.

There were weeks without smiles. Linda used to sit on the stairs a lot. I didn't know why. Nor did she. We were both confused. What we needed was a great big hug. And we got one—our daughter, Talia.

daddy's song

*"I guess it's nice to have some-
one to love while you're looking
for someone to love."*   —Davy—

I thought that having a baby and getting married would be a good responsibility. I thought it would make me take the initiative, be decisive. But when you've never done it before, it's not so easy.

Linda travelled to England with her sister, Janet, to have the baby at the London Clinic. Dual citizenship, English passport—nice, I thought. Meanwhile I was halfway around the world—we were touring Australia and Japan, September/October, '68.

"A girl," Janet said to me over the phone.

"A girl? Oh, no!"

I don't know why I said that. Probably nerves. . . the excitement of a first child, y'know. A girl? Oh, boy!—was what I was really thinking. I celebrated with a bottle of Saki. Maybe two.

Talia was born on October 2nd. Two weeks later, as soon as the tour was over, Davy flew straight to London. But instead of being able to rest and savour the happy event, he was greeted with the news that his father was very ill. He flew immediately to Manchester just in time to see his dad being carried on a stretcher into an ambulance.

He always used to joke about how they'd have to give him a shot to put him away. 'As I climbed into the ambulance and knelt next to him, he shook his head.

"I'm done for, son—tell 'em to give me the shot."

Then he smiled.

Davy's father knew very little about Linda, and nothing about the baby. He hadn't even known that Linda was pregnant; Davy had been waiting for the right moment to tell him. Now that Talia was born, he had hoped to present his father with his grand-daughter, but because of his critical condition, the time was not right.

He flew to Manchester to visit his dad in the hospital every day, and back to London each night to be with Linda and Talia. This went on for about a week and then, the day before he was due to return to the States for a commitment, his father seemed much improved. Davy, Linda and Talia flew to Los Angeles. The moment they arrived they got the news that Harry was dead. Davy turned around and flew straight back to England, alone.

Beryl Jones—
"We were all at the house in Manchester. Hazel had made the funeral arrangements for the following week. We were going to have a wake, as with mother.
David arrived, white as a sheet, and gave us a wink, saying,
"He's alright now."
But he didn't cry."

I was so angry at myself. Sure, I had commitments back in Hollywood—but were they more important than my dad, ill in hospital? If that had happened today I'd have said, "Screw the shows—I'm stayin' with me dad!" But I was a kid being led around—do this—do that—don't say a word about being married—don't mention about your dad dying. AND I WAS STUPID ENOUGH TO OBEY! I didn't know any better—but I *should* have. The day before he died he gave me the thumbs up and a wink—he always used to do that—it meant, "Go get 'em, son—everything's fine." And I just thought—okay, go—it's alright, y'know?

Davy would hear nothing of a wake. To him it was no time to sit around with a bunch of people, drinking tea. He'd experienced that when his mother had died and wasn't about to go through it again. Consequently, he offended many members of the family by rushing the whole thing through within a day of his arrival, and then leaving the country as abruptly as he had arrived. But it was the only way he could deal with the situation.
Years later, after the ill feelings had mostly worn off between him and his sisters, Davy visited the grave a few times with Beryl. He has a plot already purchased for himself, next to his father and mother.

I try it each time I go. Beryl gets embarrassed and starts looking around to see if anyone's watching me, lying down there among the graves—but it's best to check these things out. I don't want a grave that doesn't feel right. After all, I'm gonna be there for quite a while.

One day we're there and an incredible thing happens. I'm lying in my spot, just testing it as usual, and we hear this announcement over the public address system of the nearby railway station:
⋅"Harry Jones. Will Harry Jones please report to the main office? Thank you."
Beryl and I look at each other in amazement. We both hear it—far off, and clear as a train whistle. We decide there must be a lot of Harry Jones's. But then we realize the railway station has been closed for years. There's nobody there.

Whether the determining factor in Davy and Linda's marriage was his father's sudden death, Talia's birth, or his impending U.S. Draft Induction, Davy cannot accurately recall. They had planned to marry anyway, and presumably all these factors helped to precipitate the event.
*Certainly they had delayed until now partly because of the pressure of Davy's image of **availability**. (The network made it clear that neither they, nor the fans,*

were going to like it if their most desirable Monkee were suddenly to become ineligible.) In any event, Davy returned from burying his father and, only five days after the death, on his parents' wedding anniversary, October 31st, he and Linda drove over the Mexican border to wed secretly in Tijuana. Davy's friend and business associate, Lindy Goetz, was best man; Talia, aged four weeks, was the only bridesmaid.

I guess you could say we got the rush job special. They didn't have too much time to clean up or anything, so there were still a couple of jacked-up cars outside, and bits of engine lying around the hallway. Weirdest church I've ever been in. Maybe it was a garage, I don't know. On the way back I told Linda I was sure the guy had read the service from a mechanic's manual. We laughed hysterically that night—all the way home.

I don't know if the guy was for real or what. He hadn't shaved in about a week and I'm sure we got him out of bed. I could only understand the odd word here and there and he kept making mistakes and looking at his watch. It was great. We probably got the three-thousand mile service instead of the wedding one—who would know?

The American Draft Board had a similar opinion about my marital status. They'd been trying to convince me for some time that the Army was a man's life. I kept ignoring the invitations they sent me. (Well, you know how bad the mail is.) But finally, I had to go along for the medical. I tried everything—

"I'm an only son."

So did they—

"They'll be proud of you."

"I'm allergic to bullets."

"We don't use bullets any more. It's all napalm these days."

Finally—

"Married with a baby!"

"Well, you'll be glad to get out of the house then." Real funny guys. They should've been writing TV scripts.

They found me A1. Better than I ever did at school. Just goes to show you—if you're physically fit enough to die, you can go. It dawned on me that they were serious—their country needed ME? Then *I* needed Harry Schtumm. Harry was a Hollywood lawyer, of sorts—well-known for fixing things like this. He protested strongly on the marriage and child grounds, but the army delved into that and claimed the marriage to be null and void. It was—but the ceremony too?

Off to church again. This time to Winterhaven, California, (Linda's birthplace), on the Nevada border. Baptist. December 15th, 1968. David Pearl was best man this time, and Talia stayed at home.

It's a bit more difficult being secretive in California. I kept imagining telephoto lenses hidden in the hillside, waiting to snap that special picture that would front-page all the trades and nationals the next morning. . . "Another Monkee Bites the Dust." But somehow we were in luck, and managed to keep it quiet.

This wedding was almost as much fun as the first. At one point Linda laughed herself into one of those 'point of no return' states. It started 'round about,

"And will you, Dixie Linda Haines, take. . . " She catches my eye and has a little suppressed chuckle, which quickly changes into a barely supressed cough, which, by the time ". . . to have and to hold" comes 'round, has become heaving, gasping, choking—and eventually full-fledged, hysterical laughing with tears and nose-blowing thrown in for good measure. She tries twice to say, "I do"—but no way will it come out. There's just too much else happening. The minister is clearly not amused.

"Young lady," he says. "This is a very serious matter." More giggling.

"Are you ready to continue?" Sniffles.

"Yes," she manages—eyes riveted about a foot above his head.

So there we were, married. Twice.

Itish schoolgirls, protesting at the U.S. Embassy in London, were appalled at the possible conscription of Davy Jones of the Monkees.

Back in England hundreds of girls held vigil outside the US Embassy in London, waving banners that read, "DON'T DRAFT DAVY". But the army was not moved. They wanted ed him, and they were determined to get him. Davy, however, was equally determined that they wouldn't. . .

No *way* man! D'you think I'm bozo or something? This is not playing north, south, east, west anymore—these guys are for real. North and South Vietnam. Eat versus West. With guess who in the middle? Not the Manchester cowboy, that's for sure. There's no way I'm going any further east than Pasadena. I make this clear to Schtumm and he says,

"No problem—give me three grand, I'll take care of it."

Not bad. Hey, I'd have paid anything to avoid a Viet-cong shampoo, I admit it. It's a lousy system—that I could do that and some poor GI Joe Schmo who doesn't have the three grand, or the connections, has to go. But I'm not going to apologise for using the system to save my neck. As it turned out I inadvertently got a few others a brief reprieve in the process, anyway. . .

. I didn't find out 'til years later what Schtumm had done with the money—I assumed it was just his fee. But actually he got some blokes who were stuck for some excitement at the weekend, and paid them to break into the draft building and steal my records. Only it turned out that the filing cabinet was a bit tricky to crack—so what did they do? They took the whole cabinet, of course! All the 'J' files—out the window. Incredible. Thousands of James's, Jeffries', Johnstons' and Jones's got an instant reprieve. For a while, at least. They were all at home waiting for that call, getting stoneder and stoneder—

"Hey, man. . . I thought we were going to 'Nam. . . what happened?"

I suppose they had a central filing system somewhere. Anyway, six months later they sorted the whole mess out and were onto me again. I got the papers through the mail. . . an invitation from Lieutenant Nadel, US Army. Nice stationery.

The interviewer was a real split personality. Nice as pie during the preliminary exam—even asked for my autograph—"for the wife". So I gave it to him. (How did *I* know I was signing up?) Then he turned real unhelpful and insisted that travelling would be good for me.

This time Schtumm told me to just go along on the prescribed date (only three weeks away), and he'd investigate more legal avenues in the meantime. Pretty unusual avenues for *this* lawyer, I thought. I didn't trust it—sounded too risky to me. I had my own plan. I decided to lay off food for a while. Three weeks to be exact.

Sounds a bit drastic, I know, but—so is war if you ask me. And I heard if Charlie caught you there was rarely a choice of second vegetable anyway—so this seemed by far the least uncomfortable course of action, in the long run. I had lots of dinner guests that three weeks. It was the only way I could do it. Every night I'd cook loads of food for everyone, then sit there with my grapefruit juice and watch them all gorge themselves. If you've never tried this—next time there's a war on 'round your way, I highly recommend it. You get real high—your breath smells the pits—and not even the Italian Army will take you. As I said to the U.S. Army doctor, just before I fell down,

"But I feel fine, sir. Let me at the bastards—please, sir! SEND ME!"

"We can't take you, boy. You're a ninety-nine pound weakling."

"But, *sir. . .*"

A funeral. A wedding. A close-shave with the draft board. Now, if you don't think everything's happening at once, forget it. Back on tour I go. Thirty-eight days, thirty-six concerts.

"Hi, honey. Yes, it went fine tonight. How's my baby? Did she ask where her daddy was?"

No. That question would come later.

MONKEES Licensee List

Abon Mfg. Co., Inc.
92 Narragansett Avenue
Providence, Rhode Island 02907
(401) ST-1-4100 (Victor M. Kindlund)

A MONKEES-identified charm bracelet and pendant

Alaid Distributors, Inc.
165 West 46th Street
New York, N. Y. 10036
247-1045 (Sidney Beckerman)

MONKEES souvenir programs (for personal appearances only)

Art Award Co., Inc.
3900 West Side Avenue
North Bergen, New Jersey 07047
(201) 864-0100 (Al Schwartz)

Paint and pencil by number sets

Bland Charnas Co., Inc.
869 Macon Street
Brooklyn, New York 11233
HI-3-0400 (Harry Panzer)

masks, wigs and costumes

Debs Sunglasses Corp.
13158 Saticoy Street
N. Hollywood, California 91605
(213) HO-9-5911 (Steve Boxer)

MONKEES sunglasses

Dell Publishing Co., Inc.
750 Third Avenue
New York, New York 10017
YU-6-6300 (Helen Meyer)

Comic books

The Donruss Company
1013 Kansas Street
Memphis, Tennessee 38102
(901) 946-1616 (Bailey Wiener)

Bubble gum and trading cards

Ed-U-Cards Mfg. Co.
60 Austin Boulevard
Commack, New York 11725
(516) 543-6711 (Irving Brambier)

Poker-type playing cards

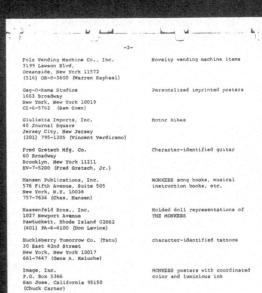

...this is without question,

that ever has happened

-2-

Folz Vending Machine Co., Inc.
3199 Lawson Blvd.
Oceanside, New York 11572
(516) OR-8-3600 (Warren Raphael)

Novelty vending machine items

Gag-O-Rama Studios
1663 Broadway
New York, New York 10019
CI-6-5762 (Sam Coen)

Personalized imprinted posters

Giulietta Imports, Inc.
40 Journal Square
Jersey City, New Jersey
(201) 795-1305 (Vincent Verdiramo)

Motor bikes

Fred Gretsch Mfg. Co.
60 Broadway
Brooklyn, New York 11211
EV-7-5200 (Fred Gretsch, Jr.)

Character-identified guitar

Hansen Publications, Inc.
576 Fifth Avenue, Suite 505
New York, N.Y. 10036
757-7634 (Chas. Hansen)

MONKEES song books, musical instruction books, etc.

Hassenfeld Bros., Inc.
1027 Newport Avenue
Pawtuckett, Rhode Island 02862
(401) PA-6-4100 (Don Levine)

Molded doll representations of THE MONKEES

Huckleberry Tomorrow Co. (Tatu)
30 East 42nd Street
New York, New York 10017
661-7447 (Gene A. Keluche)

character-identified tattoos

Image, Inc.
P.O. Box 5366
San Jose, California 95150
(Chuck Carter)

MONKEES posters with coordinated color and luminious ink

King-Seeley Thermos Company
Thermos Division
Norwich, Connecticut 06361
(203) 887-1671 (Donald C. Eccleston)

lunch kits consisting of vacuum bottles made of metal and/or plastic

Laufer Youth Marketing Co.
1800 N. Highland Avenue
Hollywood, California 90028
(213) 467-3111 (Chuck Laufer)

Monthly MONKEES magazine and various one-shots

Sparta Graphics
434 E. Williams St., Suite 103
San Jose, California 95112
(408) 297-9253 (Dave Schiller)

MONKEES color lithographed posters
approximately 17" by 22"

Sta-Well Hat Corp.
12 East 22nd Street
New York, New York 10010
AL-4-0515 (Gene Graff)

Novelty hats

Standard Plastic Products
450 Oak Tree Avenue
So. Plainfield, New Jersey 07080
(201) 756-7300 (Leo Miller)

Record cases, notebooks, wallets,
ring binders

Thom McAn Shoe Company
67 Millbrook Street
Worcester, Massachusetts 01606
(617) 791-9271 (Victor P. Mangini)

Men's and boys', women's and
girls' shoes and boots

Topps Chewing Gum, Inc.
234 - 36th Street
Brooklyn, New York 11232
768-8900 (Woody Gelman)

picture flip-books

Transogram Company, Inc.
200 Fifth Avenue
New York, New York 10010
OR-5-1500 (Jerry Goldstein)

Traditional-type boxed board game

FOR FURTHER INFORMATION, PLEASE CALL OR WRITE:

Edward L. Justin
Screen Gems, Inc.
711 Fifth Avenue
New York, N.Y. 10022
(Pl-1-4432, Ext. 572)

the biggest thing of its kind

in this business.

Mattel, Inc.
5150 Rosecrans Avenue
Hawthorne, California 90252
(213) OS-9-4611 (Jack Jones)

Various toy items

Model Products Corporation
126 Groesbeck H'way
Mt. Clemens, Michigan 48043
(313) 293-7200 (George Toteff)

hooby kit models of THE MONKEES
car

Pembroke Mfg. Co., Inc.
350 Fifth Avenue
New York, N. Y. 10001
PE-6-0752 (Robert Stevens)
(Leo Cogan)

Pop-art knitted cotton sweatshirts
and T-shirts and MONKEES berets
Selling Agents:
Kay IV Enterprise
Post Office Box Six
Glencoe, Illinois 60022
(312) 835-1430 (James E. Kaplan)

Personality Posters Mfg. Corp.
74 Fifth Avenue
New York, New York 10003
929-1271 (Martin Geisler)

30 x 40 decorative posters,
novelty buttons

Popular Library, Inc.
355 Lexington Avenue
New York, New York 10017
MU-7-2800 (Frank Lualdi)

One-shot magazine and paperback
books

The Poster Master Enterprise
1250 25th Avenue
San Francisco, California 94122
(405) 681-2691 (Marty Jacobs)

MONKEES posters

Publix Shirt Corp.
350 Fifth Avenue
New York, New York 10001
OX-5-4700 (Dick Golub)

Boys' shirts (cut and sewn and
knitted) and vests

Screen Gems Merchandising
711 Fifth Avenue
New York, New York 10022
PL-1-4432 (Ed Justin)

MONKEES buttons and pins

Sixteen Magazine
745 Fifth Avenue
New York, New York 10022
PL-5-9466 (Gloria Stavers)

MONKEES column and one-shots

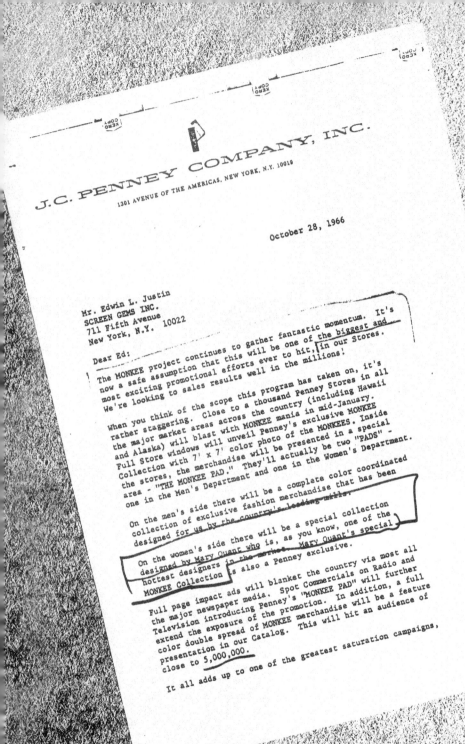

J.C. PENNEY COMPANY, INC.

1301 AVENUE OF THE AMERICAS, NEW YORK, N.Y. 10019

October 28, 1966

Mr. Edwin L. Justin
SCREEN GEMS INC.
711 Fifth Avenue
New York, N.Y. 10022

Dear Ed:

The MONKEE project continues to gather fantastic momentum. It's now a safe assumption that this will be one of the biggest and most exciting promotional efforts ever to hit, in our Stores. We're looking to sales results well in the millions!

When you think of the scope this program has taken on, it's rather staggering. Close to a thousand Penney Stores in all the major market areas across the country (including Hawaii and Alaska) will blast with MONKEE mania in mid-January. Full Store windows will unveil Penney's exclusive MONKEE Collection with 7' x 7' color photo of the MONKEES. Inside the stores, the merchandise will be presented in a special area - "THE MONKEE PAD." They'll actually be two "PADS" - one in the Men's Department and one in the Women's Department.

On the men's side there will be a complete color coordinated collection of exclusive fashion merchandise that has been designed for us by the country's leading mills.

On the women's side there will be a special collection designed by Mary Quant who is, as you know, one of the hottest designers in the market. Mary Quant's special MONKEE Collection is also a Penney exclusive.

Full page impact ads will blanket the country via most all the major newspaper media. Spot Commercials on Radio and Television introducing Penney's "MONKEE PAD" will further extend the exposure of the promotion. In addition, a full color double spread of MONKEE merchandise will be a feature presentation in our Catalog. This will hit an audience of close to 5,000,000.

It all adds up to one of the greatest saturation campaigns,

ever to hit. As you can well imagine, our advertising expenditures for this promotional effort will far exceed the $100,000 mark.

The promotion as it now stands is great! However, there is one element that can actually double the impact. That is the tie-in with a new MONKEE Album. A new Album released in our coincide with the promotion with the MONKEES dressed in our exclusive Collection on the cover could be fantastic. If this could be accomplished, we would adjust all of the aforementioned promotional efforts and bring in the record as a feature component of the total promotion. The 7' x 7' color photo in the windows would become the actual photo on the Album. The Albums would be displayed in all of the windows, along with the merchandise. Within the MONKEE PAD we would set up a highlight display of this Album.

All of our advertising, Radio and Television Commercials, and Catalog presentation would include the record.

Beyond the benefits to the overall promotion, the exposure that the record would get would probably be the largest ever seen in the business. In addition, no small by-product would be the hundreds of thousands of record sales that Penney Stores would generate.

Time is now of the essence. If we're going to have this Album tie-in we've got to have a decision fast so that all of the adjustments necessary to bring the Album into the picture can be accomplished.

So as to give you a visual impression as to what we had in mind relative to the Album tie-in, we are enclosing a Mock-up Album utilizing one of the photos we took.

Please bear in mind that this print was done fast via cheap color process strictly for the purpose of illustrating the tie-in. If this particular shot were used, the finished product would come up a lot clearer and brighter after the experts got to work in retouching. The record title and cover copy would naturally be developed by your record division's art department. The main thing we're interested in is the picture of the boys wearing our merchandise. We would, if possible, like to have a credit line on the back of the cover indicating that the clothes are from Penney's exclusive MONKEE Collection.

Ed, we cannot emphasize enough the important part this Album tie-in can play in this very exciting promotion. Everyone involved---most assuredly Screen Gems-Colgems-and R.C.A.--- have got to benefit greatly from this proposed tie-in. If the proposal is accepted, we should certainly want to get together with R.C.A. And determine what additional publicity or

advertising they might want to consider as part of this total effort.

SCREEN GEMS
A DIVISION OF COLUMBIA PICTURES INDUSTRIES, INC.
1334 BEACHWOOD DRIVE
HOLLYWOOD, CALIF. 90028

HOLLYWOOD MAIN OFFICE
Bank of America
NATIONAL SAVINGS ASSOCIATION
6300 SUNSET BOULEVARD
HOLLYWOOD, CALIFORNIA 90028

12244

16-321
1223

April 29 19 70

Exactly $0 AND 00 CTS _____ DOLLARS $ -0-

PAY_____

SCREEN GEMS

TO
THE
ORDER
OF

David Jones

⑈012244⑈ ⑉1223⑈0321⑈ 03735⑈000060⑈

DETACH AND RETAIN THIS STATEMENT
THE ATTACHED CHECK IS IN PAYMENT OF ITEMS DESCRIBED BELOW. IF
IF NOT CORRECT PLEASE NOTIFY US PROMPTLY. NO RECEIPT REQUIRED

SCREEN GEMS
A DIVISION OF COLUMBIA
PICTURES INDUSTRIES, INC.
HOLLYWOOD, CALIFORNIA

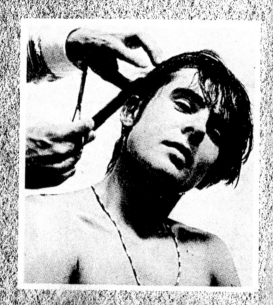

zilch

"Son—take the money and run."
—Harry Jones—

The letterhead of Ed Justin's business stationery bore the legend, 'Monkee Business is BIG Business'. 'Honest' Ed Justin, as he liked to be known, was in charge of merchandising. And everything that could possibly be sold with the name 'Monkees' on it, (no matter how tenuous or improbable the connection), was sold. In the first year alone, revenue from Monkee merchandising grossed an estimated thirty-five million dollars. The arsenal of Monkee-associated stationery, toiletries, clothes, foods, kitchenware and other knick-knacks, was impressive—and the market was so glutted that it would probably be easier to name the one or two items that didn't feature in the nation's shop windows, or mail-order ads...

Enquiries have revealed no 'Monkees Enema Bag', and it seems that the United States Government really missed out by failing to clean up with the 'Micky Dolenz Ground-to-Air Tactical Nuclear Missile'. But that's it—just about everything else was covered.

Of course, the fan magazines helped the merchandisers' cause tremendously. But Justin was such an astute businessman that he managed to set a precedent by getting magazines like 'Tiger Beat' and '16' to pay a fee, just to use photos of the Monkees in their issues. It was a short-lived coup, though surely lucrative while it lasted. After a while the magazines refused, claiming they were helping to make the Monkees a phenomenon, and that they certainly shouldn't be paying for the privilege.

Still, Justin kept a tight rein on any and all promotional schemes that came across his desk, and made sure that anyone who stood to profit from a connection with the Monkees, was licensed by him first. There was certainly no shortage of ideas... the ingenuity (or the greed?) knew no bounds:

'WIN THEIR HAIR!' proclaimed one tabloid of the day. 'In packets with GUARANTEE signed by their hairdresser!' And for those who couldn't risk not being one of the lucky winners, there was a fail-safe—'BUY A PACKET- be sure to specify whose hair you want—JUST ONE DOLLAR EACH!' Yes, each hair that is.

I noticed one of our studio hairdressers used to sweep up everyone's hair into a big pile, laughing himself silly. We wondered why he was so happy all the time. He was always asking if we needed a trim.

"But I just had it done!"

"No, dearie—looks *terrible*, love. Here, allow me." Snip, snip.

Then we saw what the magazines were selling. It was a button with *one* hair taped across it. You had to look hard to see it. His haircuts sucked but he was great with a broom.

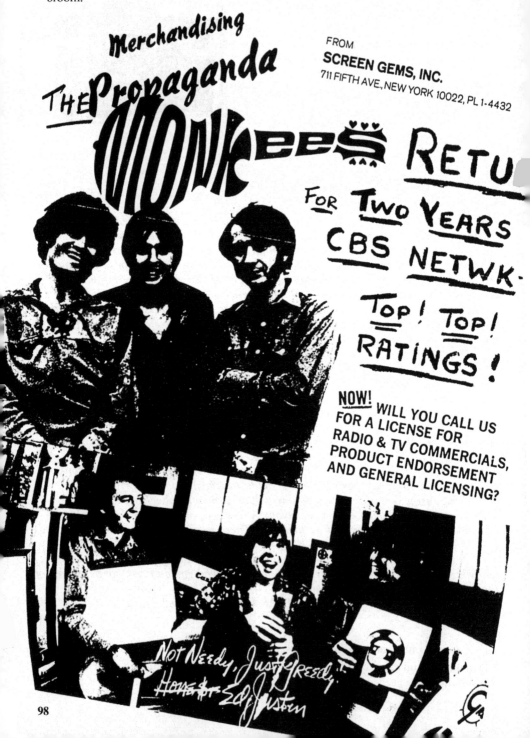

Merchandising

The Propaganda

MONKEES RETU

FROM
SCREEN GEMS, INC.
711 FIFTH AVE., NEW YORK 10022, PL 1-4432

FOR TWO YEARS
CBS NETWK·
Top! Top!
RATINGS!

NOW! WILL YOU CALL US
FOR A LICENSE FOR
RADIO & TV COMMERCIALS,
PRODUCT ENDORSEMENT
AND GENERAL LICENSING?

Not Needy, Just Greedy,
Hours Ed Justin

TO   Don Berigan

FROM   Ed Justin

RE

DATE   March 28, 1967

Check ... ...
... ...
... ...

TIGER BEAT
16
DATEBOOK

Dear Don: *I NEED LIST OF*
ALL LICENSEES

First, let me wish you luck with THE MONKEES.

Ward asked me to give you a general outline of the publishing –
licensing situation as it exists with respect to THE MONKEES
and it follows:

1. It is the custom in the teenage magazine field to steal
everything and when we began with THE MONKEES, the teenage
magazine publishers followed the usual arrangements. They
got pictures from the studio and they proceeded to write whatever they chose to write and to use THE MONKEES as they chose
to use them and they had no licenses and they paid no royalties
on anything. When I began calling them, they protested that no
other organization had ever asked for licenses or for royalties
and they told me that they had no intention of paying. After
a series of complicated legal maneuvers, I converted many of
them to religion:

1. Chuck Laufer of Laufer Youth Marketing Co. has become a
fantastic licensee. He has a license for a MONKEES-identified
column to be regularly printed in his TIGER BEAT magazine and
as you know, he also publishes a regular monthly MONKEES magazine
and in addition, he is publishing a series of MONKEES one-shots
and offering MONKEES photos for sale via mail order. Chuck
Laufer is a first-rate client. He submits everything to Ward
Sylvester for approval as he is supposed to and he pays royalties
on THE MONKEES column which appears in TIGER BEAT and on the
monthly MONKEES magazine and on the one-shots and on the mail
orders and on the photos which he offers for sale. So far as
I know, we have no problems with Chuck Laufer and I am sure
that he will end up paying us a tremendous amount of money in
royalties. He should be given <u>every possible cooperation</u>.

cont'd...

2. 16 Magazine (Gloria Stavers) has a license for one MONKEES
column per issue. She also has a license for the sale of photos
and for the sale of one-shots (which are still being created).
All of the licensed material is supposed to be submitted to Ward
for prior approval. (Gloria has not been honoring her commitments
and you will find that the most effective weapon we have with her
is to threaten that she will be barred from the set.

Please understand that it is the opinion of our Legal Department
that the execution of our rights against publishers would be extremely difficult and so, we have been using this threat of barring
from the set with great effectiveness. It is more useful than
legal action.

I was in this office in New York once—more like a supermarket, actually—rows and rows of Monkee stuff. Clothes, pots and pans—anything you could think of. Well, they didn't just all of a sudden come up with a warehouse full of Monkee love beads and calenders, did they? Most of it was all merchandise that was just sitting there, waiting for the next big name to be slapped on it. They'd used it for The Beatles and Elvis—probably used it for Elvis again when he died. It's just whoever's in office at the time.

We were very foolish about all that stuff. Even Mike and Micky, who usually handled their money properly, were green as far as merchandising rights were concerned. We were all handled by different managers, so there was no strength, no unity between us.

As it started to happen—and it started happening pretty quickly—we were none of us prepared. I mean, the guys behind the scenes knew only too well—they had their game plans ready. They asked us what we'd like from the merchandise sales—a lump sum cash advance or a deferred percentage? We looked at each other and shrugged. Cash didn't seem like too clever an idea—we'd only spend it, so we said okay. . . percentage.

SCREEN GEMS, INC.	
TO	
DAVID JONES	
MERCHANDISING INCOME - MONKEES SERIES	
INCEPTION TO SEPTEMBER 30, 1967	
STATEMENT #1	
NET PROCEEDS FROM MERCHANDISING IN WHICH ARTIST SHARES	$346,726.37
5% OF ABOVE	$ 17,336.32
PRO RATA REDUCTION (MERCHANDISING USING ARTIST WITH OTHER "MONKEES"	13,002.24
AMOUNT PAYABLE TO DAVID JONES	$ 4,334.08

But what we didn't stop long enough to think about, was that all the limousines, the lear jets, the five-star hotels, the whole life-style—the *image*—was being charged to us. Everything—even phone calls we made from the office— it was all knocked off the top. So it often ended up that there was little or even no percentage left.

We should have taken the up-front cash first and let them get it back, but that was our own fault. For myself, that came from my childhood—we never had anything on HP (Lay-away). . . if we couldn't pay for it outright, we wouldn't have it.

Something wasn't quite right, though. I missed out on all sorts of investments that I should have been in on—and those I *was* in on, well. . .

We did one episode where we were Errol Flynn-type pirates. It was filmed on an actual galleon. The four of us were so impressed by the ship that we offered to buy it for a hundred thousand dollars. But the ship was booked for one more film project, so we couldn't take immediate possession. Anyway we had all the papers drawn up and the next day the ship sank.

Another situation Davy got himself into was a rather ambitious project. There was talk of building a shopping centre, under one roof, to house a group of artisan's stalls and shops. . . much along the same lines as an English flea market. To help the artisans get things started, Davy fronted the necessary capital and paid the initial few months' rent (at $2,000 a month) on an old warehouse in Los Angeles. It cost $35,000 just for the renovation.

The old building had been used for making the shells of bombs, or some such thing, during World War Two. With Davy's help it was transformed into a little village with twenty-six shops, jewellery stalls, home-baked food stands and a fountain. All in 60's, gaily coloured, hippie-style decor, with wooden fixtures in abundance. They called it, 'The Street'

Everything was set for a grand opening on New Year's Eve. Then the L.A. County Fire Officers came in and told them they couldn't open because everything was made out of wood. Davy forked out again and replaced the wood with metal. By now the total cost of getting it open was around sixty-thousand dollars. All Davy had asked of the tenants was that they pay him 10% of their profits, which, at the beginning of the venture, would probably only just cover the rent. But the decor was not the only thing about it that was 'hippyish'; the organization was so loose that after three months of waiting for some kind of payment, Davy called a meeting, told them he couldn't help them anymore, and left them to it. Shortly afterwards, 'The Street' closed.

A more successful project, though not for Davy personally—he was just helping his friends get it off the ground—was a trendy New York boutique called 'Zilch'. The proprietors were Herb and Miriam Neal, who had been very kind to Davy, letting him live at their place for over a year whilst he was in 'Oliver!'

'Zilch' opened on October 27th at 217 Thompson Street, and Davy flew to New York for the grand opening. He was mobbed by two-thousand screaming fans outside the shop. As a boutique for the latest 'in' clothes, it was very successful but Davy didn't get involved with the business side of it. As far as he knows it remained successful for a number of years.

It's funny to look back on the money side of it. It was just like Monopoly. There were so many people advising—all talking and nobody saying anything. Ward Sylvester was my manager when I first came to L.A., then, as The Monkees started, he became associate producer of the series and I had to pretty much fend for myself. I then had a whole string of managers who, in my opinion, had no great concern for me personally and were just in it to make a fast buck.

Al Conn was classic. He wouldn't let anyone near me. Any newspaper wanted to interview me, he'd say to them, "I AM Davy Jones! Speak to me." I gave him sixty-three thousand dollars one day—to go buy me a house that I'd seen. I didn't have time to mess with all that business stuff myself—we were filming, rehearsing, touring, saying 'cheese' all day.

Anyway that's what you pay a manager for, right? So I'd been living in the place for a few months when I notice a bank statement one day and I see there's these payments going out every month that I don't know anything about. I ask Conn,

"What are these?"

"House payments," he says.

"But I own the house."

"Err, no. Not exactly."

"What do you mean, not *exactly*? What happened to the sixty-three grand?"

"Well. . . orange groves. . . in Florida. A great investment, David."

I never saw one orange. And I had to pay a mortgage too!

This sort of thing was happening all the time—a little bit here—a big bit there. He brought two women out from New York to work for something he'd set up called, 'Davy Jones Enterprises'—he wanted me to think about going solo. So these girls are in L.A. working on some promotion thing. . . *My Favourite Monkee—Davy Jones*. . . something like that. Anyway, I'm in the office and Conn's out on a business lunch somewhere—Hawaii, I think. And these two girls start telling me about all these things he's up to—sort of putting me straight, y'know?

Suddenly I see the light. I'm real pissed—they're telling me incredible stuff about where the money's been going, so I figure I'll empty our joint account so he can't buy any more fruit over the weekend, right? Only I don't have my bank account stuff handy, and my bank's in New York anyway, and they're closed by now—so I know it's dumb but what can I tell you?—I put it in one of these girls' savings account—safe until Monday, surely?—then I'll transfer it and fire my manager.

Well. . . Monday turns up. . . but the girl doesn't. (It's difficult y'know. So many lights. I just happened to keep seeing the wrong one.)

Meanwhile, the remaining girl, Helen Kensick, who had been my fan club secretary during the 'Oliver!' days, asks me whether I'm aware of the fact that I had just recently bought thirteen thousand dollars' worth of furniture for my manager's pad. (Well, the place needed it—all he had before was orange crates.) I figure I need help for this one.

There was this guy I used to call the Inspector, who'd been wanting to represent me—I knew he'd love to see Mr. Furniture out of the picture, right? So he has a plan.

We go around to the sheriff's office, explain the situation, post a bond of thirteen thousand dollars, and take a ride over to my manager's place. He's still out, right?—it's a long lunch. They're having dessert in Tokyo.

The sheriff helps us load the truck up with all the furniture—he loves it—thinks this is real funny. And I leave a note: "You shouldn't take such long lunch breaks."

Eventually my soon-to-be-ex-manager and his wife, Sally, get back from China. ("Egg Foo Yung—to take away, please.") They notice something's up right away—the place is clean! ("Boy, that new maid is thorough.") Well, he figures it out—from the note—and sends two sheriffs round to my place, with Sally along for the ride. I'm at the studio but Linda is home and she lets them in.

They know that they can't get the furniture back—I've got a bond on the stuff. But Sally claims that I've got this set of six gold-plated mixing sticks—drink stirrers—that belong to them. They're not on the sherrif's list 'cos they're not part of the furniture that he bought. (Actually, I had given them to him as a gift and I was so pissed off at what he'd done that I took them back.)

So while they're walking around looking for these mixing sticks, Linda calls me at the studio. Of course, I blow up.

"Get them out of there. They've got no right to be in there nosying around!"

"Well, they said they just want the mixing sticks."

So I tell Linda which drawer they're in and she goes and gets Sally and they look through the drawer—not there. . . second drawer—not there. . . third drawer—shit! There's a little seive in the corner with just some seeds and stems in—no grass. But Sally sees it and she goes into the other room to tell the sheriffs. Linda's back on the phone to me and tells me what's happening.

"THROW THE STUFF OUT!" I'm screaming down the phone.

Poor Linda's scared stiff but she goes and gets it and throws it in the kitchen garbage. Sally tells the sheriff it was there a minute ago. They ransack the place. Linda's hysterical. I'm on the other end of the phone wondering what it'll be like in San Quentin.

Well, they find it—big deal, eight seeds! Sheriff gets on the line.

"Mr. Jones? We'd like you to come over here and help us find these mixing sticks."

Sure. . . and the Pope's Jewish.

"Yes," I say. "I'll be right over."

Shock. Horror! The studio immediately closes down. Everybody goes straight home—the producers, the crew, technicians, the tea lady—I mean EVERYBODY. Ten o'clock in the morning. . . finished. Paranoia. Mass flushing of toilets. Nothing like this had ever happened in connection with the Monkees. Paul McCartney had told everybody that he'd taken LSD, fine. . . but if the press asked if we took drugs we were told to say, "Yes. . . aspirin." Once I think I admitted to taking a little Exlax, maybe.

So the whole set was closed down for the day. Linda was arrested but I spoke to her first on the phone.

"Don't worry about it," I said. "Don't say a word—you don't know anything. I'll set the wheels in motion."

I immediately got hold Harry Schtumm again. In exchange for handing over six thousand dollars to pay off certain people (he wouldn't tell me who and frankly I didn't particularly want to find out), Linda wouldn't spend the night in jail. Sure enough, she was released from Sybil Brand Prison at ten that night.

I stayed in hiding at the Bel Air Hotel for three days while Schtumm sorted things out. I had to write another cheque for $14,000. Where that went, I don't know. (Boy, did his fee jump up. He must be getting the hang of this lawyer business.) $20,000 altogether—but for that everything was kept quiet and I didn't get busted.

(Some months later, Micky was motorcycling down Sunset Boulevard, committed a minor traffic violation and was stopped and searched. They found half a dozen joints on him. I heard it cost him $3,000. No prosecution. It's true what they say—money talks. But how come his speaks so much louder than mine? Pisses me off.)

All that because I took the advice of the Inspector and went after a few sticks of hideous furniture—which just ended up in my garage for months. Eventually I gave it all away to Goodwill, anyway—wouldn't have been seen dead with stuff like that in my house. I mean my rented house.

So the Inspector was the next one. Peter had introduced me to him. He didn't buy phantom orange groves or anything like that, but he did make a few business decisions which, it seemed to me, were not too smart. Mind you—so did I. I gave him power of attorney and, against the advice of my dear friend, Fred Harris, turned over my New York bank account to him. Will I ever learn?

He gave some brilliant financial advice, I must say. Only my opinion, of course—but I think ten percent of Jeans West would be worth a few bob by now, don't you? I was offered that deal for only $10,000 when they were just starting up, but the Inspector didn't like the sound of it—

FRED HARRIS
Theatrical Representative

CABLE ADDRESS: HARRGENCY, NEWYORK

119 WEST 57TH STR
NEW YORK, N. Y. 1001
(212) CIRCLE 7-3025

Dear Davy:

Aug. 26, 1969

Sorry that I awoke you last night, but I had called and left my number earlier. Anyway, it was nice speaking to you.

I thought that you were going to be in Toronto two days and was thinking of flying up there today to say hello. I could not very well fly up yesterday without first making certain that it was okay and where you were staying.

It was lovely seeing you in London and meeting your charming wife and baby. You have the best behaved baby I have ever met, and a real charmer.

I looked over my accounts and at your request I sent $77,311.02 to the inspector which was deposited in the Crocker Citizens' National Bank. A separate $5,000. I deposited in the Irving Trust Co. here in New York, which completed the $82,311.02 I had in your account here. Besides that, more than $20,000. was turned over to the inspector's London representative. Altogether this makes quite a substantial sum to entrust to a stranger and that is why I suggested when I saw you at the opening party for "HEAD" that you authorise me (or anyone else you chose) to inspect his figures.

In case you need me if the Conn matter comes to trial I shall drop everything and come out there. Having issued the various cheques and having been an unwilling participant, I feel that I might have much to contribute to the testimony.

I have a feeling that one of these days we shall get together again.

Please give my love to Linda and a kiss to the baby.

Take care, mate. All the best.

Blessings:

PS Regards to David Pearl.
PSS I still have all of your financial accounts right f... ning if you ever need them. I only sent ... copies and kept the originals.

"Jeans? No way—they'll never sell," he said. Same again with Fuji Film and Mattel Toys. Thanks a lot.

Then one morning I go down to my mailbox and open up a royalty cheque for $240,000. I'd made almost a quarter of a million dollars before breakfast! Went back to bed—I'd had a hard day.

But the point is—when you get money like that it should be invested, sheltered, deferred. It seems to me that's a manager's job—but no such advice was given—and I just paid a huge amount of tax straight off the bat. Dumb. Now, when it came to some poor gardner trying to get $37.00 out of me for some dichondra—that was a different matter *altogether*. No way was the Inspector gonna let anyone get away with that sort of thing—he could write letters all day about *that* stuff—no problem.

So I think it was a matter of priorities, y'see.

> I have just received your statement of November 13th made out to Davy Jones for maintenance plus the purchase of dichondra which was $37.00 alone.
>
> I am sure you will recall a telephone call you received from Esther in our office some weeks ago instructing you not to plant any further items in David's home without first clearing it with this office.
>
> I am authorizing the payment of this bill because our relationship has run too long for us to become hung up over $37.00 worth of dichondra. I think it should now be very clear to you, however, that you are not authorized to plant anything further for David unless you first clear it with this office. We will not be responsible for any expenses you or your associates undergo from this point on, and I would appreciate a telephone call from you at your convenience confirming that you understand this new arrangement.

He was pretty busy working on another project at the time—a low-budget film that Peter Fonda had made. The Inspector did a deal with Raybert and Columbia to distribute the film. It did pretty well—it was called 'Easy Rider'.

I didn't see much of the Inspector after that. Or Bob and Bert. They got their easy ride and took it. Can't blame 'em. Bob and Bert had put up a quarter of a million dollars of Monkee profits for a share in that film and thus launched a whole new career for themselves in movies. Rafelson became a respected director with 'Five Easy Pieces' and 'Drive, He Said'—and together with Schneider and Steve Blauner formed BBS Productions.

BBS. . . be back soon

Blauner was Vice President of Columbia in New York when I first signed to them in '63 or '64. He said I'd never make it because I was too short. Anyway, later on he loosened up a bit and started wearing bell-bottom trousers and long hair—the whole ageing hippie bit. Actually I started to like him more when he got into that. We had some fun occasionally.

Like on July 4th, 1968, with the long Independence Day weekend ahead—all of America is on holiday—I wake up, go to the bathroom, and what should come out of the tap, but nothing! No water. Not only that, there's no electricity. . . no heat. . . no anything. It's all off. Then I remember something Blauner said—just a little hint.

And I realize—it's him, the bastard—he's had the whole lot turned off as a joke.

So I have a date to go riding that morning at Pickwick Rising Stables in Burbank. All morning I'm trying to think how I can get him back. And then I see it. . . a dump truck, full to overflowing—with horse manure!

I find the guy whose truck it is and I tell him what the deal is—he can't believe it— but I've *got* to have that truck. Well, what's in it. I pay him for his, err. . . services. (Does this guy recognize me or is he taking lessons from Schtumm?) Then we drive to Mr Blauner's luxurious home, very carefully, so as not to lose any of my precious investment.

He's gone away for the long weekend. Shame. I'll just have to leave my message on his doorstep. The whole lot!

I'm laughing myself crazy as the guy takes me back to my car. I couldn't help thinking of all those other front doors I would have *loved* to deliver that message to. But it just wasn't possible—the price of shit being what it was.

Well, I guess they all knew who they were.

"A lot of people would be surprised
that you came out of that whole
thing with so little—
compared to the millions
that The Monkees generated.
Does that bother you?"
—A radio interview, 1973—

"Not at all.
Can you lend me a fiver?"
—Davy—

monkees is ze craziest peoples

Linda used to seemingly have all kinds of fun in the months leading up to Talia's birth. But whatever it was—it was no longer. Whereas before she used to tolerate my beer-drinking and pot-smoking, now it was a pain in her side. We were growing apart— fast. We had rabbits, cats, dogs, a goat, a monkey—anything to busy ourselves and avoid the issue.

"Darling. . . I've bought some chickens so you'll have some company while I'm at the studio." My idea. Great—now we'll have something in common—we can clean out the coop together. Linda is excited. "This will save us a fortune on eggs," she says. "I'll call the store and tell them to cancel our weekly order."

I suggest that we hold off a while—see if they lay first. But it's like, all of a sudden she gets really serious about economy. Which is fine, y'know, but a couple of weeks ago there's a cheque for a quarter of a million and now she's getting excited about saving three dollars a week on eggs.

Anyway, for some reason, best known to themselves, the hens won't lay. I begin to suspect it's got something to do with the monkey who also lives in the coop. We were looking after it for Phil Ochs. The monkey had his own place but seemed to prefer the coop. So the hens are getting a touch paranoid. And personally I don't blame them—the monkey's none too subtle. But that's nothing compared to Linda who's out there every morning, bright and early, checking for new arrivals.

All things considered, the hen's aren't going for it. Eventually, after five weeks, Linda's getting bored with the whole thing—and more than a little disappointed. So one morning I decide to cheer her up a notch or two. I sneak out before she's awake and place a supermarket egg under one of the birds (who's none too thrilled because the egg is fresh from the fridge and probably feels like a block of ice under its arse).

Back to bed. Two hours later, Linda half-heartedly goes down to survey the situation once more. I'm chuckling to myself and counting up to twenty—slowly. Round about fifteen all hell breaks loose. Linda comes running in like she herself is the proud mother of the egg. She holds it up like a trophy, rattling on about how she *knew* they would — you've just got to give them time to get comfortable in their new home. . . bump di bum.

"Great!" I say. "Three minutes, medium boiled, please." Over breakfast she remarks how different it tastes.

Well, I've started something now. Next day I put two in. And then three and so on—until by the weekend I'm laying half a dozen at a time! Linda, needless to say, is ecstatic. Now she's going to call the store and cancel our milk, cheese, *all* food. We're going to become eggtarians.

I figure this has gone far enough, so next morning I'm up bright and early and slip a fried egg in. Linda comes back to the house after her inspection and proceeds to bang everything in sight—except me. Boy, is she pissed off!

"What's the matter, dear?" I ask innocently.

"You know darn well what's the matter!" More slamming, banging, stamping.

"You've probably made those poor hens neurotic with a trick like that!"

"Neurotic? It was only a joke, Linda. Get it?" Nothing.

"And the other eggs too, I presume. . . "

"Cheered you up, didn't it, dearest?" She didn't talk to me for days. Neither did the chickens.

A very neurotic chicken

Everywhere the Monkees went they were front-page news. In London, during the Wembley concerts, the fans outside their hotel prompted that letter from Princess Margaret and caused total chaos for the traffic. Davy's arrival at London's Heathrow Airport caused a riot of such proportions that it was mentioned in Parliament and resulted in a government inquiry. In America, scenes of hysteria greeted them wherever they appeared and their concerts were sell-outs within hours of tickets going on sale.

*It's easy to see why Tork and Nesmith felt they could use their popularity to twist certain arms and win the musical freedom they had been promised. They needed to prove to the critics, who were crucifying them for having hits that they didn't write or play on, that they were capable of creating far more artistically valid material. It's also easy to see that Kirshner's expertise in choosing **commercially** viable material had been a governing factor behind their phenomenal record sales.*

A clash of interests was inevitable, nerves were frayed, and some of the resulting tension started to erupt on the set between the boys themselves.

Peter Tork—

"We were getting on each other's nerves, and suddenly Davy was shouting and cursing everybody in general and whoever was in his line of fire, specifically. I went over to try to calm him down.

"Get out of here, you twit!" he screams.

I didn't move, and the next thing I know he hits me in the mouth with his forehead—a nutter, as the English call it.

Pretty lethal.

So, we started at each other—arms flailing. The crew broke us up. We were held off each other by about three men apiece—still glaring, and struggling to get loose. Finally, we calmed down.

"Okay, Peter?" "Okay."

"Okay, Davy?" "Okay."

But we're good actors, remember. As they loosened their grip, I got free first and slugged him as hard as I could. I was surprised. It felt good."

Davy had to go to hospital and had seven stitches above his eye. Filming continued in his absence—without four-shots. When he returned three hours later, all smiles and bandages, he simply quipped,

"Nice shot, Pete,"

and went straight back to work.

STATEMENT

Re: David Thomas Jones

11/14/67 Minor Surgery at Cedars of Lebanon Hospital. Out-patient. $75.00

Paid.
12/30/67
 # 302

The talented comedian, Hans Conrey, who was filming with them on that episode, was amazed by it all. He kept walking around saying, "Monkees is ze CRAZIEST peoples!" That ended up caught on film but nobody watching could have known just how much he meant it.

That was the trouble. We were on so much of the time, we couldn't switch off that easily. He was right—we *were* ze craziest peoples. I mean—one time, Mike actually tried to beat up the elevator operator in this hotel they put us in. Why they booked us in there, I'll never know—it was like a retirement home. I'm sure they'd never seen anybody under sixty-five and they put us four crazies in there.

Anyway we're on the second floor waiting for the lift. One of those old-fashioned gate affairs. You could actually look down to the first floor through the grills. We see it coming, but it goes right past. Mike gets furious—runs down the stairs, six at a time.

The place is dead, y'know. Nobody's been in the elevator all month—they're all joining hands trying to contact the living. So for excitement, the guy just rides up and down all day. Suddenly it looks like premature retirement for the poor guy. Nesmith is waiting for him, and as the gate opens he grabs the guy—

"If you ever do that again, ar'm gonna knock both your teeth out, old-timer!"

The poor guy is having three coronaries—he's a hundred and eight y'know—but we're too busy singing to put anybody down! Bloody right. Mike wasn't putting this guy down—he had him about a foot off the floor, pinned up inside his own elevator. That incident alone should have shown us what was happening there. *Definitely* time for a day off.

Mike could be quite tall when he wanted to be. Not to mention rude, arrogant, belligerent and aggressive—and that was on a *good* day. He threatened both Micky and Peter on a number of occasions when things got kind of tense around the set. I intervened once—suggested he choose me instead.

"Pick on someone your own size," I said.

I don't think he could figure that one out. I was looking him straight in the stomach, seemingly fearless, so he slips into his southern twang and says,

"Ar didn't mean anything baa it. Ar'm just a simple *couuuntry* boy."

I was very lucky, I guess. The one time I saw him really let go was that highly publicized thing where he put his fist through a wall at the Beverly Hills Hotel. He and Peter were demanding more musical control over what we recorded, and what got played on the show. We'd been allowed to do one or two of our own numbers, but let's face it— it was unheard of for hired actors to start dictating network policy. Kirshner wasn't going to give up his control to *us*—no way. Wouldn't have mattered how successful we'd become.

The point was, we weren't disputing the fact that he'd done a great job picking songs for us—he was pretty much *revered* in the business for his 'ears'—and frankly, he'd been largely responsible for putting us right up there in the record side of things. But from our point of view that was the whole argument—we were trapped in what we'd become.

Anyway, we're all at the hotel. Don's lawyers are there too, getting heavy and pointing to clauses in contracts and all that stuff. Suddenly—BANG! Plaster. . . dust. . . *tension.*

"That could have been your head!" shouts Mike. And he storms out. I made a quick mental note never to call his bluff again after that.

Lester Sill and I left together and I remember us looking at each other in the car— both close to tears. We knew the end wasn't far away. Lester was, and still is, a very sensitive, brilliant, music business exception. . . a real gentleman.

Mike Nesmith—
"Tell the world we're synthetic, because, damn it, we are! Tell them we were wholly man-made overnight, and that millions of dollars have been poured into this thing. Tell the world that we don't record our own music. But that is *us* on television. The show really is part of us. They're not watching something invalid."

Yeah, Papa Nes could really warm to a subject once he got going. He and Peter *had* been promised more musical control all along—they were the two real musicians, after all. I could see both sides of it. But there were no shades of grey. . . only black or white. The big guys were coming on so tough. It was like telling a painter he had to paint by numbers because that particular method, that particular combination of numbers, had been successful in the past.

We defused a lot of the tension with humour, naturally. On the set, and on the road, we had a game we used to play called *Killer*. Jim Frawley invented it. The idea was each person was allowed three shots per day. You could shoot whoever you liked—you just mimed it with your hand as a gun, like kids do, y'know—*tssshhh!* And whoever was shot had to die.

But you couldn't just fall down, nice and simple—it had to be a spectacular death. You had to moan and kick and fall over furniture and people and take about three-quarters of an hour to do it—like they used to in all the best westerns. And if you didn't die loud enough, or long enough, or imaginatively enough, or, if say you just didn't die at all, because you were being introduced to The Queen Mother at the time, then you lost a *life.*

And if you lost three lives—you were out of the game. Forever. No second chances. That was as good as really being dead.

So of course, we'd look for the best moments to shoot each other—when it would cause the most commotion. Not everyone was included. It was a clique of about eight. Sometimes we'd have a different director—we used to have a guest director do one or two shows. They'd be in the middle of a scene and somebody would get shot and the whole scene would be ruined because this was very serious business—you couldn't lose a life.

The game produced no end of possibilities for going right over the top. In the middle of a love scene once—I had the stars coming out of my eyes, the whole bit—I'm walking over to the girl with my arms outstretched and she says, "Oh, Davy!" We're just about to kiss when. . . *Tsshhh'*—Peter shoots me. I have to go into an epileptic seizure routine for about five minutes—knocking lamps over, falling over a drum kit, out the door, roll around the parking lot, up the stairs, across the president's desk—"Oh my God, are you alright, David?"—"Aaargh! Shot, sir!" Back out the door, down the stairs, onto the set, —collapse in a heap at her feet. Wild applause.

One time in Australia, in front of about five million fans at the airport, Micky got shot and he fell all the way down this gigantic escalator. People were stunned. They thought he'd been assassinated.

It was very rarely someone wouldn't die—not even a token head-slump. One time was the Emmy Awards. I think it was Bert Schneider stepped up to receive the award for 'Best New Comedy Show'. We shot him, but the moment was too special for him to spoil it. He won an Emmy and lost a life.

Towards the end of the second year—to show you how badly things were going—even Frawley couldn't be persuaded to die anymore. Everyone had been up all night, as usual. We were on the set—first diet pill of the day—started fooling around, messing up takes as always. But somehow it wasn't the same. Nobody was laughing. Frawley was so mad. The only thing we could do was shoot him. Dolenz shot him—he didn't die. Mike shot him—still standing. I shot him—nothing. What a bummer. All the feeling was gone. The beginning of the end.

"Kirshner felt that by giving us the royalty checks for the first album, he could win our undying loyalty. He had no idea what was important to us."
—Peter Tork—

The predicted clash of interests between the Monkees and Don Kirshner was now well under way. The boys started demanding their creative freedom.

The Monkees were riding the crest of their wave of popularity, and faced with Mike's resolution to quit unless his demands were met, Schneider had no alternative but to supply pressure to Kirshner's unbending will. A month later Abe Schneider sacked Kirshner from his position as President of Colgems Records, and then Don personally handed in his resignation from Screen Gems Music. The **official** reasons given for his dismissal included: refusal to turn over finished masters; generating self-adulatory publicity demeaning to the Monkees; issuing an unauthorized third single; and denying Raybert a share of the publishing income. His $35,500,000 suit was settled for an undisclosed amount.

Lester Sill, the old head of Colpix Records, and one-time partner of Phil Spector in their Philles Records venture, now took Kirshner's place as President of Colgems. This new situation certainly gave Nesmtih and Tork the musical freedom they had been fighting for. Mike brought in his old pal, Chip Douglas (from the Modern Folk Quartet) to produce the third album, 'Headquarters', and presumably Peter and Mike were pleased with the result of their newly-won freedom. Certainly two and a half million kids liked it enough to put it at the number one spot in the American charts. (Although this was only half as many as had bought The Monkees' first album; from a strictly business viewpoint there was justification for some concern in the executive ranks.)

FRI.	JULY 7	ATLANTA, GA.	BRAVES STADIUM
SAT.	JULY 8	JACKSONVILLE, FLA.	SPORTS COLISEUM
SUN.	JULY 9	MIAMI BEACH, FLA.	CONVENTION HALL
TUES.	JULY 11	CHARLOTTE, N.C.	COLISEUM
WED.	JULY 12	GREENSBORO, N.C.	COLISEUM
FRI.	JULY 14		
SAT.	JULY 15	NEW YORK CITY	FOREST HILLS STADIUM
SUN.	JULY 16		
THURS.	JULY 20	BUFFALO, N.Y.	MEMORIAL AUDITORIUM
FRI.	JULY 21	BALTIMORE, MD.	MEMORIAL AUDITORIUM
SAT.	JULY 22	BOSTON, MASS.	BOSTON GARDENS
SUN.	JULY 23	PHILA., PA.	CONVENTION HALL
THURS.	JULY 27	ROCHESTER, N.Y.	WAR MEMORIAL AUDITORIUM
FRI.	JULY 28	CINN., OHIO	GARDENS
SAT.	JULY 29	DETROIT, MICH.	OLYMPIA STADIUM
SUN.	JULY 30	CHICAGO, ILL.	STADIUM
WED.	AUG. 2	MILWAUKEE, WISC.	ARENA
FRI.	AUG. 4	ST. PAUL, MINN.	MUNICIPAL AUDITORIUM
SAT.	AUG. 5	ST. LOUIS, MO.	KIEL AUDITORIUM
SUN.	AUG. 6	DES MOINES, IOWA	VET. MEMORIAL AUD.
WED.	AUG. 9	DALLAS, TEXAS	MEMORIAL AUDITORIUM
THURS.	AUG. 10	HOUSTON, TEXAS	SAM HOUSTON COL.
FRI.	AUG. 11	SHREVEPORT, LA.	HIRSCH MEM. COL.
SAT.	AUG. 12	MOBILE, ALA.	MUNICIPAL AUDITORIUM
THURS.	AUG. 17	MEMPHIS, TENN.	MID-SOUTH COLISEUM
FRI.	AUG. 18	TULSA, OKLA.	ASSEMBLY CENTER
SAT.	AUG. 19	OKLA. CITY, OKLA.	STATE FAIR ARENA
SUN.	AUG. 20	DENVER, COLO.	COLISEUM
FRI.	AUG. 25	SEATTLE, WASH.	SEATTLE CENTER COL.
SAT.	AUG. 26	PORTLAND, ORE.	MEMORIAL COLISEUM
SUN.	AUG. 27	SPOKANE, WASH.	COLISEUM

They started a tour in the Summer with The Jimi Hendrix Experience, who had the unfortunate position of having to open for them. On the next tour, The Fifth Dimension had that unenviable spot and fared no better in front of fans who would have considered any opening act merely an annoying obstacle between them and their heroes.

Filming for the second series of the TV show got underway even before the end of the first tour. On top of this, Colgems were hounding them to record another album to capitalize on the imminent Christmas spending spree. 'Pisces, Aquarius, Capricorn and Jones Ltd' also made the number one spot, but only (only?) sold a mere million copies.

Company heads were now claiming that giving the group artistic freedom had been a big financial blunder, and the boys found themselves in the ludicrous position of having sold 30 million records world-wide, yet being pushed to come up with something 'commercial'.

They didn't. Their fifth album, 'The Birds, The Bees and The Monkees', released in March 1968, only reached number three, and **only** sold half a million copies. The Monkees were almost has-beens. All it required was the final touch, which came in the form of Bob Rafelson's brain-child: the Monkees' first and only feature film, 'Head'.

Dear Mr. Jones,

We are enclosing a final accounting of the Far East Tour that took place last Fall.

You will note that the tour report attached reflects a net loss and, consequently, there will be no distribution due you on this Tour.

If you have any questions with regard to the attached, please advise.

Sincerely,

SCREEN GEMS

A. G. Feder
Controller, West Coast Operations

AGF:ps

Enclosure

cc: Art Frankel

2/17/69

RECAPITULATION OF MONKEES
FAR EAST TOUR
AS OF FEBRUARY 1, 1969

Income			
Australia	68,512.23		
Japan	90,000.00		
Total Income			158,512.23
Less: Expenses as follows:			
Cost of advertising	6,591.55		
Cost of equipment rental	8,580.90		
Cost of land transportation	6,101.71		
Cost from travel expense reports	4,729.25		
Miscellaneous Costs	8,779.19		
Salaries	39,482.54		
Salaries of Monkee Actors	68,160.00		
Musical Instruments	1,027.29		
Tour Preparation Cost	2,541.38		
Cost of air transportation	(131.97)		
Cost of hotels	15,333.86		
Taxes Withheld Japan	9,000.00		
S.S. Taxes, Comp. and Fringe	2,343.66		
Total Expenses			172,539.36
Net Loss to Date			(14,027.13)

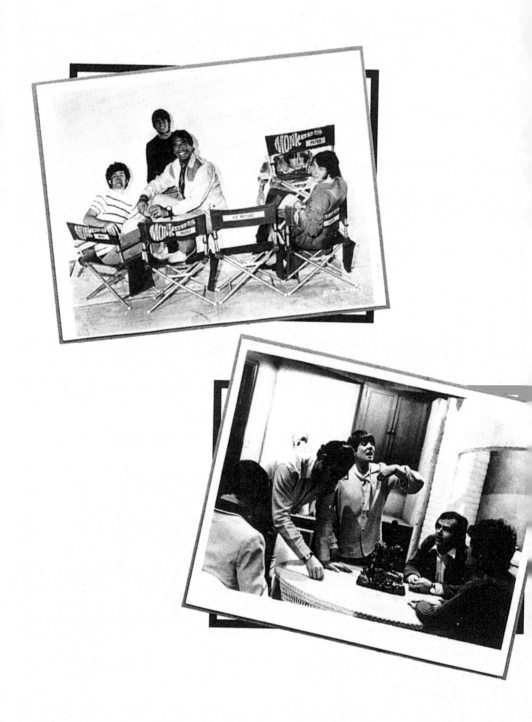

head

"['Head' is]. . . either an unrecognized masterpiece of cinematic achievement, or a huge ego-trip by stoned hippies with money to spend."
—Glenn A. Baker,
  music journalist—

"Head' shows the internal dissension and individual frustration that heralded the end of the group, in much the same way that 'Let It Be' foreshadowed the demise of The Beatles. The irony was though, that because Rafelson couldn't resist using the opportunity to take his extemporaneous style, born of the TV show, to its most bizarre limits (such as intercutting live Monkees' concerts with horrific Vietnam footage) the film received a Restricted rating, and thus, the Monkees' largest audience and truest fans, the teenagers, could not get in to see it.

The movie features some strange guest appearances by Annette Funicello, Frank Zappa, Victor Mature, Jack Nicholson, and the late, ex-heavyweight champion of the world, Sonny Liston (with whom Davy goes three rounds, just about).

But for all this, towards the end of '68, the Monkees were clearly going out as fast as they came in. Their May release, 'D.W. Washburn' had become their first U.S. single not to make the top three, peaking at #19. The TV show had been officially dropped in June, after serious conflicts between the group and the network, concerning the style of the proposed third series. Their eighth U.S. single, 'The Porpoise Song', taken from the film, failed to reach the top fifty, and 'Head', suffering from its restricted audience rating, poor promotion, and a general rapid decline in the group's popularity, died an instant death at the box office.

"Ah, yes. . .
'but aside from 'serious conflicts', 'restricted rating', 'poor promotion' and 'instant death'. . .
what have the Romans ever done for us?" We'd done two series of the TV show. We'd got very slick—we knew what we were doing now. They'd given us more freedom on the music side—now we wanted more on the TV side of it. We wanted to expand it into more of a 'Laugh-In' style of thing, (before there even *was* a 'Laugh-In'), introducing name guests each week—stuff like that.

In fact we'd already started on that during the second year. We had Bobby Sherman on (who subsequently became a big star), Frank Zappa, Charlie Small (who later did 'The Wiz'), Liberace, Deanna Martin, and many others—it became a sort of *hip* thing to guest on our show.

The concept we had *would* have been the right way to go—I think the success of 'Laugh-In' proved that. But the network wouldn't risk it and we wouldn't compromise—I guess we pushed too hard. We were so unhappy with this manufactured image that the press wouldn't let us shake off. We wanted out of it, total freedom—no half-measures.

Micky had been allowed to direct one episode in the second series, called 'The Frodis Caper'—now all of a sudden he wants to direct *all* the shows of the third series. And Mike wants to write *all* the songs. And Peter wants to give *everything* away. In fact he *demands* not to be paid—ever again. And I want a bigger tambourine.

I don't know what I wanted actually. Part of the time I was being Henry Kissinger, trying to get everyone united, and the rest of the time I just wanted to go home and sleep for a few years. But we were not together at all—we were all giving different ultimatums. So the network people just thought—wow, these guys are cracking up—which was pretty close to the truth. So they decide it's more trouble than it's worth. They see the record sales are down to *half* millions, y'know—they probably only sold eight thousand hairs last week.

Anyway—onward and downward. Let's write a movie. . .

"It was one of the projects I was involved in that I was most profoundly proud of. I was just humbly grateful to be involved in one of the most sensational space movies of all time. I think it's Rafelson's definitive work—better than 'Five Easy Pieces'. . ."

—Mike Nesmith—

The idea came about when the four of us, plus Bert Schneider, Bob Rafelson, Jack Nicholson, and about two pounds of prime Hawaiian pot, passed a memorable weekend in a hotel in Ojai, California. We left the tape-recorder running all the time—and between us we wrote the whole film in two days. Raybert and Nicholson worked on the script afterwards—but essentially we all wrote it.

The idea was to blow the whole image—kill 'The Monkees'. We wanted it to have lots of cliches and it did. Plus it had all the behind-the-scenes cliches, too. Like—we weren't going to get a credit for helping write it—that sort of thing. Damn it. . . it was our grass!

"What a load of bollocks!"
—Davy Jones—

Well, Nesmith had this manager, Jerry Perenschio, who was going to make sure Mike didn't get ripped off, and that he got credit as one of the writers. Micky and I decided to sign with him also—and for the first time ever we almost got united. But Peter wouldn't go with him. I don't know why. Maybe Perenschio wouldn't give him *no* money.

So the day before filming was to start, Perenschio tells Raybert he's withdrawing us from the movie—we're going on strike unless we get writers' credits. Raybert calls his bluff and shooting goes ahead, and the only one there on the first day is Peter. He's got to really spead himself around.

Anyway we didn't get the credit but it was negotiated somehow or other and we went to work. I didn't have a salary—I said I'd take a piece of the movie, yet again. We all did. (Would I *never* get it right?)

It was fun though. Everything we could send-up, from the TV show or from our image, we did. We wanted to show how unreal the Monkees' world was, so we'd break reality in the middle of a scene, walk through a backdrop. . . Micky gets shot with an arrow and pulls it out—"I've had it with this—fake sets—fake arrows." I go fight Sonny Liston—we play the dandruff in Victor Mature's hair, ('The Big Victor')—anything and everything. Subtlety? Never heard of the word.

But the central idea, if you can spot one, is the Black Box. We're all kept inside this great big black box, which is supposed to represent society, right?. . . HEAVY. And we've each got our own way of getting out, right? Mike's way is to con his way out—he's always the business man. Peter thinks he can meditate his way out—probably could have, come to think of it. Micky jokes his way out—and I'm the fighter, see? Anyway, the interesting thing about this is that the black box is for real. It's what we had on our sound stage during the second year's shooting of the TV show—they really had us locked away there. Not literally, but that's where we had to be so they could always find us.

It started out we had four dressing-rooms, which were really four caravans, lined up down a wall on the studio set. Nesmith—no, Tork facing that way—Nesmith facing *this* way (he'd turned his around)—me facing this way (otherwise I'd be facing the wall) and Dolenz facing—no, Dolenz just had a chair—he'd rented his out. I forget.

But anyway, the deal would be, whenever they wanted us they'd call and we could be straight onto the set. My door was just three steps away from the living room set—Micky was just three steps away from the garage set—Peter was three steps away from God knows where. . . Nirvana, I think. Anyway—it was all nice and compact. They had bunk beds, refrigerators—the whole bit. We were always inviting technicians in for drinks. It was cosy.

So one time they're filming some extras or something—I've got half an hour off and I'm in my caravan with this young lady and I hear,

"Quiet on the set! Cameras rolling. . . ACTION!"

Well—I can't resist. I step out of my door, just my shorts on, and I shout,

"Could you keep it down, please? We're trying to screw in here!"

"CUT!!!"

Well, they were pretty mad. *Something* has to be done about this—we can't work this way—this is *disgusting*—bump di bump di bum, y'know.

So what they did is they built this huge black box—sixteen feet by twelve feet by eight feet high. Giant meat freezer door—completely sound-proofed—carpet on the walls, pillows everywhere, and a light in each corner with our name under it. So whenever they wanted one of us, they just flashed our light. It was great. We had everything we needed. If we had a guest arriving and we were shooting, they'd automatically show them into the black box. So that was for real—and it was featured and expanded on in 'Head'.

I don't know what their idea was with the promotion for this film. It was the first time the actual name, 'The Monkees', was not used to sell the product. They had an ad on TV—just a face with dark glasses, and a voice saying, "Head. . . Head. . . Head. . . ", real monotonous, over and over. Weird. And our fans couldn't even get in to see the film 'cos of the restricted rating. It was stupid.

After 'Head' the Monkees did only one more thing together, as a group. (Or as together as it was ever going to be.) It was a TV special, '33 1/3 Revolutions per Monkee', with Little Richard, Jerry Lee Lewis, Fats Domino, Brian Auger and Julie Driscoll. It was directed by Jack Good and received favourable reviews, especially from 'Variety'. But incredibly NBC put it on against the 1969 Academy Awards presentation.

I didn't see it—I was watching the Oscars, like everyone else. But it was during the filming of this show that Peter told us he was quitting the group. He couldn't stand it anymore. It's funny—throughout the whole Monkees thing I'd always thought that what Peter was doing was just something to do with his age, and that the brown rice and water beds bit would come to me *next* year. But it didn't happen that way. I realize now that we all have our own way of doing what we're here to do.

It wasn't quite the end when Peter left. We tried to keep going for a while—first as three—then just Micky and me. (I heard there was a joke going 'round Screen Gems that eventually, one of us would be left billing ourself as 'The Monkee'. I guess recent events have shown *them*. Although actually there is one left billing himself as 'Not A Monkee'—but that's another story.) Really though, it would have been less painful back then, to have followed Peter's example and just called it a very long, full day.

I still believe we were right not to do a third series in the same old style. We'd have ended up parodying ourselves. But whether the direction we each took was right or not, who knows? We took it anyway. North, south, east west. Micky flew north for the winter (he never was real smart); Mike headed Magnetic South; Peter went Far East—right up his navel; and the Manchester Cowboy rode off into the sunset. My dad used to say, "Go West, young man—and don't bloody come back!"

Peter had his own reasons for leaving when he did, although it appears he was not so concerned with making sure he had a life-jacket handy before abandoning ship as was Nesmith, who had signed a solo production deal in 1968 with DOT Records.

For a short while, Jerry Perenschio continued to act on behalf of the group (now minus Peter). For the first time since they had been doing live appearances, Columbia/Screen Gems were not doing the bookings, so it looked like the group was going to make money from their concerts at last. Screen Gems however, claiming they owned the name, 'The Monkees', demanded fifty per cent of all gross monies that the three made.

Perenschio worked a way around this by having the contracts made out in his name and all fees paid to him, and then he paid the group. "Let them sue you," was his advice.

'All this was academic though, since the popularity of the group had dwindled so much, so suddenly, that they were now drawing only half-houses. A sad touch of irony, because they now had probably the best live show they'd ever put on. Utilizing back-projected silent film footage shot by the group themselves, the revue-style show lasted two and a half hours and even got glowing reviews from many of their past detractors.

Backed by a seven-piece band, 'Sam and the Good Times', their disastrous last tour in 1969 ground to a halt at a ten-thousand seater venue in Forest Hills, New York. The promoter came to their hotel room and, almost embarassedly, told them they'd only managed to sell three-thousand tickets. They decided then to make an official announcement that they were quitting touring—purportedly to concentrate on recording .

120

Perenschio read the graffiti on the wall and phased-out his connection with the group. Not wishing to leave show-business altogether, but searching for a less cruel genre, he ventured into promoting boxing matches. He did closed-circuit television coverage of big fights such as the Muhammad Ali/Joe Frazier Heavyweight Championship.

With the television show and live concerts over, all that remained to keep them together was recording. The seventh album, and first as a trio, 'Instant Replay', contained some previously rejected material. Screen Gems were now quite clearly ashamed to be connected with the group and announced that they had given them what they had been demanding for so long: complete artistic control. This, in view of their situation, was kind of like giving them the keys to the city after it had been evacuated. They even put out, for the first time ever, a single whose 'B' side was not a Screen Gems copyright, thus forfeiting half of any potential publishing royalty—a pretty fair indication of how disinterested everyone was at the label.

Inbetween 'Instant Replay' and their eighth offering, 'The Monkees Present: Micky, David and Michael', Colgems cannily released a 'Monkees Greatest Hits' album—in those days, always a sure sign that a group's hits were a thing of the past. Nowadays, that doesn't necessarily follow, but it's still a matter of the shrewdest timing to release such an album so as to maximize sales, but not jeopardize the chances of the next 'originals' set. But in 1969 Colgems didn't care about how obvious it looked. They just wanted to make what they could off the old stuff, which wouldn't cost them anything, rather than spend money promoting the new, which they didn't believe in anyway. Consequently, 'The Monkees Present. . . ', a superior album in many ways, was left to die a death.

At this same time Davy at last announced that he'd been secretly married to Linda for a year, which outraged the fans. Hurt and disillusioned, they stayed away from the record stores in droves.

Towards the end of the year, Linda Ronstadt's drummer, John Ware, approached Nesmith about forming a band. Mike's buddy, bassist John London (who played on the ill-fated '69 tour and had been Nesmith's constant companion since well before The Monkees) was going to be in the band, so it was right up Papa Nes's country road. And as the Monkees were sadly at the end of theirs (one would have thought) no one blames him for accepting the offer and joining 'The First National Band'. Soon afterwards he commenced his critically acclaimed solo career with the 'Magnetic South' album on RCA. Since '75 he's run his own successful label, Pacific Arts Corporation, recording and releasing albums conveying his own unique blend of country/rock-oriented philosophy. High points in his solo offerings include 'The Prison' and 'From a Radio Engine to the Photon Wing'.

Currently, Nesmith is one of the pioneers in the wide-open field of video and in fact, in 1982, won the first ever Grammy Award offered in that category, for ·'Elephant Parts'.

Meanwhile. . . and then there were two. The last L.P., 'Changes', was a half-hearted effort from the acting half of the group; a contractual death-rattle. The album was being recorded in New York and Davy wanted to take his daughter, Talia, with him. But Colgems wouldn't pay Talia's ticket—and wanted to give Davy only $20 a day expenses. Second-class all the way. . . and less than two years before it had been lear-jets and limousines.

All the tracks were already laid when Davy got to New York. He had no say in the choice of material and only sang one song. Micky sang all the rest, which comprised a rather dismal collection of poor bubblegum songs written by producers Jeff Barry and Andy Kim.

That was the official end of The Monkees, but Davy still had one more disaster to go before he finally broke with Screen Gems in 1971. They got him a deal to do one album on Bell/Arista, with Screen Gems publishing. He was teamed up with Jackie Mills, Bobby Sherman's producer, who still saw Davy as a bubblegum singer. He wouln't allow him to break out of that mold into something a little more challenging, in the way that he was attempting to do with his live shows. The result was one more unoriginal piece of vinyl, from which four singles were released. Only the first, 'Rainy Jane', made any impression on the charts.

Davy was very upset with the way the whole thing was handled. He didn't have a manager at the time and was therefore at the mercy of the record company executives. He asked for just his picture and name to be on the cover, but he obviously didn't ask loudly enough. They put out a cheap-looking thing that had the song titles and company logo on the front cover. Davy complained, but to no avail. By 1971, having the face of a Monkee was more of a liability than an asset. It had been a sobering few years.

That's when I started drinking.

"Ever have that sinking feeling?"

a little bit you,
a little bit me

So a couple of years fly by—'69/'70—what am I doing? I don't like this responsibility business. I was always driving off somewhere. Turning my back on it. Leaving her crying on the stairs—some stupid thing I'd said to hurt her.

I had a '67 Cadillac convertible, a Mini Cooper, a Pontiac black-top convertible (courtesy of the studio), a Honda 450 (courtesy), a Honda 800 Coupe (courtesy), a Velocetta '500' scooter. Hell, I could drive off every day of the week! North, south, east, west.

I went off to Yosemite for three or four days once—came back to find David Pearl and Linda riding one of my motorbikes. She'd never ride on them with me.

I was very jealous—always imagining the worst, thinking that they were together when I was not around. I was suspicious of any communication between them. I never really forgave her for going with him—and he never forgave her for marrying me. Jealousy on both sides. She was trapped no matter which way she turned. David Pearl was still around all the time, working for me. I should have fired him, but. . . maybe there was another way 'round it? What could bring us together again?

I suggested another baby. She didn't go for it a hundred per cent. Maybe my timing.

"Pass the peas, dear?—I've been thinking—err, carrots?—I suppose there's no chance of—potatoes *would* be nice, yes, thank you—another baby?"

"We can't afford it," she said.

"Come on, what's one more little mouth going to cost?"

"Let's gid rid of some of these people," she said, ignoring the issue again.

We had a spring clean and lost about four house guests. But it didn't really help. I didn't know how to be with *just* Linda. There had always been a crowd around. About the only difference was, it was a treat not having to wait for the bathroom. And maybe having the bedroom to ourselves might have helped too—a few weeks later, little Sarah was on her way.

I felt great. Linda didn't. She went to Hawaii to get away from me for a while. I missed her terribly but I didn't exactly hang about waiting for her. The press, as always, were keen to make any of my friendships into torrid love affairs—it must have been hard for her.

When she came back I cooled out completely. She moved the bed downstairs into the drawing room and the stereo was moved outside to the guest house. You could have put the entire Encyclopædia Brittanica between us most nights. Eye contact went south and total breakdown was not far away. Still, we salvaged what we could 'round about the eighth month. Got it together to go to England and prepare for Sarah Lee.

It was becoming fashionable for a wife to ask her husband to be present at the birth of their child. But as I pride myself on being somewhat *old*-fashioned, (and a bit of a coward when it comes to these things), on arrival in England, I immediately booked a tour. Ten days in Ireland.

As it turned out Linda wanted her sister, Janet, to be there with her again, anyway. For once we both wanted the same thing. Necessity played a part too as I had no agent working for me and lucrative engagements were now few and far between.

We had arranged to stay in London with Anton and Morna Rodgers, not knowing that they too were in the middle of heavy struggles and Anton was on the brink of moving out. When we arrived at the airport—no Anton, no ride. We took a taxi to a hotel and tried for a couple of days to reach them. Finally we met.

Turned out Anton had heard I was into heavy drugs. 'Strung out' was the expression he used. And he didn't want his kids exposed to that kind of thing. Quite right too. . . except that I obviously wasn't, never had been and never will. It was just another of those vicious rumours that people love to start for no apparent reason. And anyway, if ever you hear that a friend is 'strung out'—go *to* him, not away from him.

· Things are cleared up anyway, and we stay with Anton and Morna. Big mistake—fights all the time. It was horrible but. . . I was off to Ireland and Linda was left in the middle of it. Must've been pretty rough for her. On one of my trips back to London it looked like all go for the baby—then, no go—so off I go. Again.

Back in Ireland and straight off the plane I hear, "Davy Jones. . . paging Mr. Davy Jones. . ." My sister Beryl gives me the news this time—it's another girl. I'd missed the birth once more.

Well, I finish my stint in Ireland and off we go again—the new family returns to America. But instead of a new start it's just the same old thing, only heavier because there's four people involved now. Linda did a great job with Talia and Sarah. And I did manage to communicate on some levels—I loved to take care of them—shot loads of movies of Talia. But Sarah Lee—well, I wasn't really there—I was working.

I missed picking her up like I did Talia. I hope she's on film. I got her at one and two, but those other years—Sarah needs to be captured—she's important, special. That's what dads do—they capture the past for the future. Well, they should. I took a picture of about twelve mothers and their children at Talia's first birthday party. Seventeen years later they're *all* divorced: a 60's statistic on film.

There is only one kind of love
That lasts forever
This is something I'm sure of
There is only one kind of love.

There is only one kind of life
The life that I am living
This is something I am sure of
There is only one kind of love

And life goes on and on and round and round
Some day you're going to fall in love
Love comes easier second time around
But there is only one kind of love
That I am capable of.

Loving you, girl, isn't easy
Knowing just exactly what you need.
Putting back the pieces
Of our lives together
I hope that what we've done
Is what you feel.

— David and Talia Jones —
February 19th, 1977

I guess I never really gave our relationship a chance to grow—I didn't know how. Linda was the first person I'd ever lived with. (You call this living?)

Well, she'd had six years of being in the background with two babies so, finally she needed to make a move to where she could be her own person. That's when we moved to Santa Barbara—1974. Her security was there, her mother and two sisters. She got a job

127

working for Sheffield Records, a small outfit at the time, but at least she was working. I wasn't.

"I'm fed up with being, 'Mrs. Davy Jones'," she said once. Or twice.

Fair enough. Once in Santa Barbara she could be, "'Linda Haines Jones.' And this is my husband, David."

Leaving 8571 Franklin Avenue was a big move. I had very mixed emotions but all I could do was turn to the house and say, "Thanks a lot". At her tender age, Talia had much more flair for capturing the moment. She did a little soft-shoe shuffle ending with, "dum diddley dum dum. . . dum dum!" Cheered me up a couple of notches.

The last load was packed tightly on top of the VW. Stuff I really had no use for, but packed full of memories. When I reached Sunset I gave one last look up the hill. I knew it was the final break from a Hollywood that had served me so well. I'd come there ten years before—collected an Emmy for the Monkees TV show—bought and sold a beautiful home (or orange groves. . . not sure which)—rubbed shoulders with the rich and famous—and lived every childhood fantasy. What more could I want?

Plenty. Off down the Ventura Freeway we went. Talk about the Beverly Hillbillies! I was very tired. With the help of Linda's brother, Jim, I'd painted the house inside and out, and done the same in Santa Barbara to the new place. When the move was first discussed it was exciting—another house, another town. But now, feeling tired and alone, it seemed that the best was behind me. Linda had developed an attitude over the last few months. She'd wanted to break away for so long. Now her plans were in motion. I was driving towards a volcano that had threatened to erupt for so long.

Santa Barbara at sunset made a pretty picture. We passed a sign that said, 'Montecito City. Population 9988'. I'll change that, I thought. But I never did. When I looked back at the same sign on the day I left—it was as though I'd never been there.

I drove up the road off the freeway, past the kids' future school, the Montecito Union. Very grand. My spirits jumped another few notches. Around a few curves and then there it was. It seemed so peaceful and safe in this neighbourhood. One thing about the old house was it was very hard for the kids to play—every road went right down to the Hollywood traffic. The new place was one of only four houses on a dead end street. Perfect for the kids. But a dead end just the same.

I drove 'round the back and into the garage. There was a hideous, crunching sound. Not too good a start to the beginning of the end. The rack on the car! "Quick, stop!" cried Talia. Just in time. I backed up with a deep sigh that started ages ago. One of the memories grabbed hold of the edge of the garage roof. The rack slipped down the front of the car, screeching over the windscreen—took the wipers over the bonnet and left two tramtracks before it came to rest in front of the car. I tried to think what all this junk was that I had packed. I couldn't. I put the car into first and gunned it over the whole lot. Sat back and finished my sigh.

"What the hell are you doing?" —the wicked witch of the west.

"What?" I'd hardly heard her.

She got on her broom and flew into the house. Once again my timing was off. I didn't think. I just put my head back on the seat. Linda would have her edge just enough to keep me on the other side of the bed once again.

Kenya, my forever faithful Labrador, and Diablo, the neurotic Doberman, were soon at the car window, happy to see me and eager to show me the new garden. That was more the welcome home I needed. Well, 'home' was not quite the right word—but at least my daughters were there And I had real-life neighbours, not just 'stars', that I could talk to for the first time since I left England fifteen years before—half my life ago.

The first neighbourly encounter took place immediately I stepped from the car. Just what I needed.

"Hi, I'm Leigh. I live next door."

"I'm David."

"Yes, I know. Come on over."

I climb the tree and jump over the fence.

"Want a valium?" asks Leigh. Talk about coming straight to the point. I didn't need much persuasion.

"Smoke?" Leigh lights up a joint. Well that, plus the valium, plus a Budweiser that his sister, Moira, gave me. . . no problem.

"Play table tennis?" Three out of three so far. In the state of mind that we're rapidly approaching—if anyone returns serve it will count as a pretty fierce rally—but nevertheless, we have great fun. Mostly looking for the ball. This was the start of a year-long competition we called the 'Table Tennis Championship for the Mentally Absent'. I tried to get Leigh to share my passion for real tennis but he couldn't understand my wanting to spend so much valuable smoking and drinking time out on the courts.

Eventually I did get him to come along and play. Turned out he liked it—until one day he lost his temper over an old memory—one of his famous 180° turns. He suddenly hit a ball that landed somewhere in Canada. Then followed that with a convincing impression of The Who doing their end-of-gig smash up—using the racket I'd lent him as Pete Townsend's guitar. I decided not to stick around for the encore. We met up later that night for tea and valiums in the garden. Never even mentioned the racket—we were good at avoiding issues.

Leigh had lived in Santa Barbara all his life. He knew all the best spots for several sports—fishing and drinking are a couple that come to mind. Two or three days a week we'd go fishing. Took Talia with us once and she caught her first fish—a perch. We let it go.

"Why, daddy?"

"It's good luck to let your first one go," I told her.

"But it will tell the rest of the fishes we're here." Makes sense. We didn't catch any more that day.

The other sport Leigh was handy at usually took up the other four or five days of the week. He introduced me to some pretty interesting bars—straight out of spaghetti westerns. And pointed out several others that we couldn't actually go in together, as he was banned from them. One night, after one of our sessions, we decided to race each other home—he on his bike and me in my van, 'Harry'.

Well, Harry had a bit of an argument with an island in the middle of the road—spun into the air—and seemed to hang about there for. . . quite a risky length of time, actually. Fortunately the road broke our fall and Harry bounced on his roof until he came to rest, right way up, in the middle of three huge boulders in some sort of park area.

My seat belt was nice and tight—which saved my life. . . but then so was I—which is how I almost lost it in the first place. Harry, on the other hand, was in pretty poor shape. Looking at him I should have been just another statistic that night, but it was obviously not my time to go. I was glad. It's a lousy idea to be plastered when meeting one's maker. . . first impressions are so important.

Leigh came back for me.

"Need a ride?"

"No thanks. I'm pretty beat—think I'll just crash here for tonight."

Stuck a note on Harry's windshield: 'OUT OF ORDER'. I figured facing Linda in that condition, at that hour, would be tempting fate once too often for one night, so. . . back to Leigh's for a nightcap. Rather deal with it tomorrow. Rather not deal with it at all, actually.

Leigh was an ex-fisherman, ex-plumber, ex-carpenter, ex-serviceman, ex-fireman, ex-gas-station attendant, ex-mechanic—but forever my friend. He'd inherited some money, which his mom only let him have in dribs and drabs. So when he ran out he'd do his Oliver bit and ask for more. But he had his own peculiar little ways of asking. One that I remember was he burst in on his Mom's yoga class—with his double-barrelled shotgun cocked and aimed—and threatened to start wasting her students if she didn't write him a nice cheque. She screamed for help and I leaped over the fence. Gradually. . . slowly. . . I was able to convince him that killing the students would only complicate things further. He was a little over the top was Leigh.

One sunny morning, after mowing the huge lawn all around the house, (he was neat, I'll say that for him), he climbed the oak tree, put a rope round his neck, and jumped. Broke the branch and gave himself a nasty rope burn. He was quite proud of that burn, but I didn't like it too much—I guess I took it on myself to feel responsible for him. Stupid, I know, but. . . we weren't seeing as much of each other then—I was up and down to L.A. a lot of the time, trying to get a tour lined up with Dolenz, Boyce and Hart. When we finally went on the road, Leigh came along and helped out—but he was still spending all we paid him on booze—and occasionally having to ask me for twenty dollars here and there.

One time he asked me and I asked him if it was for drink or food. I was trying to look after him in my way—but I guess it came across like a parental trip—made him feel awful and so off he went to Oregon in a huff.

After a couple of weeks I joined him up there. He had this cabin out in the middle of nowhere. It wasn't exactly the Hilton. It had hot and cold running nothing. We made our own water supply with a couple of hundred yards of hosepipe—went up the hillside to the stream—rigged up filters and barrells and did stuff I'd never done in my life, before or since. It was great for a while. Down the river a way there was this natural pool with a Tarzan rope that you could leap off from and deer running around—the whole bit. It was magic. If only we could've just enjoyed the place. Poor Leigh—he was a hell of a nice guy, really. . . just crazy. And I wasn't far behind. We just ended up drinking all the time. After four or five days I couldn't take any more—I had to leave.

Back in Hollywood, Thanksgiving Day—Leigh calls me from some bar up there in Oregon.

"Hey, man—I'm having my Thanksgiving dinner. You should be here. Cheese sandwich. Split it with you." He was feeling sorry for himself. I told him I was thinking about coming up again soon.

"Maybe in a couple of weeks—okay, man?"

"Yeah, okay." He was still down, I could tell—but trying to cover it up. A week goes by and he calls again,

"You gonna be coming up soon, man?"

"Yeah, real soon."

"Great. Great."

Another couple of days go by and he calls me again. I remember it was a Sunday night. He says he's got great news for me.

"Oh, yeah, what?"

Says he won't be needing the valiums any more—he's given them up.

"Great," I say. Then he tells me he's quit drinking, too.

"Give me a break, man. I'll believe *that* when I see it."

"No, really. Honest."

Okay, so we talk about this and that for a while but—I've got people arriving and I guess maybe I sound a bit distant. I wind it up a bit abruptly.

"Gotta go now, okay?" Hang up.

DAMN IT! The minute I hang up I know why he called. And I can't call him back because I don't know where he is. All I know is he's in some bar in Oregon—and I know what he's going to do.

The next morning my worst fears are confirmed. His mother calls me.

"Leigh shot himself last night."

He'd called to say goodbye. To tell me he wasn't taking the pills any more because he was going.

The funeral was in Santa Barbara. I came into town and went up to the cemetery. Weird seeing all those people standing around. He'd finally got the whole family together again. I threw some dirt on the coffin, just like with my dad, and that was that.

His mother said to me,

"Well, I think this is best for all of us, don't you?"

"What?. . . "

"Would you like to come back to the house for a cup of tea and a talk?" Oh, sure. All sit around and talk about Leigh in front of his back.

"No. I don't think I can make that, Mrs. Norton."

dolenz, jones, boyce & hart & talia & sarah

$\mathbb{T}$hat tour that Leigh had come on with me came about, quite out of the blue, when Tommy Boyce called me up one morning and said,

"Jones. . . idea! Great Golden Hits of The Monkees. The guys that sang 'em and the guys that wrote 'em. 'Dolenz, Jones, Boyce and Hart'. What do you think?"

Long pause.

"Who is this?" I ask. I love teasing him. He breaks into hysterical laughter, which is what I want from him anyway—he's such a great laugher. That same old line gets him every time. Finally he gets back to normal.

"No, but seriously. . . " he tries again.

"Sure," I say. "But who're these Dolenz and Hart guys?" Off he goes again. That was the start of a magical mystery tour around the world.

"It's really nice to be here at Disneyland."

"Indeed it is. Do you know what a treat it is not to have to pay to get into this place?"

"That's only because they thought you were Dopey."

"It's really nice to be here in Tokyo. . . " We got a standing ovation there and didn't even know it.

"It's really nice to be here in Sydney. . . Hong Kong. . . Abbadabbi. . ." Bump di bump di bum. And so on, around the globe.

It was a much needed change. I'd felt as though I was stagnating, ninety miles from L.A., surrounded by all Linda's fashion-conscious people in their trendy wine-bars. We were pretty much leading separate lives by now, tolerating each other only for the childrens' sake.

So while I was on the road with Micky, Boyce and Hart, I did all the things I never did when I was fifteen. . . sixteen. . . twenty-one. Women, booze. . . I went crazy. Boyce and I really hit it off together, both on and off stage, in and out of the sauna (with selected females), from the Far East, China—to the far east, New Jersey. Great times.

We were at the Golden Banana in Boston for one week. The club had strippers during the day, and in the evening it was a 1,000 seater theatre. On this particular morning, Boyce and I had our breakfast—eggs and beer—and set out across Boston. We skipped from bar to bar until we realized it was heading-home time. The show was only an hour or so away.

"One more cocktail!" was our collective cry.

We straightened our ties and fell into a hotel lounge bar. A wedding had just taken place. The bride and groom were dancing and Tommy boldly walks over to the groom and taps him on the shoulder—

"Excuse me old chap, do you mind if I cut in?"

Boyce is dancing with the bride, to everyone's bewilderment and amusement, and when the dance ends Boyce takes the mike.

"Ladies and Gentlemen—can I have your attention please? It gives me great pleasure to introduce to you at this time. . . a man amongst men. He's been picked up by so many girls—he's starting to grow handles. Yes, you've guessed it—The Manchester Cowboy himself. . . Davy Jones!"

Oooohs and aaahs, like he's just announced the star prize on a quiz show.

"Davy would like to present his gift to the lovely couple. . . a song."

He sits down at the piano and starts into, 'I Wanna Be Free'. Hardly appropriate I thought, however. . . the people love it. We finish to thunderous applause, and leave triumphant, smiling, walking arm in arm and doing the famous Monkee walk.

Osaka, Japan, now. Ten minutes to showtime and I decide I need a drink. I pop next door for a quick one. It's cutting it close, so Micky starts to prima-donna around—

"Well, we'll just have to start without him," he tut-tuts.

"We can't start without him, Micky. Just wait—he'll be back."

They try to explain to the Japanese MC just what's happening. He thinks they're telling him to go ahead with the show.

"No-no-no! Davy. . . NOT. . . ah, *HERE*!" says Micky, in his best Japanese dialect.

"Ah-so. Very good. . . yes?" says the MC, grasping the situation immediately. "You do show now. . . so?"

"Nnnnooo—you don't understand. DAVY. . . has GONE. . . for quick. . . aah, *DRINK*. . . " making best Japanese drinking motion with hand.

"Aaaaaaah. . . you want DLINK on stage. . . very fine." He runs after somebody to get a drink, shouting, "Quickry. . . showtime—showtime!"

Micky throws up his arms in despair.

"Ladies and Gentlemen. . . I give you. . . the faburous. . . Dorenz, Jones, Boyce and Hart. . . *Golden Gleat Hits of*. . . thaah MONKEES!!!"

They have no choice. The band strikes up and they're on.

Now—my opening number is 'Daydream Believer', and I can be quite possessive about things like that when I want to be, especially when I've had a drink or three. So when I return to the theatre, walk backstage, and hear Micky doing MY song!. . . I get him in my line of fire, go running on stage like Bruce Lee, and leap into the air, arms and legs flying—all set to drop-kick Skillet Face. Except, that at the crucial moment, Micky does a little Cyd Cherise and I go flying over him—end up in the front row of the audience. Tumultuous applause, Boyce throws me a mike—and I'm on. We should have kept it in every night.

Ten thousand people came to our first show in St. Louis and, twelve months later, at the same park, just the same amount of people with just as much enthusiastic applause. Success followed us on that tour from concept to conclusion, and after the events of the few months leading up to it, it tasted real sweet.

After a year on the road I came back and there was nothing there between Linda and I, so I stayed in L.A. with Micky at his place, up on Lookout Mountain in Laurel Canyon. On the night of the Grammy Awards, Linda came back there and started talking about getting a separation. I said, no—it's divorce or nothing. Then out of the blue she said,

"Well, it's coming up to my birthday—why don't you get me a divorce?"

At that moment, the whole move to Santa Barbara seemed to me to have been just premeditated divorce. She said to me recently, it doesn't have to be all or nothing—we were talking about the kids. But father/daddy means, to me, *being* there—taking part in the children's lives.

Something did come from Linda and David, though. . . Linda and David and Talia and Sarah. And my love for us will never die. It was meant to be.

I have a lot to thank Linda for and I'll always love her in a special way. The affair was over in a night, but our friendship will last forever. She would probably see our relationship differently but you'll have to wait for her book to find that out. I notice she still has a picture, taken on our wedding night, sitting on the piano. No, wait a minute—it's here—

P.S. Talia — Personal Aches

I was much smaller than I am right now
I was so dirty from playing and really somehow
I didn't stop to spend the time with you
But I can right now
Don't you remember me, daddy?

You know all my friends say you're really the thing
And when you step out on stage to dance or sing
That people look happy and jump up with joy
But don't you remember me, daddy?

Well now that I'm married and have kids of my own
I know you're singing and dancing like in times that are gone
Somehow it's strange that over the years
I'll always remember you, daddy.

But there was one time when to no-one else you would give
And that was when you used to rock me in my crib
I know there were more girls than me to be with
And I know that your heart's warm and you love to give
But don't you remember me, daddy?

I'll never forget you, daddy.
And no matter what happens between
I'll always remember you, daddy.

—a song I gave to Talia after Linda and I split—
(for her to give to me, someday)

136

Song for Sarah's birthday –

You have grown up right before my eyes
And it comes to me as a surprise
The things I thought I'd have to tell you
You already know
I try to give you sound advice
That you already know
And you're only ten years old.

You might think it's pride
Or protocol
Maybe too parental
Yes, that's all
Everything's the same to you
Does that include me?
Before we grow too far apart
How can I make you see
When you're only ten years old?

You have memories just like me
You have feelings just like me
You have freedom just like me
And you're only ten years old.

reviewing the situation

In December of 1973, Davy was offered a six-month theatre engagement back in England. It was a welcome respite from his domestic turmoil back in California; far easier to immerse himself in work once more, and to receive the acclamation of the crowds, than to stay and face the work needed in a one-to-one relationship. So off he went to appear in Peter Nicholls' play, 'Forget-Me-Not Lane'.

My life with Linda seemed ages away, and I was glad to be back in England working in the theatre again. But somehow I missed her, damn it. The smell and the atmosphere took me back to the Dodger—the West End and Broadway. But there was a guy in the play, Edward Chapman, who took me back even further—to Abdullah and the school play.

He was a great guy, old Edward, but he had a terrible habit of suddenly jumping whole lines of dialogue, right in the middle of what was usually the most important scene of the play—the one that slots it all together, y'know. Sometimes he'd jump whole pages—even entire scenes—and I'd be ad-libbing like crazy to fill the audience in on what they'd missed. And then, just when it seemed I'd caught up to where he was at, he'd jump back to before the part I'd just filled in for him—and we'd go through it all again, and the audience is thinking—boy, this Peter Nicholls sure likes to make a point! It was madness. But it was lovely madness. That's the beauty of live theatre. That's why I went back to the boards—and always will.

There was a whole portion of the play where me and this other guy, Tom Owen— we had to go off to war, see? So we'd just nip 'round the corner to the pub and leave old Edward and the rest of the cast to it.

One night, Tom and I are 'at war' in The King's Arms—I've had a few bevvies more than everybody else put together—and I tell Tom I'm not going back on. I mean, old Edward could be doing RICHARD III by now—you never knew. And I don't know that one, so I'm not going back. I refuse. Tom has to go back without me. War can be hell, sometimes. That's when I started drinking.

At the end of the run I asked Tom to come back to California with me. We'd shared a houseboat together, picked up a few Norfolk broads together—I'd got used to having him around. Looking back, I guess that was my way of avoiding the issue with Linda again.

*Years later, while driving through London with his secretary, Bobby Wade, (now Bobby Boyce—she married Tommy), Davy suddenly yelled out, "Stop the car!" He'd spotted Tom Owen in a crowd of people and just leaped out of the car in the middle of rush-hour traffic. She didn't see him again for two days. It transpired that Tom and Davy were going to be working together on a couple of episodes of an English TV series called 'Horse in the House'. Neither of them had known that the other was in it, so they had gone for a drink together to celebrate. For **two days?***

Yeah, well—I had to give him some training and moral support, y'see? In the show, I played a crooked jockey, Frank Tyson, and Tom played the good guy. Both roles required a certain amount of riding ability. Tom could stay on okay, but—he was a bit nervous about having to shoot the race scenes—especially one where he had to ride a real race-horse—in a real race, at Kempton Park. I wasn't in the scene they were shooting that particular day—I went along just to watch and to take care of Tom's wife, Mary, who was expecting a baby. . . like, yesterday.

Well, we're standing at the side of the track—watching and drinking, and making encouraging faces and noises to help Tom through his ordeal. The race sets off and Tom's doing just fine—he's approaching the end of the circuit, which is all they need to film, and he's still aboard. We're all relieved and we start applauding and laughing and I'm getting ready to order the congratulatory round of drinks when I look up—and I stop laughing. This is suddenly *very* serious.

All the horses are easing off, gradually slowing down—except Tom's. His is getting faster. Much faster. *And* he's heading straight for the paddock—for the member's enclosure where all the television cameras are. This is no joke. The only way Tom can survive is if the horse suddenly dies. I turn Mary away 'cos she's going to give birth right now if she sees what's happening. It's terrible—everybody's scattering—light's are falling all over the place. The horse thinks it's in Ben Hur. Tom's got his eyes closed—he just figures he's a gonner, y'know—this is it.

I don't know to this day how he survived, but by some miracle—by the grace of God—the horse stopped. Knocked some stuff around but there were no dead technicians— it was unbelievable. Tom staggers over, really shaken—but alive. We're all relieved, and breathing again, and Mary hasn't had her baby yet, and I'm about to buy that round, when the director comes over and says,

"Great, Tom—absolutely great. The race, I mean—not that bit at the end. Anyway, we almost got it. Just once more and we'll be finished for the day."

The sequel to this is that about a year after we did 'Horse in the House', I was living in a lovely little farm house, out in the middle of nowhere, down in Sussex—'Burnt House Farm' it was called. Nothing but fields as far as you could see. And over the brow of a hill was this little village with a great pub that I liked to visit—whenever it was open. I had two Jack Russell terriers, Doris and Harry, and in a field adjoining, there was this old horse, Magpie. I loved that old horse—he used to come over every time I stepped out of the house, and I'd give him carrots.

So one night I'm crawling back home from the pub. I mean, literally—on my hands and knees in the snow. Doris is not doing much better—she's been drinking lagers all night—so we're both well out of it, making our way across the field. Suddenly I have this great idea.

"I know," I say to Doris. "Perhaps Magpie would like to see where we live."

Doris's ears go back and she starts to whimper, but I take no notice. I call Magpie over and there's all three of us outside the front door looking for the key. It takes forever but eventually somebody finds it. Doris, I think. I open the door and invite Magpie in. He doesn't quite understand so. . . very gently, I tell him that my place is his place, and if he's ever stuck for anywhere, y'know—not to feel bad about asking. Then I pull him inside.

Well, he's only thirteen hands—but then, it's only an eighteen hands house, and that doesn't leave much room for rearing and jumping and kicking and all the other stuff that horses generally like to do. I let him get the feel of it while I put the kettle on. *I'm* thinking this is great—but nobody else is too impressed. Doris is cowering in the corner. I go over to her and I say, with a big fanfare—

"Look, Doris. . . da-daarr! . . . *Horse in the House!"* Nothing. Not even a yelp. I can see this is just another idea way ahead of its time, so I turn Magpie around and walk him out again. He was too bewildered to complain either way, but I rather think he liked it 'cos every time from then on, whenever he was taken past the barn, he'd break away— through the garden gate—and stand outside the front door, waiting to be invited in.

When Tom Owen and I returned to Los Angeles in '73, I was soon back in the theatre again—a revival of 'Oliver!' at the Music Centre. The only reason I said I'd do it was because the great Ron Moody was supposed to be directing it. There were troubles and in the end he didn't direct—but it was tremendous fun acting with him.

After six weeks in L.A., we moved to the Curran Theatre in San Francisco. I'll never forget the last night when Ron was doing his solo scene. He was 'reviewing the situation'. He's opened his box, he's counted his money—he's bitten his pearls to test them. He's packed his hankies, he's unpacked his hankies—he's banged his pans. Just a minute. Banged his pans? That's not in the script. . . but there he is, still banging his pans. All over the walls, and the counters, and the floor—he's banging his pans. The audience are loving it—he's magic.

Now he's packing his hankies again. Now he's *unpacking* his hankies. Packing them. . . unpacking them. Still reviewing the situation—or, more precisely, the last verse. And the band are now reviewing *their* situation—faking like crazy, trying to keep up with him. The management are wringing their hands, mopping their brows, and generally panicking backstage. I'm loving it. Moody's still at it. . . packing, unpacking, banging, packing, more banging—reviewing, revamping, remarkable!

david jones

I know I've got to do something and as I turn around there's this fireman's axe on the wall behind me—so I take it down and march on stage. I look out at the audience—they're in hysterics now, still laughing at Ron, who's just sitting there making Fagin faces. I hand him the axe.

"'Ere y'are, Fagin. You can change the scene yerself."

He has a glint in his eye that says, "thank you, me boy—*perfect!*" He takes hold of the axe and starts breaking up the set. Chops the whole thing down. Hilarious. What a finish to the show!

Mind you, the management didn't think so.

"You'll never work here again!" they screamed. Of course, they said that to me in '65, and there I was. Come to think of it though. . .

Ron said the most fun he'd ever had doing it, was with me. Likewise, Mr. Moody. When you're working with good people it's easy to be good. Mind you, you can be *too* good sometimes—or so I've been told. On Broadway I was so young and enthusiastic that I'd sometimes overdo it a bit. Georgia would come off stage and scream in my face—

"Who the *hell* do you think you are?"

"The Dodger."

"Well, watch it, 'Dodger'—or I'll report you to Equity."

Actually, it was decorated with a few more colourful terms than that—but I never took it seriously. Did just the same the next time. I suppose my genuine innocence helped me get away with more than most. Clive Reville used to get hold of me and say,

"Don't you *ever* do that again on stage!"

"Do what?"

"You were doing *this*, while I was doing *that*."

But I wasn't thinking about it. I didn't know when I was upstaging anyone, or when I wasn't supposed to. I thought it was just, y'know—for the good of the show, the overall thing. One time when Fagin was going for the money, doing one of his counting scenes, a coin landed at the foot of the stage by the curtain. So at the end of the show, at the curtain call, I kneel down, Oliver kneels, Bette kneels—we're singing, 'Consider Yourself'. I spot it and I know what I'm going to do, and I make a face like, y'know. . . *corr*, look what *I've* found! . . . knowing full well that Clive Reville will take it out of my hand and give me one of his looks, see?

Well, the audience got an extra laugh that night, and that bit was in the show for the next three years. Even if sometimes there wasn't a coin there, I'd mime it and the audience knew what it was anyway. Things like that are made by just *doing* them, without thinking about upstaging or anything. That's the magic of live theatre.

It was also the magic of The Monkees, come to think of it. I mean, we worked around a script—there was always that structure—but they gave us the freedom to ad-lib like crazy *within* that structure.

Ad-libbing like crazy is something Davy is known for, of course. It's definitely one ingredient in the indefinable magic of any of his performances. As he is fond of saying, "It's no different from the school play. Whether it's for millions of television viewers, or for one neighbour in the living room—it's the performance that counts".

*He means it, too. It's one of the most striking things I've noticed about Davy in all the time I've worked with him—he gives a **performance**. Even if he's just strumming a guitar in a hotel room, running down an idea for a song, or if suddenly he remembers something that he wants to turn you on to. He does it the same as if he were on stage, opening night. It's invigourating.*

Some performers find that hard to work with. It's almost funny to see sometimes, because you know that Davy is trying to pull out of a fellow performer, that same kind of spontaneity, that willingness to risk. And if that fellow performer is at all insecure in their art, they'd better watch out because he'll try anything to force them to stretch and be better than they thought they could be. Well, that's the theory anyway. . .

Davy was appearing in pantomime once in Swansea, south Wales. 'Panto' is a wonderful, unique style of theatre in Britain, for which there is no equivalent in the States. It's essentially for children, but performed throughout the Christmas season for family audiences, in intimate, mid-sized theatres.

This particular season I'm thinking of, Davy was in 'Puss in Boots' playing 'Colin', the miller's son. In the story he's in love with the King's daughter but cannot be seen with her because he is a commoner. He gate-crashes the Royal Ball in order to see the princess—and his usual disguise is no more than a handheld mask which he removes when he gets near to her. He reveals himself on the line,

"Isn't this a wonderful night? The night was made for dancing!"

"Oh, Colin. . . it's you!" cries the princess. "But my father would be furious if he knew we were together."

They argue and she leaves him, in a huff—

"I never want to see you again!"

This girl was rather stiff in her performance as the princess, and she would hardly ever look Davy in the eye, particularly on that line. Always her sight was trained, for some reason that Davy could never fathom, on his left shoulder. Even when they were in a close embrace. So he started doing things to try to get some reaction out of her.

*One night he took his mask down and he was wearing a large, red, clown's nose. No reaction. . . nothing. Left shoulder—and not even a smile. Next night he wears the nose again, plus some clown make-up, and is **pointing** at the nose as they're doing their dialogue. She doesn't even see it. This really starts to become an obsession for Davy—he's going to **make** her see him, whatever it takes.*

Next evening's performance sees young Colin turning up at the Ball wearing an old-man's mask. And then, nightly, a series of masks and various bits of costuming, all for her benefit, and all completely missing their mark. Except that the rest of the cast are falling about and generally losing it at inappropriate moments. It's a running gag now, and they're all keen to see what he'll come up with next.

Finally, Davy can't take it anymore. He tells me he's going to borrow my gag

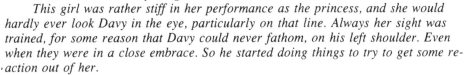

that I'd cracked him up with on tour one time. If this doesn't do it, nothing will.

Scene: the Royal Ball. All the ladies are in flowing gowns; the men are in leotards, ruffles and wigs. Nobody is supposed to suspect he's there; he must blend in if he is to see his fair maiden without getting caught.

"Isn't this a wonderful night? The night was made for dancing!"

"Oh, Colin. . . it's you!" cries the princess—her royal gaze rivetted firmly on the left shoulder of Davy's scuba-diving outfit.

"Which way to the beach?" asks Colin.

Nothing.

"But my father would be furious if he knew we were together." Left oxygen tank.

Some people just won't loosen up.

Yeah, it was great. The producer was up in the bar with the mayor of Swansea—and the mayor was saying, "Oh, it's a beautiful show, boyo—beautiful. But tell me—it must get awfully hot on stage—especially for that boy in the wet suit."

The producer comes to my dressing-room, fuming. . .

"Jones! Were you wearing a wet suit in tonight's performance?"

"A *wet* suit?" I say, perplexed. "Don't be ridiculous—have you any idea how **hot** that would get up there?" Then I open my closet and hang my leotard up next to my wet suit. He's furious.

"Don't you *ever* do that again, Mr. Jones. You're not supposed to be funny in that scene."

"Oh, really? Try telling that to the 1200 people who were laughing themselves silly."

Davy loves that 'live' element of surprise. I've seen him totally bewilder an audience by coming out with some philosophical one-liner, utterly out of context. Once, in Ireland, he reminded the spud-farmers that, "Success is never final. Failure is never fatal. It's courage that counts! And now. . . 'I'm Not Your Stepping Stone'."

He was doing a guest appearance on a television show called 'Star Games', in which celebrities battle against each other, and the weather, on an outdoor obstacle course, to win money for charity. The match was over, and Davy and Peter Duncan (host of a children's TV show called 'Blue Peter') were in front of the cameras, soaking wet and covered in mud, after quite a gruelling race. The scores came up and the host, Michael Aspel, announced—

"Plucky little Davy Jones lost by just one point. What have you got to say for yourself, Davy?" Immediately Davy grabbed the microphone and preached to the camera, very gravely—

"Yes, I lost. So, always remember. . . "Success has a thousand fathers—Failure is an orphan"."

Michael Aspel was dumbstruck for a moment, and then he started to turn to Peter for his victory speech. But just as he did so, the scoreboard changed, a correction was made, and due to a penalty awarded against Peter, Davy was now declared the winner—by one point. Aspel exclaimed—

"Oh, Davy—you WON! How about that?"
Davy grabbed the mike.
*"Oh, well—**you** can have that saying then, Peter."*

"Energy is eternal delight!"
—Davy Jones—
(quoting somebody or other)

The Gospel according to Jones

It's now '77 and it's time to review my situation once more. I've got the travelling bug again—the Boyce and Hart experience had strengthened me no end—thanks guys, for everything. Maybe it's time to go home. Home, England, I mean. I'd lived more than half my life in America. I decided to give it a try.

My plan was to tour for a while, on my own, and end up on the east coast—closest departure point. Off I went. But before I'd got to the end of the block, Micky decided he wanted to tour, too. My solo became a duet. We created a show—singers, musicians, costumes, staging, lighting—hey, wait a minute! This was turning into quite a production. Oh, well. . . go for it.

We opened in a punk club in L.A.—four nights, got the act together, then headed for Reno, Nevada, where Micky fired the brass section and two of the singers—leaving his sister, Coco, and his girlfriend, Trina, who he'd met on the DJB&H tour in Chicago. (She was shooting pictures for a Playboy spread and Micky went all over town buying up every copy he could lay his hands on.)

Harry Nilsson decided he couldn't live 'without me' playing 'Oblio' in the London production of 'The Point', and Micky decided we should keep the partnership intact. "Hey—we could be like Crosby & Hope, Martin & Lewis, Morcambe & Wise." So Micky was written into the show.

It was a privilege and a pleasure doing Harry's wonderful fantasy.

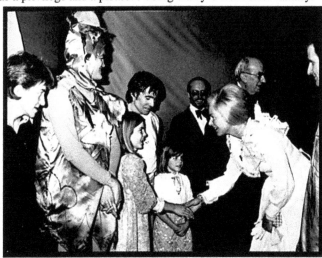

147

she

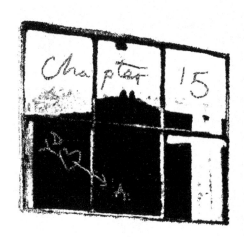

> "God won't turn His back on us just because I'm divorced. . . He hasn't got a back!"

It was clear from the start that there was a unique chemistry between Anita Pollinger and David Jones. Anita is a playful lady who loves to exercise her oneup-womanship on anyone who, like Davy, loves to be the centre of attention. So he'd barely got into his inimitable brand of story-telling when she started throwing back witty retorts, right on the nail and sharp as can be. Davy raised an eyebrow in my direction.

He pulled out all the stops, his best stories, the 'if-all-else-fails' jokes. Anita closed her eyes, slipped slowly down in her chair, and started making loud snoring sounds. I was stifling my chuckles; Davy gave me two eyebrows.

The coup de grace was when, only a couple of hours after they had met, in the middle of the best bit in his whole repertoire—the stuff he usually saves for on screen or blind drunk—Anita walked right past him in mid-punchline, rummaged around in his kitchen cupboards, and came out with a two pound bag of flour which she emptied over Davy's head. He, long past trying to match verbal wits with her, then poured a bucket of cold water over her. . . and they were off.

If it's possible that any one, single act can so influence a person that their fate is sealed by it, I'm sure that the flour incident did the trick for Davy. Whether it registered consciously or not, it's at least interesting to note the connection with a similar incident in Chapter One, between Doris and Harry (which Davy told me with barely concealed admiration for his parents' playfulness). I think it's safe to assume that this rang some subconscious bell for him. In any event, it was certainly clear that if they were to go on meeting like this they would end up either killing or marrying each other. Fortunately it was the latter. . . on January 24th, 1981, at 10:30 a.m., in Swansea, south Wales.

They had wanted a church ceremony, but were told they couldn't have one because Davy was divorced. (We British can be terribly stuffy about such matters sometimes.) So they agreed on a civil ceremony at the Town Hall, to be followed by a blessing at the church.

It was all set. And then, the day before the big day, the vicar said that Anita couldn't wear white in his church because it would be 'hypocritical'. After a heated debate he relented, but with the stipulation that if she did, she was to cover herself with a cloak, and they had to enter through different doors! Davy was furious. He ranted and raved that they didn't need to be in his church to have God bless them:

"He's blessed us already by giving us each other—so stick your church!" he shouted. "God won't turn His back on us just because I'm divorced. And do you know why? Do you?! Because He hasn't got a back—he faces everyone—sees everything!"

So it was a civil ceremony with only God's, and not the vicar's, blessing. The intended church congregation were now told to simply meet afterwards at the reception because there wouldn't be room for them in the tiny registrar's office. (Not that the tiny registrar would have minded, but that's beside the point.)

Secretly however, the entire cast of the pantomime Davy was appearing in, plus the lighting and sound crew—even the orchestra musicians—all turned out, on a cold and miserable Saturday morning, and waited patiently in the pouring rain for the newlyweds to emerge. And as they did, trumpeters played 'Here Comes the Bride'; stage hands held decorated stage props and swords aloft to form an archway; others cheered, applauded and threw confetti and rice. It was a lovely gesture from so many who wanted to show Davy and Anita how much they cared.

A reception followed at a local hotel. Davy's sisters, Anita's family, and my mum, all cried their eyes out happily. Davy gave a moving speech, (several of us moved into the next room) and I played an original piece for them which is reproduced here, but which loses much in the translation from the Manchester dialect into the typewritten word.*

**"Don't get me wrong—
I think marriage is a wonderful thing. (Don't I, dear?)
But I don't need a minister to ask me—test me—as to
whether or not she is my choice, or me hers."**

.

---

*(Anita has suggested that many of Davy's faithful fans and friends might want to hear the original recording. If there's enough interest maybe we'll make that available. . . please write to us and let us know.)

'The Day the Artful Dodger

From Manchester to Fareham via Hollywood
Such a round about way to here and now
But in the strangest places fate lurks
When she wants to do her great works
You can never tell just when she'll take a bow

From Fareham to Manchester via Swansea
Not the most direct approach that one could pick
But as a cure for the grumbles,
Honeymoonin' in The Mumbles†
—then a tumble in the hay should do the trick

So, off to the Registrar they went, so picturesque
With the whole pantomime tagging along
And, "Do you take this man?" asked the vicaress⁺
"Oh, yes I do," said the blushing bride
"Oh, no she doesn't!" the cast replied◊
There were not a dry eye in the house
She were every Mother's Pride
The Day the Artful Dodger Didn't Dodge 'er

From the Far East to the West Coast via everywhere
Our Cowboy searched for the cowgirl of his dreams
But it seems no matter where 'e went
He could not find lasting merriment
Until 'e met our 'Nita—she's a scream!

From Lancashire to here via California
Our hero in 'is search, really persisted
Little Willie did the rounds
He played every major town
Aye—and a few that no-one even knew existed

But when at last he met our heroine they both knew it
Their destiny were written in the stars
And though no-one knew quite where or when they'd do it
I could feel it in me bones
That she'd be plain old, 'Mrs. Jones'
But when the fans find out—
God 'elp 'em answering the phones
The Day the Artful Dodger Didn't Dodge 'er

Didn't Dodge 'er'

From Manchester to Fareham via Broadway
Our kid could hear his dad's words to this day
"Son"—said our 'Arry
"Make sure you never marry
And always bring your kids up t' same way"

From up north to down south via the airwaves
Our Davy were a right Monkee, it's true
But he swore he'd never leave her
And she said, "Now, I'm a Believer"
And they'll take the last train to East Grinstead
Just as soon as the show is through

And while we're on the subject of the theatre
It's not only the groom who has that flair
or Anita, too—the footlights are very dear to her
You should hear her impressions
She's got fifty-six expressions
But I've never seen her looking quite like that—
(Sort of a cross between being told she was on
'This is Your Life'. . . and acute indigestion!)
The Day the Artful Dodger Didn't Dodge 'er

Oh, we all like to be beside the seaside
Do you think you'll live in Blackpool, by the sand?
Then if you have a son named, Rio*
He'll be Rio by the sea-o
And everyone'll say, "Ee—in't Rio grand?"

And if you do, don't forget who introduced yer
On that fiery, fateful day one year ago
When she covered you in flour and then seduced yer
Well, now you're in the thick of it
And if some day you're feeling sick of it
Don't put up with 'out like that
Just hit her with your Rhythm Stick a bit°

Well this is all I've got you for a gift
So if you don't like it—sod yer
This message comes right from my heart
I hope today is just the start
Of the happiest life either of you have ever had
So from your friendly, faithful lodger
I'm glad the Artful Dodger Didn't Dodge 'er

Some helpful hints to understanding the 'in' jokes:—
† 'The Mumbles' is the name of the small town where most of the cast were staying.
+ I had been told, whilst composing this piece, that they would be married by a woman cleric.
◊ It's a custom in English pantomime for the audience to respond to the cast by negating, *loudly*, any statement
   that begins, "Oh, *yes*. . ."
* Davy had always said that they would have a son—and he wanted to call him, Rio. Stay tuned for further
   information.
° 'Hit Me with your Rhythm Stick' is the name of a somewhat lewd pop song that was
   quite big at the time and which Davy had frequently performed during our tours in '79/'80.   **153**

As most of you know, Anita gave birth to Jessica Lilian Jones on September 4th, 1981. When I first saw Jessica in Los Angeles, early '82, Davy said to me—

"I make great girls, don't I?"

He keeps telling me I really ought to say something myself about Anita. (I'll never forgive you for this, Alan!) But don't they say a picture paints a thousand words? Don't we have any more pictures?

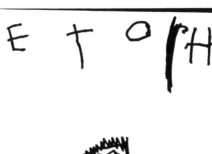

DADDY BY JESSICA
MAY 11th 1986

157

Oh. Are we still on this chapter? Well, it's hard, y'know. She's a very shy lady—I wouldn't want to embarrass her.

Like at the 'Caddyshack' Premiere?

Well, that was different. . .

Davy and Anita were at the Premiere of...

I'll tell it. . . this is *my* wife we're embarrassing here.

("We're"?—Ed.)

We were at the British Premiere of the film, 'Caddyshack', starring Chevy Chase. Anita and I had been invited along by the Playboy Organization— she'd worked for them as a Bunny girl and then, a few years later, as Press and Public Relations Officer.

Anyway, we go along and we're sitting a few rows up from the front with the whole Playboy mob—and the usual celebrity stuff starts—everybody getting up and saying how nice it is to be seen here— and then they're invited to hit a golf ball up a ramp to a bucket, and whoever sinks it wins a car or something. I'm not paying too much attention to be honest—I'm bored stiff and all I can think of is that if they introduce me (I'd just gone along for a quiet night out—and they didn't even ask me if I'd mind. . . but I'm preparing myself, just in case)—then I've got to do something outrageous to wake these people up. If you believe in life after death, that is. So it happens, anyway—

"And heeeeere's. . . Davy Jones!"

I go up and take the mike and I start to say what a pleasure it is to be here in my own country again—bump di bump di bum—and before I know it I'm elabourating like crazy and I know what I'm leading up to and even *I* can't believe it—but once these things start, it's difficult to stop. . .

"Y'know, ladies and gentlemen. . . being successful does have inevitable rewards. For instance, where I live in Hollywood, I have a big mansion with a pool—and tennis courts. . . " (I catch Anita's eye and she's like, "What's this??")

". . . but the nicest thing about my success is that I can play golf whenever I like— on my own golf course." (All the Playboy brigade are cringing in their seats by now.)

"In fact, it's not generally known, but I am a very accomplished player. . . " ("What IS he doing?")

". . . but there's just one thing. When I play at home—I wear just my socks, so. . . I hope you'll understand if I make myself at home." And I strip off. Tuxedo, bow tie, shirt, shoes, and lastly—leaving my socks on—I face away from the audience and I pull my shorts down. (Anita is under her seat now—literally.)

Then I take the putter and stroke the ball. . . yes. . . yes. . . straight all the way. . . rims the bucket twice and falls out again. Nobody can believe it—the shot or the spectacle of my arse mooning the whole theatre.

I turn and take a bow, cupping my credentials in one hand and picking up my bundle of clothes with the other. Back to my seat. Anita wouldn't even look at me.

I think I accomplished what I set out to do though. It certainly woke everyone up. Anita didn't want to be seen with me at the party afterwards—and none of the so-called 'liberated' Playboy set would even speak to me. Another idea ahead of its time.

Bill Kenwright, the West End producer, couldn't believe they hadn't paid me to do that. And Record Mirror gave me a great review—they said the floor show was far better than the movie. Anita, on the other hand. . .

Well, she got me off my arse, I'll say that for her. My life was a disorganized mess when I met her—now it's a very *organized* mess.

Seriously, she bought me one of those 'organizers' while we were on tour. You put everything in it—addresses, phone numbers, appointments, all the usual stuff—*plus* notes that you make throughout the day. . . who called, what was said, what to think, where to go, what to wear, who to sue. . . it's just like having a manager. And then you've got everything all in one place and you're not looking for bits of paper all over the house. Now I just lose my organizer. So I have a back-up. Anita.

As my manager she's worked wonders. You've go to be hard as nails in this business, outwardly—or they'll walk all over you. That's something I've never been able to do myself—the management bit. And although Anita is a sweetheart and a softie deep down, ("Yes, darling—I promise I'll do the dishes—can I finish this chapter first, dearest?") and not a tough task-mistress at all, ("No, dear. . . no, I won't forget to fold the laundry. This bit's about you, my love—can I dust tomorrow?") still she can put on a surprisingly stern exterior when it's needed at the negotiating table. Anyone who can go up against David Fishof, our producer on the Anniversary Tour, on a daily basis, and still be a loving mother and wife when the day is through, has my deepest respect.

In Fishof's book, 'Putting it on the Line', he spells out, in detail, the strategies he employs in high level negotiations in the big leagues of sports, and more recently, entertainment. He's no lightweight. He deals in millions and has a reputation for being tough. So Anita's job, in representing her husband, fleshing out those fine details that may mean a considerable difference when the paycheck arrives, was not an enviable one. Many times throughout the tour, tempers were frayed as complications would inevitably arise—and hard bargaining, coupled with subtle diplomacy, were needed to keep everyone happy and working under optimum conditions.

During one particularly gruelling test of patience and strength, Anita was trying to field phone calls, pack to leave the hotel, instruct the road manager, sort photos for Davy to sign, and answer fan letters. . . plus deal with a dozen other things that were crowding in. Jessica was feeling a little neglected. She'd been asked to amuse herself for a while until the rush was over—but she was tired and a bit niggly and, inevitably, she started to cry. Both Davy and Anita stopped what they were doing to ask her what the problem was.

"It's not easy being on the road," she said. "Sometimes you treat me worse than you treat David Fishof!"

After hugs all 'round, Jessica was reassured that she was loved very much, and that mummy and daddy were sorry.

Another example of Anita's organizational abilities, harnessed to her love for David, was the fulfillment of a life-long dream for him—to actually ride in a race. It came to fruition just before they were married, as a result of Anita's connection with the Playboy Organization, and her pushing him to re-awaken his belief that he could in fact still do it, even starting so late.

All the time I was at Basil's stables I learned a lot about riding, but I never actually took part in a race. So what if it's a bit late to start—it's something I've always wanted to do. Shoemaker's in his 50's—Piggot's in his 40's—why not? I finally got my Jockey's license, and it was all systems go.

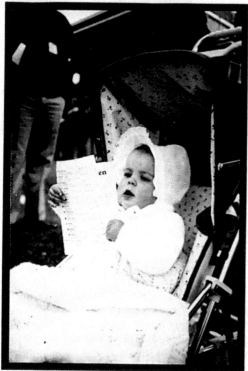

"Okay. I'll have £1 each way on daddy."

September 19th, 1980, at Newberry race track. I'm riding Speed of Light. And we're off! Straight away those other guys are way out in front of me—I'm definitely last, but I'm enjoying it and improving, slowly. God, this is hard work—they're turning the bend—am I getting any closer?

It's head down and eyes up, and I think—hey, wait a minute. I don't want to be looking at all these horse's arses. This isn't the movies—this is for real! So I kick on, and Speed of Light's starting to live up to his name a bit, and I'm getting real close now. I'm nose to tail with Tim Thompson-Jones, and he's making his move—

"Oh, shit!" (That's me.) Tim's made his move alright—to the ground. He's a faller, so I pull around him and I'm making good ground—I'm leaving some of them behind me. This feels good. I leave some more standing and now it looks like I'll make a decent showing, after all. There's the finishing post. . . Bravo!

I went out thinking, 'Win, place or stay on will do.' Well, my legs finished way before the end of the race but I finished fifth and I'm happy. Thanks, Anita—for pushing me, and helping me live up to my potential. I still want to win the Grand National, though. Keep pushing, will you?

Davy's band, 'Toast', on the '79/'80 Tours

pieces of toast

I first met Davy in Los Angeles, September, 1979. This guy, Dennis Larden, called saying he was a guitarist and that they were stuck for a musical director/ keyboard player for the 'Davy Jones Alimony Tour' (as we came to call it). Could I come along and rehearse?

"When do you need me?" I asked.

"Oh, no big rush," he started. "Not for an hour yet."

Maybe I seemed overly anxious—I got there early. Met the band, got through about half of the material, and then Davy arrived. We seemed to hit it off right away. Coming from the same area of Manchester we share a local humour that is, sometimes, rather difficult for non-'Mancunians' to follow. Maybe having worked with Americans for so long he missed sharing that certain kind of 'in' joke—the Manchester dialect, the north country simplicity. Whatever it was, I got the gig anyway, and the next night we were all on a plane headed for Middle America. . .

. . . and madness.

There were no giant road crews like on the current, record-breaking Monkees 20th Anniversary Tour. We played small clubs or mid-sized halls to enthusiastic, mostly hard-core fans. Halfway through the first leg of the USA our only road manager had to be fired for skipping us out of a couple of towns without paying the hotel bills. So. . . on to the next gig with no road manager.

Davy now found himself having to deal directly with the agent in Los Angeles. We were supposed to be playing a town in Alabama, which, according to the news, was about to be hit by a hurricane."We ain't going down there man—have you seen the news?" Davy shouts down the line.

The response is that if we don't play that gig, we lose a week's salary. Nobody likes the idea of flying into a hurricane but, being true musicians, the idea of no pay is even more devastating. We board the plane and it's a terrifying flight—change of underwear all 'round. And when we land the town looks like a hurricane's hit it—

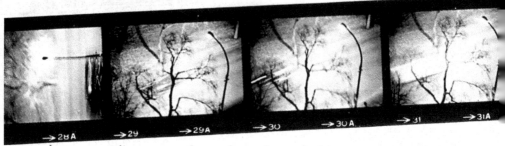

trees down, power lines across the roads, roofs smashed in.

We arrive at the motel—no electricity and half of the windows are blown out. On to the gig, where the club owner is most surprised to see us.

"What are you guys doing here? Didn't you see the news yesterday? We **knew** this was going to hit."

"Yeah—we saw the news but, err. . . we're professionals."

—Mobile, Alabama
"Where's Davy? We're on in two minutes."
Somebody had seen him sneaking into the dressing-room, wrapped in the limbs of a fan.
Only one way to get him out. . .
"Ladies and gentlemen— we're proud to present a young man who came up from nothing—and he's brought it here with him tonight. . . " (Screams)
". . . DAVY. . . JONES!"

Into 'Clarksville' vamp. Davy bounces onstage, goes to take the microphone from its stand. . . more screams, bordering on pandemonium. He has no trousers! Vamp continues. Davy feigns surprise, about turns and rushes off. Moments later he stumbles back on, buttoning up. Into 'Clarksville'.

—Washington, D.C.
Davy and the bassist are writing a song in
the dressing room:
"Had some champagne in St. Tropez,
drank some saki in Japan.
I got a girl in Reno
but I keep movin' if I can.
Singin' in the rain in Spain,
having tea in London town. . ."
Davy turns to me and says,
"I'm too knackered to go on tonight,
cowboy—
I got jet-lag just writing that song."

Trenton, New Jersey—
"Where's Davy? We're on
in two minutes!"
"He's in his dressing
room—but I'm afraid he's
covered in woman."
"Ladies and Gentlemen—a
young man who is so short-
sighted, he hardly recognizes
his girlfriends until he's
practically on top of them. . .
David. . . (drum roll). . .
THOMAS— ("pssst—is he
ready?")
—JONES!"
(Screams)

—Shreveport, Louisianna
'Monkees Theme'—screams.
'I Wanna Be Free'—more screams and even
the occasional fainter.
Into Randy Newman's, 'Short People'.
The song starts and a midget climbs
onstage to complain.
(This gag is a set-up but the midget
gets more than he bargained for.)
Davy jumps on him and starts pretending
to beat him up, arms flailing.
This bit is planned, but
then Davy picks him up and throws
the poor guy into the arms of
a security cop.
One very surprised cop—
*and one **extremely** surprised midget.*

Nashville, Tennessee—
"Where's Davy? We're on in five."
"He's lying down for a while. On the pool
table."

"**That's** when I started drinking."

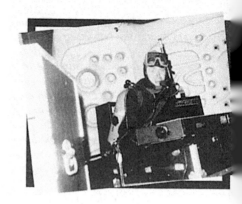

Little Rock, Arkansas—
It's the last night of a week's engagement.
A fan has baked a huge cake for the band.
She foolishly brings two pieces up onto the stage
and gives one each to Davy and me.
We look at each other.
It's too obvious but neither of us can resist. . .
so we do. . . squarely into each other's face.
Goodnight, everybody!
Into, "I'm A Believer."

(Screams.)

—Belfast, Eire
First night in Northern Ireland with a new
band. I'm the only one who knows the show
properly and in the middle of the second tune
the electric piano dies on me. Not a sound. After an embarassing pause whilst we try, unsuc-
cessfully, to fix it—Davy fills in by telling IRISH
jokes—and they all laugh!
It's that magic again—with Davy you
forgive a lot, y'know?
Even jokes against your own race.

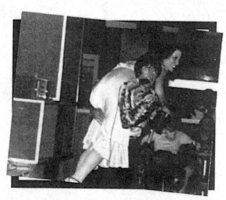

Manchester, England—
"Where's Davy?"
"He's, err. . ."

It's amazing that in most places we played there was a whole new generation of Monkees fans who probably thought that The Monkees were a new group. They would watch the TV re-runs and come to the shows and scream, just like their mothers did. Some were only eight or ten years old.

And then, of course, there were the original Monkees fans who were then in their late twenties, early thirties. They came out of loyalty and a hankering after nostalgia. All seemed more than satisfied.

But, that was then. . .

. . . this is now

It's September 7th, 1986. And when Mike Nesmith walks onstage at the Greek Theatre, Hollywood, to join the other three Monkees—it's the stuff dreams are made of.

*Five days short of the 20th anniversary of the first airing of 'The Monkees' TV show—the impossible, the improbable. . . the inevitable happens. The boys come home to tinsel-land—to the town that made them and then threw away the mold. And they play and sing together, just the way we always hoped they would, confounding their critics and delighting their fans. Dreams **do** come true. And good guys win in the end.*

Just a couple of days prior, they had been on the MTV Music Awards show featuring such stars as Tina Turner, Mister Mister, Whitney Houston, David Lee Roth and Genesis. And there they were on our screens again—as bubbly and instantly recognizable as when they originated the whole music-video style with the first Monkees episode, 'The Royal Flush', September 12th, 1966.

Now, in retrospect, we know that they were, undeniably, the first TV video band. They started a whole style which today is virtually the only way an act breaks their new record to the public. Twenty years ago today—they were all but crucified for miming their records on TV. Yet here they are in MTV-land, lip-sync city, the act we've known and loved for all these years—breaking the rules again. Singing LIVE!

Talk about pop history coming full circle. . .

From Florida to California to New York—Davy, Micky and Peter played big towns, small towns, 700-seater halls and 40,000-plus stadiums. They fulfilled, with a vengeance, their promise of coming to your town. What started out as a six-week summer jaunt escalated into a six-month marathon as the demand of the fans grew and grew. Promoters found themselves swamped with an unprecedented rush on tickets. More and more concerts were added and still the fans were turned away from overflowing houses. It was clear that the passage of twenty years had not dulled the attraction—in fact, absence had made millions of hearts grow fonder, and the guys found themselves in the middle of Monkeemania Phase Two. The only difference?. . . their act is sharper, funnier, musically more accomplished—and, of course, seasoned with that indefinable chemystery of nostalgia.

For the current weeny-boppers, the songs are as fresh and new and exciting as they were when they were fresh and new and exciting. They will become, for them, what they are for us oldie-boppers now—the common bond of our uncommon memories.

*Funny—as I wrote that last paragraph I immediately pictured Davy reading it and saying, "What a load of bollocks!" After all, they're just pop songs, it's true. But I've seen it from both sides. As part of the band, I've played the songs and felt the excitement of a performance. But as part of the audience—particularly say, an eighteen-thousand strong audience who are singing along to every song, catching every nuance, well. . . that's something else. They **are** more than pop songs. They're some sort of magic.*

*And apparently we all want that magic right now. As this is written, The Monkees have **seven** albums in the charts, plans for new recordings in 1987, a new tour already in the works, a Broadway show being talked about, and TV movies a possibility. Let's hope the guys continue to work together and we don't have to wait another twenty years for more of their magic.*

Could it possibly have been that long? It seems like only seventeen or so. Well. . . as the saying goes, "What goes 'round, comes 'round". And except for a few cuts and bruises we're all in one piece.

Mike asked if he could join us at the Greek Theatre, Los Angeles. What a buzz he must have had. I know Peter, Micky and I were just as excited as the audience was to see him back on stage. He'd seen our Arlington Stadium concert—in disguise. He came as Colonel Sanders, I think. Imagine—the only Monkee ever to have seen a Monkees concert from the audience.

The tour has brought many memories flooding back. To see old fans and new fans listening and singing together—what a sensation! The press have had a very positive field day all around. And apart from eating our dinner at a State Fair under a mortuary tent— it's been great. That and the driver we had at one place who announced to the whole of the towns' CB owners that he had the Monkees on board! We're trying to get back to the hotel after the show and before we know it—we've got a convoy! Trucks, cars, fans—all following our white limousine like a full-page ad procession through town. . .
"MONKEES THIS WAY!" "GET YOUR MONKEES HERE!"

"Lose them!" we told him.

No problem, he says. Sorry, he says. Takes a few lefts and rights and shakes the cars off his tail, down a couple of one-way streets the wrong way, a few 'U'ies thrown in for good measure. "Don't worry—I know exactly where we are," he says. Starsky and Hutch have got nothing on this guy. He's looking over his shoulder to see if we're impressed yet.

172

"Yeah, great. There goes my supper, but. . . great."

Well, we lost the convoy, alright—we're back at the stage door! Hundreds of fans climbing on the car and the show finished an hour ago! (If anyone says, "I know *exactly* where we are," again. . .)

Sometimes after a large concert, in order to avoid death by affection, it's necessary to drive out of town and just play cops and robbers for a while so as to make the game more interesting and the odds a little more favourable to the guys. Usually ninety-nine percent of a crowd can be deterred that way. (The other one percent will always find their heroes, and then the guys don't mind signing autographs in the lobby for the valiant few.) But the Texas School of Limo Driving obviously doesn't train their personnel in the fine art of Escape.

*At Arlington Stadium, Dallas, on June 22nd, 1986, the 41,000 fans were thrilled to see their idols on the hallowed Texas Rangers turf—ecstatic to cheer them when the limos did a victory lap of honour around the field—and positively **surprised** when those same limos drove out of the stadium and pulled up right across the street at the Marriott. No 'now you see us, now you don't' stuff. Almost spoilt the game, really. How simple! Now all 41,000 of them could come and party.*

Meanwhile, Davy's bodyguard and aide, David Lewis, was walking to his car with the show clothes over his arm, and a couple of fans ran by and made off with Davy's gold jacket. David jumped into the limo and told the driver to chase after them across the parking lot.

There followed a real-life chase for about five minutes—weaving in and out of parked cars. Finally the girl carrying the jacket dropped to the ground, weary and repentent, crying hysterically, and offering the jacket back. David very sternly told both girls to get into the limo.

*He's really a very sweet-natured man but obviously the girls were very frightened of him, not knowing what action might now be taken. He tried to ease their ordeal by saying that although they'd been "very naughty", they **had** given themselves up and he wouldn't press charges. In fact, seeing that they were such ardent fans, he'd see what he could do about getting an autograph for them. He left them waiting in the limo whilst he fought his way through the besieged lobby and up to Davy's room. David relayed the story to the Manchester cowboy and asked him whether he'd mind giving them an autograph.*

"No way," he says. "Not bloody likely! I'm supposed to give them a signed photo after what they did? D'you know how much these 8x10's cost? Here. . . " Davy takes off the gold pants that go with the jacket. ". . . tell them we don't have any pictures left—they'll have to manage with these." He signs the pants—and the jacket. "And tell 'em to get it together next time—I mean, if they're gonna go around doing this sort of thing, the jacket's no good without the pants, is it?"

David Lewis—

"That's the thing I respect most about Davy. His generosity to the fans. I remember after one gig—Anita was tired and Jessica was asleep—Micky and Peter were long gone. We were about to leave for the hotel so I went to check out the fan situation, to see if we'd have any trouble getting out. The show was over an hour and a half ago, but it still didn't look good. I told Davy we may have to run for it. "How many are there?" he asked. I told him about a hundred or so.

"Okay, I'll sign autographs," he said.

"For all of them?" I asked.

"They've waited, haven't they?"

I'll say. About twenty years. . .

MONKEE MANIA

It's the Sixties all over as frenzied fans throw themselves at the TV rockers

Monkees make for happy night

By JIM SANVILLE

They haven't been too busy singing for the past 15 years or so, but at their concert here yesterday, the Monkees sounded as if they never

Review

stopped rehearsing.

The made-for-TV band from the '60s made believers out of an unusual mix of 6,500 fans at the Cumberland County Civic Center.

"I am so psyched. I can't believe this," shrieked a 40-years-old woman just before the trio took the stage. (Michael Nesmith stayed home for the tour). And a large vocal contingent of teens and preteens added harmony to the screaming.

Hey, Hey, The Monkees Are Even Better Than Before

THE MONKEES
HERMAN'S HERMITS   THE GRASS ROOTS
GARY PUCKETT & THE UNION GAP
20th Anniversary World Tour Sept. 8-14   LAS VEGAS HILTON

Hey, Hey, The Monkees Hit Town

ICD 08120

Billboard

NEWSPAPER

VOLUME 98 NO. 33

THE INTERNATIONAL NEWSWEEKLY OF MUSIC AND HOME ENTERTAINMENT

August 16, 1986/$3.50 (U.S.), $5 (CAN.)

CHART BEAT

by Paul Grein

THE MONKEES have five (count 'em) albums on this week's Top Pop Albums chart. Their "Then And Now" collection on Arista jumps 11 notches, to No. 31, while reissues of four of their old albums on Rhino Records re-enter the chart. "The Monkees" debuts at No. 139, "More Of The Monkees" bows at No. 143, "Headquarters" opens at No. 160, and "Pisces, Aquarius, Capricorn And Jones" lands at No. 177.

All four of those albums reached No. 1 on the Top Pop Albums chart in 1966-67. Between them, they held the No. 1 spot for a whopping 37 weeks. In fact, the Monkees were No. 1 on the album chart more often than even the **Beatles** in that two-year period. From January 1966 to December 1967, the Beatles were No. 1 just 32 weeks.

UPDATE...
Seven !!!
count 'em
again.

Compiled from a national sample of retail store,
one-stop, and rack sales reports.

2 WKS. AGO	WKS. ON CHART	ARTIST LABEL & NUMBER/DISTRIBUTING LABEL (SUG. LIST PRICE)*	
		★ ★ NO. 1 ★ ★	
3	4	BOSTON MCA 6188 (9.98) (CD)	2 weeks at
1	9	BON JOVI ● MERCURY 830264-1/POLYGRAM (CD)	
2	9	HUEY LEWIS & THE NEWS CHRYSALIS OV 41534	
6	7	TINA TURN	
13	6		

		...-8409/ARISTA (8.98) (CD)	
		HALEN △³ WARNER BROS. 25394 (8.98) (CD)	
		MIAMI SOUND MACHINE ▲ EPIC BFE 40131 (CD)	QUIET RIOT III
		RIC OCASEK GEFFEN GHS 24098/WARNER BROS. (8.98) (CD)	WHIPLASH SMILE
		QUIET RIOT PASHA OZ 40321/EPIC (CD)	RAISED ON RADIO
5		BILLY IDOL CHRYSALIS OV 41514	THEN & NOW...THE BEST OF THE MONKEES
		JOURNEY ▲ COLUMBIA ...39 (CD)	LIKE A RO...
16		THE MONKEES ● ARISTA AL9-8432 (9.98) (CD)	
		...OB SEGER... SILVER BULLET BAND ▲ CAPITOL PT 12398 (8.98) (CD)	
4		CHICAGO WARNER BROS. 25509 (9.98)	JAMES BROWN...ATLANTIC
5		YNGWIE J. MALMSTEEN MERCURY 831 073-1/POLY...	
49		THE OUTFIELD ▲ COLUMBIA BFC 40027 (C...	
8		SOUNDTRACK ATLANTIC 81677 (9.98)	
		BANANARAMA ● LONDON 828 013-1/POLY...	
13		DAVID & DAVID A&M...	

		ZZ TOP △³ WARNER BROS...	
84	52		WINNER IN YOU
91		...ER BROS. 25504 (8.98)	THE MONKEES
	25	PATTI LABELLE ▲ ...CAPITOL (8.98)	STANDING ON THE BEACH
	13	THE MONKEES RHINO RNLP 7...	WHILE THE CITY SLEEPS
	22	THE CURE ELEKTRA 60...	SHAKE YOU DOWN
102		...WARNER BROS. 25475 (8.98)	THE RAINMAKERS
94	93	GREGORY ABBOTT COLUMBIA BFC 40437	REAL LOVE
119	—	THE RAINMAKERS MERCURY 830-214-1/POLYGRAM	NO JACKET REQUIRED
101	108	ASHFORD & SIMPSON CAPITOL ST 12469 (8.98)	GUITAR TOWN
106	88	PHIL COLLINS △⁵ ATLANTIC 81240 (9.98) (CD)	MORE OF THE MONKEES
105	100	STEVE EARLE MCA ...13 (8.98)	FAME & FORTUNE
110	125	THE MONKEES RHINO R...	
96	96	BAD COMPA ...ATLANTIC 81684 (9.98)	
108	114	PETE TOWNSHEND ATCO 90553/ATLANTIC (8.98)	
	3	...OUDINI JIVE JL8-8407/ARISTA (8.98)	

141	188	—	...CHURCH ELEKTRA 60493 (8.98)	HEADLINE...
142	150		...ELEKTRA 60496 (8.98)	TAKE ME ALL THE WAY
143	142	13	RICHARD THOMPSON ...POR 829 728-1/POLYGRAM	THE DARK
144	146	13	THE MONKEES RHINO RNLP 70143 (8.98)	GEORGIA SATELLITES
145	129	112	...NER BROS. 25490 (9.98)	DARING ADVENTURES
146	137	128	GWEN GUTHRIE POLYDOR 829532-1/POLYGRAM (CD)	HEADQUARTERS
147	145	145	...EN △ ...858 (8.98) (CD)	TUTU
148	128		THE MONKEES RHINO RNLP 70141 (8.98)	GOOD TO GO LOVER
149	138	30	PET SHOP BOYS ● EMI-AMERICA ST 1719... (8.98) (CD)	UNDER LOCK AND KEY
150	139	127	HEART △⁴ CAPITOL ST-12410 (9.98) (CD)	...PISCES, AQUARIUS, CAPRICORN, AND JONES LTD.
151	130	117	34	LEVEL 42 POLYDOR...817-1/POLYGRAM	PLEASE

				UNDER A BLOOD RED SKY
				BREAKOUT
				THE BIRDS, THE BEES & THE MONKEES
				BON JOVI
157	151	153		THE MONKEES RHINO RNLP 144 (8...
158	148	148		SPYRO GYRA MCA 5753 (8...
			39	BON JOVI ▲ MERCURY 814 982-1/POLYGRAM (CD)
159	143	138		CHAKA KHAN WARNER BROS. 25425 (8.98) (CD)
160	178		12	EUROPE EPIC BFE 40241
161	131	119	2	LIZZY BORDEN METAL BLADE/ENIGMA ST 7327...
162	168		2	INXS ● ATLANTIC...
163	179			...SATELLITES
164	167	151	54	
165	144	126	17	

				DESTINY
				THE FINAL COUNTDOWN
				MENACE TO SOCIETY
				LISTEN LIKE THIEVES
				THE SEER
				THE BIG CHILL
				DISCOVER
				BORN IN THE U.S.A.
				SPORTS
				WILD AND FREE
				MONTANA CAFE
				THE LACE
				ISLE OF MAN
				CHANGES

171			...BENJAMIN ORR ...RA 60460 (8...	SOLDIERS UNDER COMMAND
172	NEW ▶		...LE OF MAN ...CAPITOL (8.98)	FULL FORCE GET BUSY 1 TIME
173	177	165	THE MONKEES RHINO RNLP 70... (8.98) (CD)	TURBO
174	NEW ▶		FULL FORCE COLUMBIA BFC 40395	CARL ANDERSON
175	181	185	JUDAS PRIEST ● COLUMBIA OC 40158 (CD)	SHOT IN THE DARK
176	169	172	11	CARL ANDERSON EPIC 40410 (CD)	FACE VALUE
177	158	141	31	GREAT WHITE CAPITOL ST 12525 (8.98)	I COMMIT TO LOVE
178	159	104	12	PHIL COLLINS △² ATLANTIC SD 16029 (8.98) (CD)	CHRONICLES
179	140	130	13	HOWARD HEWETT ELEKTRA 60487 (8.98) (CD)	NINE LIVES
180	190	180	159	CREEDENCE CLEARWATER REVIVAL FANTASY CCR2 (11.98)	GT...
181	185	—	BONNIE RAITT WARNER BROS. 25486 (8.98)	J MOO...
182	182		GTR ● ARISTA ALB-8400 (8.98) (CD)	STOP MAKING SE...
183	163	166	11	WYNTON MARSALIS COLUMBIA FC 40308	LITTLE CREAT...
184	157	129	26	TALKING HEADS ▲ SIRE 1-25186/WARNER BROS. (8.98) (CD)	THE BIG...
185	196	—	2	TALKING HEADS ▲ SIRE 25305/WARNER BROS. 25293 (8.98) (CD)	RAP'S GREATE...
186	192	175	71	HONEYMOON SUITE WARNER BROS. 9466 (7.98)	LIFE...
	194	171	...ETS PRIORITY SL 9466 (7.98)	THE UNFORGET...

Midnight Star 138
Mike & The Mechanics 136   R.E.M. 29
Eddie Money 23   The Rainmakers 101
The Monkees 158, 174, 143, 97,   Bonnie Raitt 183
105, 147, 41   Ratt 31
The Moody Blues 63   Regina 126

"Success is not to be measured by the position you reach in life - but by the obstacles you overcome."
—Booker T. Washington—

And these are some of the obstacles I've overcome. . .

NatWest Bank
Arista Records
Charlie White
Mr. Withington
Larry Spector
Yoshio Aayama
Hal Cone
Dick Condon
The Hollywood telephone directory

bits and pics

Reliving all this as we write it, I keep thinking of all the stories I haven't put in that I've wanted to—stories that don't fit neatly into any particular place but need to be in.

David Niven, in the introduction to his book, 'The Moon's a Balloon', apologises for name dropping but says, in effect, why write about the butler when there's some statesman or other at the dinner table—something like that. So this is my 'name-drop' section—or, as I'd prefer to call it, my 'Bits and Pics' bit.

I'm a guy who got lucky, y'know—and I've met my share of big names. Some of their photos are in here at the end just because they're nice pictures and why not? But they don't all have a story because frankly, many of them who you might think would *scintilate,* are not actually that exciting in the conversation department—not without a script. I met Linda Lovelace at one of Hugh Hefner's parties once and to be honest she had *nothing* to say. Well, that's probably a bit unfair actually—she had a sore throat. But there again, everybody's imagination goes into overdrive—wow, Hefner! But actually I was there twice and fell asleep each time. The second time I played ping-pong but I was seeing three balls so I had to let him beat me. (I want a return match, Hef.)

That's the trouble. Everyone's so wiped out at these kinds of gathering—they can't just sit and eat cake like regular Texas policemen and their wives. Everybody's saying, "Hey—did you speak or was that me?"

*Just in the interests of accuracy, Davy—when **did** you start drinking?*

I haven't yet.

Look—I joke a lot about drinking and all that scene but frankly, when it comes to raising my daughters, or giving advice to kids in general, I guess I belong to the 'do as I say, not as I do' school of thought. I'm against it.

I used to like the occasional beer, it's true. Or whisky. . . or vodka. . . gin, port, brandy, saki, schnapps, champagne. The usual stuff. But this Anniversary Tour that we've just finished taught me a lot. We did a gruelling six months and I have to own up—I just can't carry on anymore like I used to—*and* throw myself around on stage for an hour. It's just not possible.

Take this guy, Moonie. I loved him dearly but he's not around to make me laugh anymore. What a waste. I've lived through a lot of the same stuff and consider myself lucky to haved *lived* through it. Many don't. This is a warning to you kids—the jokes may be funny and all that—but the actual drinking and drugs scene is *not*. People die every day, just like my friend did. . .

Keith Moon—

I was in L.A. in '67 when The Who came into town on one of their first history-making tours. I spent a late evening with Moonie and Pete Townshend but I don't remember too much about it except Pete's nose. Remarkable the first time you see it up close. The next time I see Keith it's totally out of the blue. We haven't kept in touch or anything and when the opening night of 'The Point' comes to a close, I go backstage and there's Moonie. I'm very surprised—and very pleased.

He reaches out his hand—smiles and nods his head, and then reaches around my shoulder and gives me a hug. Doesn't say a word—just smiles and nods. He points to a Guinness that he's brought backstage (he remembers my favourite drink). He's drinking champagne, and nodding and smiling. The man's magic. Not a word. Finishes his drink and leaves, still smiling and nodding.

Harry Nilsson invites a few people back to his hotel suite at The Inn on the Park and I turn up about an hour later. The door's open so I walk in and who should be sitting there on the couch with Harry, but Mister Magic! He smiles a smile that takes up half the room—and off goes the nodding again. I just smile right back and start laughing—okay, we'll be nodding acquaintances—no problem.

Drinks are poured and mine hits my Guinness like a ton of bricks. I'm feeling pretty good. The topic of conversation is the show, naturally. Seems Harry's pretty pissed off with the sound system. Dolenz, who's co-starring with me, asks Keith if he thinks the sound was bad. Keith nods. But then, he smiles too—which seems to confuse old Skillet features.

Well, it goes on for a while—everybody complaining but nobody coming up with any answers. Finally, Keith breaks his silence. He offers to lend us some of The Who's equipment that's in storage—stuff they'd used years ago on their smaller tours and haven't used since—PA speakers, microphones, play-back monitors, a sound-mixing board—the lot. He just sort of throws it out like he's offering to put the kettle on. And then, just to cap it off nicely, he gives Harry a slip of paper and says,

"Anything else you require, old chap—just give this number a tinkle." Settled. Now he can sit back and resume his nodding and smiling in peace.

After a few more cocktails the party has dwindled down to Harry and his wife, Una, Keith and his lady-friend, and me—with the £200-worth of caviar and cream puffs.

There's a breeze blowing in from the open french windows which lead out onto a balcony with this great view of Hyde Park from nine floors up. I stand there for a while, admiring the view, breathing in the air, watching the taxis to-ing and fro-ing. I'm glad to be back in England, working in the theatre again. Great feeling. I look out towards the Playboy Club, and as I do, something flies past my face and down towards the traffic—floating, like slow-motion.

It's a sock, I think. A white sock. What would a sock be doing flying over Hyde Park Corner at this time of the morning? But then—another one. Then. . .

"That's enough of those."

Mr. Magic, ex-occupier of the socks, is at my side. We both lean over the rail and watch the two pieces of sweaty cotton land amongst the taxis. Well, I think, at least it's not the TV—or the £200-worth of caviar and cream puffs. Everyone's heard the stories about Mr. Moon. . . I suppose compared to deliberately driving his Rolls into a pool, a pair of socks over the balcony is harmless enough.

It's funny. At that moment I felt I knew what he was about. I had thrown my socks out of a railway-carriage window back in '73, during 'Forget-Me-Not Lane'. Such a feeling of freedom. I wore open-toed shoes for three years straight after that.

Yes, I knew how he felt—but why is he climbing onto the rail? This is a bit different. Why is he just sitting there with his legs dangling down over Hyde Park Lane, with that big smile on his face? Oh, my God—he's going to jump!

"Keith?" He just nods and smiles.

I walk back in and pour myself a large brandy.

"Harry. He's on the rail."

"What d'you mean?"

"I mean Keith's sitting on the rail out there, that's what." I'm shaking.

"Oh, *Keith* !" laughs Harry. "Don't worry about him—he's only joking."

Joking. Right. That's what I figured. No problem. I go back out, feeling slightly better. OH, MY GOD! Straight back in.

"Harry. He's *really* joking this time." He's hanging over the side of the rail by *one hand—SMILING*—I swear to God.

I down my brandy in one. My mind won't listen anymore. I can see the headlines, the pictures—"KEITH MOON FALLS FROM PENTHOUSE SUITE BALCONY!" "Schmilsson and ex-Monkee accused of manslaughter."

This is too much. I pour another large brandy, sit on the couch, and wait for the phone to ring or for the house detective to start pounding on the door.

The phone rings and there's a pounding on the door.

The phone is the doorman asking for the chauffeur to move the car—and *at* the door is the chauffeur. At which point Keith comes strolling in from the balcony as cool as you please—like he's been doing nothing more daring than scratching his balls.

"I say, old chaps—anyone for Tramps?" he inquires.

There's a story about Keith and Tramps, or to give it its proper name, 'Tramp'. (It was one of London's most exclusive, discotheque/restaurants at the time.) I wasn't personally involved but it's one of those famous stories in the business, destined to become a standard. A friend of mine who was there assures me that it's true—so I pass it on in dedication to a truly magic guy.

Keith would often take friends down to Tramp and treat them to a late-night/early morning bash, and he'd always run a tab for food and drink, and just sign it and have his accountants settle the bill.

So one night Moonie takes a whole bunch of his friends down there and they do the usual Roman Empire bit until the wee hours. Champagne and shrimps it is, this particular night. Comes time to go, Keith calls for the bill, signs it as usual, and hands it back—along with a handsome cash donation for the maitre d'. Suddenly, as though something just clicked in his brain, a few Dom Perignon seconds late—he calls the maitre d' back and asks to see the bill again.

Now, it wouldn't be out of the ordinary for the night's fun to have cost around two or three hundred pounds—'Tramp' is not your average cafe. But this bill was for over two *thousand* pounds! (About four thousand dollars, at that time.)

It seems that whilst Keith had been away on tour, a few unscrupulous 'friends' had been charging their shrimps to Moonie—and now he gets this night's bill plus the several that had been put on his account without his knowledge.

Keith, realizing the situation, simply says, nice and loud in broad cockney,

"Blimey! These shrimps 'ave gorn up, 'aven't they?" And hands the bill back—no doubt with a smile and a nod.

Mister Magic. May God bless you, wherever you are.

Harry Nilsson—

Doing 'The Point', with Dolenz, at the Mermaid Theatre in 1977, was a thrill and a privilege. I have many fond memories of that period of my life, and besides the Moonie incident I spent many good times with Harry Nilsson, the writer of the show.

Aside from the show we had another common interest—horses. I was very sad when he left to go back to the States and I wrote this little song for him:

Goodbye, Harry,
We hate to say goodbye, you know.
Goodbye, Harry,
You didn't have to go, you know.
Well, we'll all miss you,
You touched us all inside, you know.
England needs you,
But you crossed the ocean wide.

I'll win the Derby—if that is what it takes.
I'll win the Derby—you've put up the stakes.
I'll get you back here—if the Derby's what it takes.

Hello, Harry.
We all make mistakes.

'Dennis Larden'

FPII 856

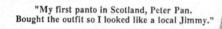

"My first panto in Scotland, Peter Pan.
Bought the outfit so I looked like a local Jimmy."

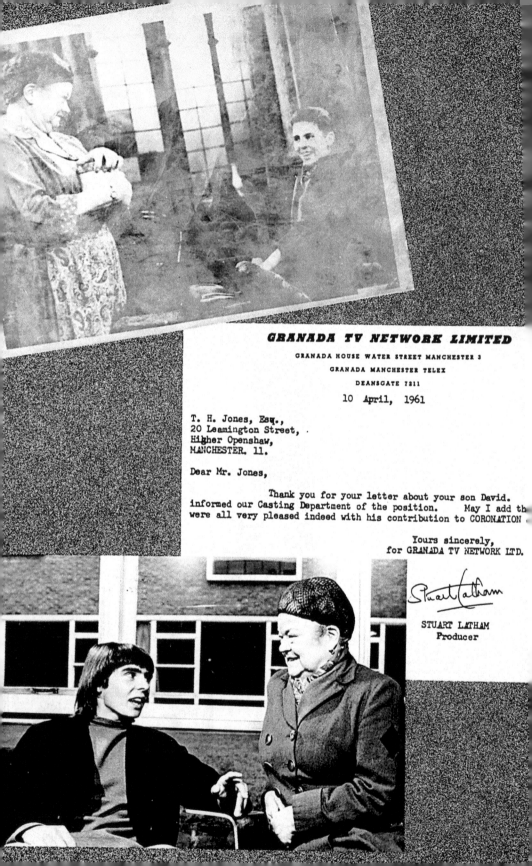

GRANADA TV NETWORK LIMITED

GRANADA HOUSE WATER STREET MANCHESTER 3

GRANADA MANCHESTER TELEX

DEANSGATE 7211

10 April, 1961

T. H. Jones, Esq.,
20 Leamington Street,
Higher Openshaw,
MANCHESTER. 11.

Dear Mr. Jones,

     Thank you for your letter about your son David.
informed our Casting Department of the position.   May I add th
were all very pleased indeed with his contribution to CORONATION

      Yours sincerely,
      for GRANADA TV NETWORK LTD.

STUART LATHAM
Producer

Jan Berry—

Jan was virtually the first person I saw when I came to live in Hollywood with Ward Sylvester in '65. We hit Santa Monica Boulevard and there was this blonde, surfer-type, six-footer, slicked-back hair, great-looking, typical California guy. Ward said, "That's Jan Berry." It stuck in my mind.

Later, when we were doing The Monkees, we were recording at RCA and there he was—Jan and Dean were recording some stuff in the next studio. And then a couple of weeks later I saw him come in the studio with a cast all the way up his leg—he'd broken it shaving or something—I don't know. He was a pretty wild guy. But he was also taking a degree at UCLA to become a doctor, or dentist—something like that.

Anyway, Jan and Dean had this song, 'Dead Man's Curve'—and a few weeks after I first heard it, Jan—who drove a Stingray—was in a car crash. He hit a parked vehicle on Mulholland Drive and was in a coma for about six weeks or so—terrible. Here was this twenty-year old, pop star doctor-to-be, with a great career ahead of him—and he Dead Man's Curved it in his Stingray.

Well, a year went by and he came wandering into one of our sessions at RCA again. But now he was this guy who dragged his leg, his hand was all shrivelled up, and he couldn't talk properly. That is, he knew what he wanted to say, but it just wouldn't come out properly. It was awful just to know what he had been and what he'd become.

He wanted to sing with us on a record but—well, it was just hopeless. His voice was gone. But anyway, we swapped phone numbers and we became real good friends. But I noticed whenever I'd go up to his house, there'd always be loads of people ripping-off his food and using his phone—doing stuff they shouldn't. So I tried to clue him in on what was happening. But he was so lonely—he wanted their company, and all I could do was watch the way everyone stroked him, and I could see what it was, but. . .

Anyway, he'd call me up and we used to talk for hours. Or I'd go over and help him with stuff—reading and writing. His hand was gone, so he was learning to write all over again.

One day I told him I wanted him to come on the road with us—on a Monkees tour—get him away from all those people who were using him. Plus, he'd been a big star himself—I thought he'd probably like to come along and watch from the side of the stage—live it again—feel the atmosphere.

He really enjoyed it. And when I couldn't give him so much time, there was Marilyn Schlossberg, our helper/secretary, on the road and off. She really helped him a lot with his reading and just giving him time and attention. A great lady.

So we took him all over the place with us and I got totally involved for a whole year, a couple of days a week—teaching, helping, talking. We used to sing a song together called, 'Laurel & Hardy'— worked out a little routine on it.

Later on I just kind of stopped seeing him. It wasn't that I forgot about him, but things were not going well for Linda and I, and my life was changing drastically at that point—'69/'70. I was getting in-volved in other things myself.

I saw him again in '74, though. He just drove up to my place one day. Wow, what a treat! He could talk a little better, still dragged his leg around, but he *drove*. And he just wanted to say how much he appreciated the friendship we had shared. For myself I felt it hadn't been enough—I could have done more—but I guess you can always go on saying that. Bottom line is, I didn't. My own life was too screwed up. *I* was hurting and needing.

I was in Lester Sill's office one day and there were a couple of Jan and Dean Billboard Awards lying around that Lester didn't want. I still have them—a little piece of Jan Berry.

It was lovely seeing him again on the Anniversary Tour—just like old times.

DAVID JONES,

WE'VE GOT TO GO ALL THE WAY. MONDAY WE WILL SING LAUREL AND HARDY FROM 10:00 O'CLOCK TO 1:00 O'CLOCK. BELIEVE IT OR NOT JAN BERRY WILL SING AND DAVID JONES TOO. STEVE WRITES WORDS SO HE COMES WITH ME.

CAN YOU DIG IT? IF YOU DO ALL THE WAY.

JAN BERRY

(PARENTHESIS)
JACKIE AT WESTERN HAS ALREADY BOOKED A SESSION. YOU BETTER GO! THATS ALL!
THIS WAS DONE BY JAN BERRY

KEN DOUGLAS & FRIEND

THIS SURVEY IS BASED ON THE
LISTENING HABITS OF THE WINN
AUDIENCE AND THE IMPECCABLE
TASTE OF WINN D.J.'s

515-39

Little Willie's in town

195

"Bert and Bob giving me my wages."

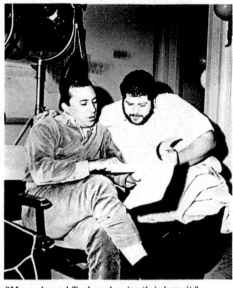

"Mazursky and Tucker planning their lawsuit."

Lulu—

In show business, or any other type of business that exposes you to the media, when you're seen out with a member of the opposite sex, the press immediately assumes that the next step is marriage.

So Lulu and the Monkees shared the same bill at Wembley in '67—and later on she visits The Monkees set back in Hollywood and straight away we're supposed to have marriage plans. Ridiculous, really. I couldn't have—my girlfriend would have punched me out.

Lulu is so sweet. There are two types of entertainment people and she slots easily into the better half.

We had lunch and dinner and our lips did meet—our hearts beat as one for ever such a short time. I was doing what I had to do and she was riding her own wave of success. I felt lonely and very much in need of her kindness and feeling but we were very young and moving in very fast times. We both came from working-class backgrounds and our feelings for each other were so true—very real.

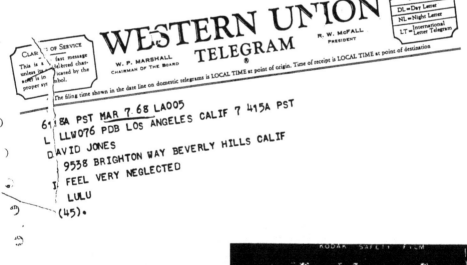

WESTERN UNION TELEGRAM

SYMBOLS
DL = Day Letter
NL = Night Letter
LT = International Letter Telegram

W. P. MARSHALL
CHAIRMAN OF THE BOARD

R. W. McFALL
PRESIDENT

CLASS OF SERVICE
This is a fast message unless its deferred character is indicated by the proper symbol.

The filing time shown in the date line on domestic telegrams is LOCAL TIME at point of origin. Time of receipt is LOCAL TIME at point of destination

6118A PST MAR 7 68 LA005
LLW076 PDB LOS ANGELES CALIF 7 415A PST
DAVID JONES
9538 BRIGHTON WAY BEVERLY HILLS CALIF
I FEEL VERY NEGLECTED
LULU
(45).

Mr. Lester Sill
Screen Gems-Columbia Music
7033 Sunset Blvd.
Hollywood, California

Dear Les:

As a follow up to our conversation of Friday, I want to reiterate that I feel it is imperative we do everything possible to protect the MONKEES' royalties so that they are not dissipated.

Based on the figures that have been given to me on sales of the single record, it would appear that the production costs of the entire first album will be recouped, and that the boys will then be in overages. At that point, every time someone goes into a studio, he is spending the boys' money. If this were a typical situation, no recording group would allow someone to go in and cut tracks without some knowledge of what they are. There are several things Tommy and Bobby have done lately that are of dubious value. They definitely cannot be used on the show and I think we all agree that several of them may have no value for records either. It seems to me that whomever the record producers are going to be on the MONKEES that there should be some financial loss to them when they go in and cut a lousy track. If Boyce and Hart or anyone else does not get charged with any costs, than he is going in with what amounts to a blank check at this point, and it is on the four boys' bank account.

I would suggest that in the future, the record producer be charged with cost of any unusable material which he creates. In that way, perhaps they will be more careful about what they do. I would appreciate your discussing this with the powers that be and letting me know what is going to be done.

Regards,

Bert

Bert Schneider

Ward Sylvester, Esq.,
Screen Gems-Columbia Music Inc.,
7033 Sunset Boulevard,
Hollywood 28,
CALIFORNIA, U.S.A.

Dear Ward,

Following up my recent cable to you concerning "Randy Scouse Git". You are no doubt aware that many English expressions have a totally different meaning in America and vice versa, and in this case it is a question of the verse being vice. To give you a perfectly straight forward translation of the title you are referring to someone as being an 'oversexed illegitimate son of a prostitute from Liverpool'. The word 'git' has been used on television in this country but only in a late night adult programme. The British press look upon the MONKEES as being clean cut all-American boys and, therefore, the title could do them a great deal of harm.

If it is not too late I would strongly recommend that you change the title in the U.S.A. also. However, my main concern is for this territory.

Kindest regards,

Sally Field—

My most favourite person who worked for Screen Gems was a nun, and a flying one at that— Sally Field.

She lived on Kings Road and I lived on Queens Road—they both led up to the same mountain. I would leave my castle on the hill and rap-rap on her door. We'd talk about the movies we wanted to see, the places we wanted to go, and the lives we wanted to live. We exchanged problems and cried on each other's shoulders.

She was then, as now, most attractive—like a doll sometimes. Childlike. Yet she could be adult and distant too. I loved to spend time with her. It was a studio friendship which the papers loved.

"Me and my manager."

Dear David—

Just use this pen & pencil to sign where I tell you to, and if you run out of money, melt them down. They should be worth enough to cover Thalia's porridge for a while.

Merry Christmas, Thomas, and a bright, successful, and prosperous 1969.

AIR MAIL INTER-OFFICE COMMUNICATION

TO   Floyd Ackerman

FROM   Ed Justin

RE

DATE   September 20, 1967

Dear Floyd:

Under our license arrangement, Kellogg's will be carrying autographed photos of each of THE MONKEES on about sixty million cereal boxes.

In view of the fact that you have a whole set of new photos, I would like to suggest that you send Bill Prag directly one autographed photo for each of THE MONKEES in the manner indicated on the enclo~~se~~

them but I don't h~~---~~

~~---~~ny, inc.

~~---~~cial Plaza

Chicago, Illinois 60601

The Monkees. Say Nothing on this. Lexis.

Ed

SG-1-1   PRINTED IN U.S.A.

Newspapers: At present, the policy is NO INTERVIEWS.

VERNON SCOTT, UPI, has done the only actual NEWSman to interview the group.

NBC has set up trade interviews (Jack Hellman w/Bert Schneider), but neither Schneider or Rafelson give a damn about trade stuff.

"No interviews?—My lips are sealed."

Phil Ochs—

During the Chicago Seven era, Jerry Rubin spent some of his on the run days at Phil's house. I'd go over there—got quite friendly with Phil and met Jerry a few times, but my head was obviously in a different place. I didn't fully understand their cause.

Phil's songs are wordy and political, but beautiful. A radical poet—he had a kindness that was visible through his deeds as well as his words. I have an album of his—well, a first-cut dub actually—he signed it, "To David—thanks for being a good neighbour."

We were at a friend's house for one flowered sixties hippie day, supposedly for the purpose of doing something constructive about the Vietnam War. You paid two hundred dollars or something to get into this pool party and the money was going to buy food for the refugees. Everybody was there—all the 'beautiful people'. Well. . . all those beautiful enough to have a couple of hundred to spare. I can't remember whose house it was, but it was pretty impressive—had two zipcodes.

So I walk in and they're all in their robes and beads and there's enough brown rice going cold to accomplish what the whole thing's about anyway. Peace, love and waterbeds, man.

Donovan's sitting on about seventy-five satin pillows singing about dew, I think it was. But it's all very nice and I enjoy it better than waiting for Linda to come back from Hawaii, or spending my afternoon at the Pussycat Theatre on Hollywood Boulevard. Certainly the intentions are good.

Probably the whole of that week's Top Forty, aside from the Beatles themselves, were there. They had great dip. Many people sang, or offered to tell you their mantra.

When it became apparent that Donovan was having no luck keeping the sun from setting behind the hills, they decided to draw a raffle and call it a decade. Why a raffle? Well—that's what Phil, who won it, couldn't figure out. They gave him his prize—a gigantic wicker basket filled with every fruit under the sun. I guess he thought—"What do I want with this? Aren't we supposed to be feeding the needy?" So he put the basket in the pool, and everybody watched it sink and probably thought, "Why did he do that?"

Phil immortalised that day in a song later on, 'Pleasure of the Harbour'.

One day I went down to his place and it was unlocked as usual, so I walked in. There was a half-finished meal, dishes in the sink, dirty ashtrays, unmade bed—but no Phil. Call again later, I thought. But I didn't get the chance. He'd just walked out and left his house with everything in it exactly as it was—flew off to New York and hung himself.

Ronald Reagan—

I hear he got a new job so I guess he's doing alright these days. But when I met him he was only Governor of California so I didn't bother to make that great an impression. My mistake.

Funny, when we were first doing the TV show, if someone fluffed a line they'd shout, "Cut!"—and there'd be a pause and recueing and all the momentum would be lost. So I said—don't do all of that and lose the pace and the flow just—if I fluff, let me turn around and deliver the line again, and you can cut it in the editing room. Okay, Mr. President, Sir. . . how about it?

I was on my way to the MGM Studios Ranch to fire a tank out on some wide-open prairie land—just out of L.A.. Deano Martin (Dean's son) had just bought this tank, a real army tank, and we'd planned to spend the day trying it out.

So on my way I pull into this gas station in Topanga Canyon and who should be parked there getting his station wagon filled up, but Governor Reagan.

Well, they take about five-hundred gallons those Governor-mobiles—a lot of gas— so I've got time to check him out. He looks like he could use some lively conversation. I mean, he's locked up there in *his* tank—at least I've got a choice—and I know how it feels anyway so, I roll down my window and I wave to him and say,

"Excuse me—can you tell me the way to the MGM Ranch, please?"

I know he knows. He must have done at least one movie there himself, but he won't roll his window down. He's pretending he doesn't see me. Maybe he thinks I'm having him on. I've never seen his movies so I don't know how much of a joke it is.

Well, I'm not having any of this. I'm gonna get him to talk if I have to get a Bill passed. I sound my horn about three times, loud and long, then I just lean on it—all the time I'm staring right at him. We're only feet apart—I'm pulled up right alongside. And I shout, full-throttle. . .

"EXCUUUUSE ME!! CAN YOU TELL ME. . . "

He's eyeing me with real suspicion, like—who is this creep? But the politician in him gives in, and he rolls down his window as I'm finishing off. . .

" . . . THE WAY TO THE MGM RANCH?!"

Sure he can. He points a finger, gives a couple of quick directions, and up goes the window again. Thanks.

"Take Two. . . and, rolling. . ."

"Mr President, sir. Would you please be so kind as to direct me to the MGM Ranch, sir? And could you possibly put in a good word for me at your old movie company, maybe? . . . Sir?

206

Deanna Martin—

Fired the tank, blew out the whole hillside—no problem.

Deano thought it was great, too. He wanted to buy a whole Panzer Division. Probably has done by now—his dad's not short of a bob or two. And Jeannie (Dean's wife) would always give the kids whatever they wanted. She was great—always treated me like one of the family.

I got to know them all through Deanna. Milton Berle had introduced us at the Whisky a Go Go one night. I think she could tell I fancied her—I kept getting down and sucking the hem of her dress—while she was dancing. (With someone else!)

Nothing came of it though, until later when we had her as a guest on the TV show. She was a fairy princess—one of the girls I fell in love with each week, stars in my eyes, the whole bit. But the stars stayed in my eyes after the show for a while there.

Thanks for those stars, Deanna.

Jackie Onassis—

There are three women in my life who, unfortunately, never realized they were supposed to be in my life: Ursula Andress, Anne Bancroft and Jackie Onassis.

I was rehearsing for 'The Boyfriend' in New York, and I needed a change one afternoon, so I decided to go to the Boat Show. As it happened, that afternoon fate was arranging one of my more improbable fantasies for me.

I'm looking around. Ooh, *that's* a nice boat—ahh, *just* what I want! All of a sudden, there she is—*just* what I (and twelve million other guys) want. I mean, even if you had been living in a mud hut for the past fifteen years—had never read a newspaper or seen a TV—you'd have to know that *somebody* had just walked in.

She's surrounded by eight Secret Service guys. I mean, *surrounded*. A good ten or twelve feet away in every direction but it's clear they're with her. They never stop looking behind themselves. One guy's got six machine guns hidden under his raincoat. They're real subtle.

But this is *my* Jackie-O. I have to do something—my dad would never forgive me.

I have to tell you—I'm in awe. I mean, I haven't been this excited since Willie first woke up to his mission in life. So, straight in the deep end. At the risk of being gunned down in broad daylight I walk up to her, my hand outstretched, and as she takes my hand I say,

"Hello. . . my name's Davy Jones. . . and I just wanted to say. . . hello."

Suddenly I know how it feels to be famous. I mean, it's like—what do you say? So what? But she gives me a beautiful smile and says,

"Well. . . hello, Davy Jones."

So I'm standing there just holding on to her hand—and it feels like forever but it's probably only seconds—and I know we have something in common and yet. . . how do you say that to someone in such a seemingly different world. And now *I'm* the fan and she's this unreachable object so near and yet. . .

I fizzle out with,

". . . and . . . . . . goodbye."

I turn, wave to the Secret Service goons, and walk straight into a boat.

Oh, well—whilst I'm dropping names—there's three guys I guess I should mention.

You'd think that having worked with people so closely for a number of years you'd get to know what makes them tick. But we each had our own little worlds going on and I'm sure never let ourselves truly discover each other as friends.

We were working partners—we each had our own little entourage of people—friends, lovers, teachers and leaches.

Like a marriage, if you're lucky enough to survive, you assess your feelings and emotions. What if I had said this, done this—why didn't I arrive at that point of view then?. . . and so on.

So I'll try now, after a twenty year relationship, to explain Mike, Micky and Peter— as I saw them then and as I know them now. . .

Peter Tork—

I'll start with Peter because he was the most well-rounded of us all. Genuine, reliable and huggable, Peter is a natural person—really gets off on talent—loves other musicians and can jam along with the best of 'em. I saw him holding his own with Hendrix, Stills, Young. He encouraged me no end. Bought me my first guitar and my first drum kit.

He went about his work as an actor in the studio, showing the same natural approach he did with his music. He would stop acting and peer through the camera lens to find out how it looked—in the middle of a take.

"Let me look. Wait a minute—I'm not there. Oh, of course I'm not—I'm here!"

Peter wore what I called, 'drain-pipe' trousers. Never really got into the fashions—he had his own. The first guy I ever met who wore different-coloured socks. Wore his belt buckle on the side. Hated boots. Always had on sandals or moccasins. He used to walk with a swagger, swinging his arms with a confident air. He calmed hysteria, and lifted depression.

"Dried banana, anybody? Piece of orange?"—smiling, waving, running his hand through his hair.

He knew all the crew by their first names. Kids crying at his feet he lifted and hugged like a father calming a child.

Health food was just starting to catch on in the sixties and Peter was kind of a forerunner of that whole scene. I'm afraid that sort of image was a little thin for two other guys I could mention, but I understood—I really did. And I think he knew it. I didn't inwardly agree with a lot of his company but it didn't keep me from dropping in on him from time to time. Great salads—and always a cold beer to wash down the tofuburgers and brown rice.

He's the most musically talented of us all by a mile. His songs are real. 'For Pete's Sake'—which replaced the Monkees Theme at the end of some of the shows of the second season—is one of my all-time favourite songs by *anybody*.

I've joked a lot about Peter giving everything away. But it was true. He was always giving his spare room to someone who needed it for the night—anyone. And he always seemed far away somewhere—in a different space. But I'm glad I know him. Of all the things he gave, he gave me lots of laughs—and food for thought.

Mike Nesmith—

Nesmith was always a true professional. He and Peter were always concerned about how it sounded, musically. Or even how it looked. When we did those tight group shots where we were miming he'd be the one to notice that we weren't plugged in—and put it right just in *case* the camera picked it up. Nesmith cared. He'd finish a day's filming by climbing onto his motorbike—or jumping into his dark blue Cadillac Eldorado that he turned up in on his first day of shooting. Nothing subtle about the Texas Kid. Actually, he had a couple of singles out on Colpix Records prior to The Monkees, so he was doing alright. He always had two or three cars at a time, come to think of it. But then he knew how to look after his money, did Mike.

He liked style. Nes and his Cadillac limousine, his English body-guard/chauffeur, Alfie Weaver, and his trained German shepherd killer-dog called Frak, who once sank his teeth into my head without leaving the ground!

Mike was always into Bigger and Better—something about being from Texas, I suppose.

"Hey, what's that?"

"It's Australia, Mike."

"How much is it?"

I remember once being over at his house in Bel Air—he'd just bought it for $250,000, or something like that. Anyway, he's showing me his pool—gigantic it was. He was real proud of it.

I'm over there again three weeks later, at a party—Frak's birthday I think—and I notice that the pool is now indoors.

"Hey, what's going on, man? This wasn't *here* before."

He's had it extended. So now it comes under the giant picture window, and ends just short of the bar.

"Great idea," I say. "It needed something."

The party's in full swing, and suddenly Nesmith decides he's got to have a hamburger, and he hasn't got any in the house. He's got a hundred thousand gallons-worth of Olympic Swimming Pool in his front room—but he forgot the hamburgers.

"Who wants a hamburger?" he asks.

Nobody, apparently. Everyone's either swimming, or getting bitten by Frak. So Nes leaves.

There's no shortage of wine at least, and though I don't usually drink as you know, I think—what the hell? It's Tuesday.

. Well, it's getting dark and there's no sign of Nesmith—but the party just keeps rolling. Much later the phone rings.

"It's for you, Davy."

I pick up the receiver. Loud traffic noises.

"Hey, you should have come with me. Great hamburgers, man."

"Sounds like it. Where are you?"

"Dallas."

He'd taken a jet to go eat at his favourite hamburger stand back home in Texas. I like that. Style.

I still maintain that at any given moment he could be Hollywood's next leading man. A truly great talent. A very funny man. He'll probably become Governor of Texas next. I wish he'd get rid of Frak, though.

Micky Dolenz—

Who?

Oh. . . Micky, right. He's a different skillet of fish altogether. If you ever saw Micky on The Monkees show—he was playing himself. A tough role—but somebody had to do it.

Micky's the kind of guy who buys a do-it-yourself Gyrocopter. He gets all these huge parts laid out in his living room—takes forever to make the thing—everybody's falling over bits of Gyrocopter for weeks. Nobody wants to visit him because they know they'll have to sit on a rotorblade or something. Finally, he gets the thing assembled.

"Right, let's take it out and FLY!"

But it won't go through the door. He has to completely dismantle the thing to get it outside. Don't think he ever did build it again. He got bored with it.

He once bought the most beautiful, incredible, 1929 Bentley. Cost him a fortune. Had it flown over from England and delivered to his house. We were all there to see it. It was gorgeous—British Racing Green, original paint job.

Well, there it was, and we're all looking at it and sitting in it, and wondering if we dare risk taking such a beautiful piece of art out onto the open road. We decide to wait.

So we're all inside having tea, and admiring how the half-finished Gyrocopter obscures the view of just about everything—when we hear this strange, squeaking, crunching sort of sound. We get to the door just in time to see The Car rolling backwards out of the driveway.

Micky goes chasing after it, but it's all downhill. It winds its way for about fifty yards, up an embankment, turns over and lands on its back. The most beautiful car in the world—dead. He'd left the hand-brake off.

Fortunately he'd bought himself a 1926 Rolls Royce as well, so the day wasn't completely ruined.

I like Micky a lot. I've got a lot of respect for him and for his talent. We rub each other the wrong way sometimes—like, whenever we're in the same country! But that's because he loves to wheel and deal, and sometimes when he starts that wheeling and dealing, he goes straight for target, and his generous nature and better judgement take a back seat. I must say though, that after doing this six-month Anniversary Tour with him, I've changed some of the opinions that I'd formed about him over those very trying years. I'm sure he had just as many difficulties dealing with me—that's probably what has made us so close on stage and so distant in life.

Just to hear him admit to me, before the Tour started, that he'd been dissatisfied with his life and career for some time—that he would wander around the grounds of his mansion in England and actually *cry*. . . I tell you, that upped my respect and feeling for him quite a few notches.

I guess none of us knows what the other has really gone through. Hey, Skillet-features—write us *your* book, will you?

THURSDAY, JULY 31, 1986 · USA TODAY

SHOW

ENTERTAINMENT, NEWS, REVIEWS AND PERSONALITIES

Madcap Monkees are swingin' again

By John Milward
Special for USA TODAY

NEW YORK — Davy Jones, the cute Monkee, now streaks his brown shag haircut with red. "People don't see the wrinkles," confides Jones, 41.

"They just see the bright colors and the other kids" packing the Monkees' reunion concerts. "We're actors, and this is fun." Or as Mickey Dolenz, 41, is fond of saying, "This is not brain surgery."

217

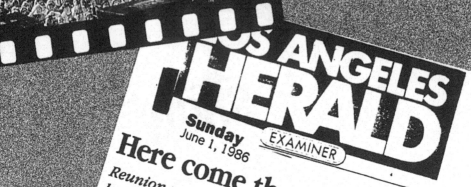

LOS ANGELES HERALD

Sunday
June 1, 1986

EXAMINER

Here come the Monkees — again

Reunion minus one leaves audience dancing in aisles

ATLANTIC CITY, N.J. (UPI) — "Monkee Madness" returned to the United States early yesterday as the pop group The Monkees opened a 20th anniversary tour to a sold-out, shrieking casino audience that danced in the aisles.

The Monkees, minus former guitarist Michael Nesmith, took the stage at the Tropicana Casino well after midnight Friday, with a new, "Miami Vice" image, but the same humorous foibles.

The sh...

Mickey Dolenz, 41, Peter Tork, 44, and Davy Jones 40, took the stage.

When the group ambled into view to a skipping record of "Hey, Hey, It's the Monkees," many in the crowd rushed the stage of the normally sedate casino showroom.

Nancy Askin and her two friends were indicative of the crowd, sipping wine quietly one minute then dancing and shrieking during the show.

"What can I say? These guys are great." Askin said, adding that while a teen-ager, she watched the Monkees "religious..." wouldn't say ho...

The sh...

albums than the Beatles and Rolling Stones. The Monkees w... Emmys for "Outstanding Comed... Series," had four No. 1 album... nine Top 20 singles.

Dolenz, the group's... said after the sho... nearly 17 y... excited ... 1969, ...

Observer-Reporter

Surprising Monkees: even the cynics should be believers now

Friday, July 11, 1986

By Terry Hazlett, *Entertainment Editor*

This is a tale of the unexpected, and it is not science fiction. It is 100% true, and it happened close to home. Just ask the 10,000 fans at the Civic Arena Wednesday night.

The Monkees headlined a much-hyped concert that evening, and the surprise was *not* that the Civic Arena roof opened all the way. Instead, the surprise was the concert itself, and the fans who attended it.

The fans were *not* yuppie mothers and their daughters, as many had predicted. There were families with teens, of course, but the Civic Arena was primarily filled with fans in their late teens and early 20s, the ones who attend concerts by Springsteen, the Grateful Dead, Motley Crue, Van Halen and Madonna. T-shirts throughout the edition attested to the fact.

In addition, the opening acts — Herman's Hermits, Gary Puckett and The Gap and The Grass Roots —

Critics of the band wouldn't believe it — and they certainly wouldn't have been in the arena Wednesday night to witness it themselves — but The Monkees are a legitimate rock and roll band. They're also entertaining, something that can''t be said about some of their '80s counterparts.

If I were a member of the Moody Blues or 38 Special, I'd be worried about my upcoming appearance at the arena. The Monkees are a hard act to follow.

The three original members — Davy Jones, Micky Dolenz and Peter Tork — bounced on stage as if they were walking out of any episode of their TV series. When the recording of the Monkees Theme "stuck," they promptly "blew up" the stage with a five-foot piece of dynamite and emerged from the smoke with "Last Train To Clarksville."

It was followed by "A Little Bit Me, A Little Bit You" and another Monkees [...]

[...] menting on the band's musical ability.

"You can't play that guitar," Peter told Davy. "Don't you know the Monkees don't play their own instruments." "Yeah, but this is not my guitar." Davy shot back. "It's Mickey's."

Perhaps it was because the trio didn't take itself seriously that the concert worked. The rock and roll songs were the genuine article, but The Monkees pretended that they were just giving rock and roll a whirl for the first time.

For whatever reason, the concert worked, including the current "That Was Then, This Is Now," an insipid song on record, but an energetic number in concert.

Having always been a Monkees [...]

"I can see it now. . . we'll do the bathroom in flamingo pink. . ."

Monkees leap into renewed popularity

NEW YORK

Young girls scream at men old enough to be their fathers; teen-agers rush home from school to see the mad antics of the mop-top pop singers on TV; and Monkees records are back on the charts.

Monkee mania has hit America — two decades on. It is bringing the group to Wolf Trap for a concert tonight.

Davy Jones, Mickey Dolenz and Peter Tork are back on stage 17 years after the breakup of one of the best-selling pop music groups of the 1960s.

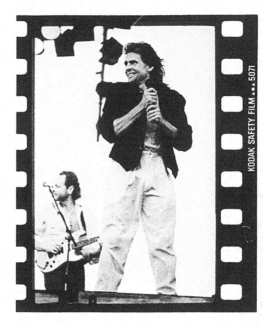

223

GET READY OR NOT...HERE WE COME

DAY	DATE	VENUE	CITY	ST.
2 WEEKS	05/09/86	CONCORD HOTEL	KIAMESHA LAKE	NY
FRIDAY	05/30/86	TROPICANA HOTEL	ATLANTIC CITY	NJ
SATURDAY	05/31/86	TROPICANA HOTEL	ATLANTIC CITY	NJ
SUNDAY	06/01/86	TROPICANA HOTEL	ATLANTIC CITY	NJ
TUESDAY	06/03/86	WARNER THEATRE	ERIE	PA
WEDNESDAY	06/04/86	STANLEY THEATRE	UTICA	NY
THURSDAY	06/05/86	SAMUEL CLEMENS CENTER	ELMIRA	NY
FRIDAY	06/06/86	SIX FLAGS GREAT ADVENTURE	JACKSON	NJ
SATURDAY	06/07/86	STATE THEATRE	CLEVELAND	OH
SUNDAY	06/08/86	THE WOODLANDS	WILKESBARRE	PA
TUESDAY	06/10/86	NEWPORT MUSIC HALL	COLUMBUS	OH
WEDNESDAY	06/11/86	NEWPORT MUSIC HALL	COLUMBUS	OH
THURSDAY	06/12/86	SANTA TERESA COUNTRY CLUB	SANTA TERESA	NM
FRIDAY	06/13/86	FORT BLISS ARMY BASE	EL PASO	TX
SATURDAY	06/14/86	OMAHA CIVIC AUDITORIUM	OMAHA	NE
SUNDAY	06/15/86	NEBRASKA LAND DAYS	NORTH PLATTE	NE
TUESDAY	06/17/86	COTILLION BALLROOM	WICHITA	KS
WEDNESDAY	06/18/86	SANDSTONE	KANSAS CITY	MO
THURSDAY	06/19/86	RIVERFRONT AMPHITHEATRE	HANNIBAL	MO
FRIDAY	06/20/86	STEAMBOAT DAYS	BURLINGTON	IA
SATURDAY	06/21/86	DES MOINES CIVIC CENTER	DES MOINES	IA
SUNDAY	06/22/86	ARLINGTON STADIUM	ARLINGTON	TX
TUESDAY	06/24/86	BAYFRONT ARENA	CORPUS CHRISTI	TX
WEDNESDAY	06/25/86	SUNKEN GARDENS	SAN ANTONIO	TX
THURSDAY	06/26/86	FRANK ERWIN CENTER	AUSTIN	TX
FRIDAY	06/27/86	SOUTHERN STAR AMPHITHEATR	HOUSTON	TX
SATURDAY	06/28/86	BEAUMONT CIVIC CENTER	BEAUMONT	TX
SUNDAY	06/29/86	AUDUBON ZOO	NEW ORLEANS	LA
TUESDAY	07/01/86	MUD ISLAND AMPHITHEATRE	MEMPHIS	TN
WEDNESDAY	07/02/86	STARWOOD AMPHITHEATRE	NASHVILLE	TN
THURSDAY	07/03/86	ALBANY CIVIC CENTER	ALBANY	GA
FRIDAY	07/04/86	ROBARTS ARENA	SARASOTA	FL
SATURDAY	07/05/86	RUTH ECKERD HALL	CLEARWATER	FL
SUNDAY	07/06/86	FLAGLER GREYHOUND TRACK	MIAMI	FL
TUESDAY	07/08/86	WOLFTRAP PARK	VIENNA	VA
WEDNESDAY	07/09/86	PITTSBURGH CIVIC CENTER	PITTSBURGH	PA
THURSDAY	07/10/86	BLOSSOM MUSIC FESTIVAL	CUYAHOGA FALLS	OH
FRIDAY	07/11/86	CHAUTAUQUA INSTITUTE	CHAUTAUQUA	NY
SATURDAY	07/12/86	ONTARIO PLACE	TORONTO M6K3B9	CN
SUNDAY	07/13/86	OTTAWA CONGRESS CENTER	OTTAWA K2P1X9	CN
MONDAY	07/14/86	FINGERLAKES PER. ARTS CTR	LAKE CANADAIGUA	NY
TUESDAY	07/15/86	LANDMARK THEATRE	SYRACUSE	NY
WEDNESDAY	07/16/86	CONCORD HOTEL	KIAMESHA LAKE	NY
FRIDAY	07/18/86	WARWICK MUSICAL THEATER	WARWICK	RI
SATURDAY	07/19/86	SOUTH SHORE MUSIC CIRCUS	COHASSET	MA
SUNDAY	07/20/86	OAKDALE MUSIC THEATER	WALLINGFORD	CT
MONDAY	07/21/86	CAPE COD MELODY TENT	HYANNIS	MA
TUESDAY	07/22/86	PIER 84	NEW YORK	NY
WEDNESDAY	07/23/86	SARATOGA PERF ARTS CENTER	SARATOGA SPRING	NY
THURSDAY	07/24/86	MIDDLETOWN FAIR	MIDDLETOWN	NY
SATURDAY	07/26/86	JONES BEACH THEATER	WANTAGH	NY
SUNDAY	07/27/86	STABLER ARENA	BETHLEHEM	PA

DAY	DATE	VENUE	CITY	STATE
MONDAY	07/28/86	JONES BEACH RAINDATE	WANTAGH	NY
TUESDAY	07/29/86	CLUB CASINO	HAMPTON BEACH	NH
WEDNESDAY	07/30/86	CLUB CASINO	HAMPTON BEACH	NH
THURSDAY	07/31/86	WOLFTRAP	VIENNA	VA
FRIDAY	08/01/86	PIER SIX PAVILLION	BALTIMORE	MD
SATURDAY	08/02/86	GARDEN STATE ART CENTER	HOLMDEL	NJ
SUNDAY	08/03/86	MANN MUSIC CENTER	PHILADELPHIA	PA
TUESDAY	08/05/86	GREER PAVILLION	MORGANTOWN	WV
WEDNESDAY	08/06/86	PINE KNOB MUSIC THEATRE	CLARKSTON	MI
THURSDAY	08/07/86	POPLAR CREEK MUSIC THEATR	HOFFMAN EASTATE	IL
FRIDAY	08/08/86	RIVERBEND	CINCINNATI	OH
SUNDAY	08/10/86	WISCONSIN STATE FAIR	MILWAUKEE	WI
TUESDAY	08/12/86	ROCKLAND COUNTY FAIR	NEW CITY	NY
WEDNESDAY	08/13/86	POWELL HALL	ST. LOUIS	MO
THURSDAY	08/14/86	FIVE SEASONS CENTER	CEDAR RAPIDS	IA
FRIDAY	08/15/86	DOUGLAS COUNTY FAIR	WATERLOO	NE
SATURDAY	08/16/86	TBA	ABERDEEN	SD
SUNDAY	08/17/86	HALL COUNTY FAIR	GRAND ISLAND	NE
TUESDAY	08/19/86	SIOUX EMPIRE FAIR	SIOUX FALLS	SD
WEDNESDAY	08/20/86	CARLTON CELEBRITY THEATRE	BLOOMINGTON	MN
THURSDAY	08/21/86	CARLTON CELEBRITY THEATRE	BLOOMINGTON	MN
THURSDAY	08/22/86	CARLTON CELEBRITY THEATRE	BLOOMINGTON	MN
SATURDAY	08/23/86	JACK MURPHY STADIUM	SAN DIEGO	CA
WEDNESDAY	08/27/86	RED ROCKS	DENVER	CO
FRIDAY	08/29/86	THE LAGOON	SALT LAKE CITY	U?
SUNDAY	08/31/86	MARRIOTT'S GREAT AMERICA	SANTA CLARA	C
THURSDAY	09/04/86	PACIFIC AMPHITHEATRE	COSTA MESA	C
FRIDAY	09/05/86	GREEK THEATRE	LOS ANGELES	C
SATURDAY	09/06/86	GREEK THEATRE	LOS ANGELES	
SUNDAY	09/07/86	GREEK THEATRE	LOS ANGELES	
MONDAY	09/08/86	HILTON HOTEL	LAS VEGAS	
TUESDAY	09/09/86	HILTON HOTEL	LAS VEGAS	
WEDNESDAY	09/10/86	HILTON HOTEL	LAS VEGAS	
THURSDAY	09/11/86	HILTON HOTEL	LAS VEGAS	
FRIDAY	09/12/86	HILTON HOTEL	LAS VEGAS	
SATURDAY	09/13/86	HILTON HOTEL	LAS VEGAS	
SUNDAY	09/14/86	VALLEY FORGE MUSIC FAIR	DEVON	
SUNDAY	09/21/86	VALLEY FORGE MUSIC FAIR	DEVON	
MONDAY	09/22/86	BLOOMSBURG FAIR	BLOOMSBURG	
TUESDAY	09/23/86	WESTBURY MUSIC FAIR	WESTBURY	
SUNDAY	09/28/86	WESTBURY MUSIC FAIR	WESTBURY	
MONDAY	09/29/86			

SECOND LEG OF MONKEES TOUR

	CITY	STATE	VENUE
ober 8	Pittsburgh	PA	Civic Center
9	Johnstown	PA	Cambria County War Memorial
10	Troy	NY	RPI Fieldhouse
11	Fairfax	VA	Patriot Center
12	Norfolk	VA	Scope Arena
13	OFF		
14	East Rutherford	NJ	Brendon Byrne Arena
15	Baltimore	MD	Civic Center
16	Richmond	VA	Coliseum
17	Chapel Hill	NC	Dean Dome
18	Atlanta	GA	The Omni
19	Gainesville	FL	O'Connell Center
20	OFF		
21	OFF		
22	New Orleans	LA	Superdome
23	Jackson	MS	Coliseum
24	Mobile	AL	Municipal Auditorium
25	Little Rock	AR	Barton Coliseum
26	Ruston	LA	Thomas Assembly Center
27	OFF		
28	OFF		
29	Chatanooga	TN	UTC Arena
30	Knoxville	TN	Civic Coliseum
31	Dayton	OH	Univ. of Dayton Arena
November 1	Evansville	IN	Roberts Stadium
" 2	Chicago	IL	Rosemont Horizon
3	OFF		
4	St. Louis	MO	Kiel Auditorium
5	Peoria	IL	Civic Center
6	Cedar Rapids	IA	Five Seasons Center
7	La Crosse	WI	La Crosse Center
8	Duluth	MN	Arena Auditorium
9	OFF		
10	Ft. Wayne	IN	Memorial Coliseum
11	South Bend	IN	Notre Dame Athletic & Convocation Center
12	Green Bay	WI	Browne County Arena
13	OFF		
14	Toledo	OH	Centennial Hall
15	Kalamazoo	MI	Wings Stadium
16	Pontiac	MI	Silverdome
17	Cleveland	OH	Richfield Colisem
18	OFF		
19	OFF		
20	Worcester	MA	The Centrum
21	Portland	ME	Cumberland County Civic Center
22	Bangor	ME	Auditorium
23	Providence	RI	Civic Center
24	Utica	NY	War Memorial
25	Rochester	NY	War Memorial
26	OFF		
27	OFF		
November 28	Hershey	PA	Hershey Arena
29	Roanoke	VA	Civic Center
30	Charlotte	NC	Auditorium Coliseum
December 1	Charleston	WV	Civic Center
2	OFF		
3	Bethlehem	PA	Stabler Arena

—PHOTO CREDITS—

Alan Green & David Jones, 1986 — Photo by Carla J. Faye
Alan Green & Carla J. Faye—"The making of the book." — Photo by Leslie Heller
David Jones, 1986 — Photo by Alan Green
Alan Green & Carla J. Faye—"The making of the book." — Photos by Leslie Heller
Davy Jones—"This was the first picture I sent my dad from from Monkees Pilot." — Photo by Bud Fraker

INTRODUCTIONS

p. 2	David Jones, 1986	§ (Courtesy of David Jones Collection)
p. 6	Alan Green, 1983	Photo by Aaron Rapoport
p. 8	Alan, Wendy Clarke & Davy Beavertown, PA., 1986	Courtesy of Wendy Clarke Collection
p. 10	The Jones Family	§

CHAPTER 1

p. 12	Harry Jones—Davy's father	§
p. 12	Davy at 18 months	§
p. 15	Davy as Abdullah, the Turkish Magician	§
p. 15	Davy	§
p. 17	Davy on the local cricket team	§

CHAPTER 2

p. 19	Davy at sister Hazel's Wedding	§
p. 20	Davy's class picture with Moira, 2nd row from top, 5th from left	§
p. 22	Doris—Davy's mother	§
p. 24	Davy in talent contest—Beryl on piano §	
p. 24	Aunt Jessie with Davy & Anita's daughter, Jessica	§
p. 27	Basil S. Foster	Courtesy of Basil S. Foster Collection
p. 27	Davy at Holland House, Newmarket—age 14	Courtesy of Basil S. Foster Collection
p. 27	Davy at Holland House, Newmarket—age 14	Courtesy of Basil S. Foster Collection
p. 27	Davy and the stable lads—Gerry, Taffy, John, Keith, Gary, Davy, Bill, Dog Willy	Courtesy of Basil S. Foster Collection

CHAPTER 3

p. 32	Davy polishing his Cockney accent	Copyright © Manchester Daily Mail
p. 32	'Oliver!'—Clive Reville, Georgia Brown, Davy & cast	Photo by Friedman-Abeles
p. 32	Cover of original 'Oliver!' Programme	The Wyndham Theatres, Ltd.
p. 35	Davy & Bruce Prochnick in 'Oliver!'	§
p. 37	Britons on Broadway—Daily Mail October 24, 1963	Copyright © Associated Newspapers, Ltd.
p. 43	Davy & Sir Harry Secombe in 'Pickwick'	§
p. 43	Davy & Sir Harry Secombe in 'Pickwick'	§
p. 43	Davy & Sir Harry Secombe in Tennessee Ernie Ford's Thanksgiving Special 1969/70	§
p. 43	Davy & Nancy Barrett in 'Pickwick'	Photo by Rothschild Photo

CHAPTER 4

p. 46	Davy & Jackie Cooper, 1965 Original Screen Gems Contract	Photo by Wagner International Photo
p. 46	Davy—"Exclusively on Colpix Records"	§
p. 51	Micky & Peter	§
p. 52	Mike	§
p. 53	Sven Helstrum & The Ryhthm Kings—from pilot episode of 'The Monkees'	§
p. 53	The Monkees—from pilot episode	§

§ - Courtesy of David Jones Collection
† - Courtesy of Joyce Supple Collection
* - Photo by Henry Diltz
• - Copyright © 1986 Michael G. Bush—All Rights Reserved
◊ - Courtesy of Linda Jones Collection

david jones

I'd gone to America in 1961 to play the Artful Dodger in Lionel Bart's musical, 'Oliver!'. I thought it was going to be just another gig—maybe last a few weeks. But it stretched into months, then years. After that came 'Pickwick'. . . Hollywood. . . and then all that crazy Monkees stuff. And always in the back of my mind was the idea of going back to my old job in the stables at Newmarket—ride some winners.

I'd come a long way. I didn't have any set ideas about where I was going—just bobbing along with the tide. But all of a sudden it was 1966 and I realized. . . *(Err, I think we've already gone through this, Davy. Why don't you take a lie down now—it's been a long book, you need to rest up for the next one.)*

No, no. . . this is important—I've got to tell everybody—err, I realized. . . bump di bump di bum. . . I'd got a whole new lifestyle, y'see—that's it. Err. . . something they wouldn't be able to imagine back home in Manchester. I was living in a big house with a swimming pool. . . free cars, free motorbikes, free cornflakes—everything we promoted, we got to keep!

Except ourselves. That's the <u>point</u>. . . err, except *ourselves*.

*We interrupt this biography to bring you one you **haven't** heard before. . .*

Err, it was a far cry from growing up in Manchester, England. . .

alan green

Alan studied piano for eight years in Manchester, England but left the Royal Northern College of Music after only one year of his four year Diploma course because of the little signs in the practice rooms which read, "Anyone caught playing jazz will be expelled."

He joined a jazz band, sailed to West Africa for a four-month engagement which turned out to be "two weeks of playing jazz and three and a half months of scratching mosquito bites whilst waiting to go home. Nobody came to hear us."

On to bigger things: Cruise ships—Captains' Parties—champagne and beautiful girls. . . sunstroke and seasickness. For two years Alan sailed the Caribbean—first as a bandleader and then, when the band could take it no more, as a solo pianist and entertainer.

On to better things: Merv Griffin recorded a song Alan wrote for his cruise ship show called, "Happy to Know You". Figuring this was it—the Big Time—he quit the ships and drove from Miami to Los Angeles to meet Merv, without an appointment. (Which only goes to show—it pays to make appointments; Merv was in Vegas that week.)

A brief appearance on Merv's show, (twelve seconds), encouraged Alan to continue his songwriting in earnest, and pursue a recording contract in manic style. "I did anything I could think of to attract attention to myself. I auditioned wearing a scuba-diving outfit (that gag's been a bit overdone in this book, I grant you!); interrupted Elton John in the middle of a press conference, to give him my tape; broke into the home of one of LA's top record producers to beg him to sign me."

Each episode paid off though. . . kind of. Alan has probably been signed to more major record and publishing companies than any other 'unknown' in the business: Damila Music Publishing, Mooncrest Records, Bell Records, Arista Records, Screen Gems Publishing, ABC Records, MCA Records, Warner Bros. Publishing and CBS Records.

He was also sued by Warner Bros. Film Company for $1,000,000.00 for impersonating Dudley Moore's "Arthur" character from the film of that same name. (But a month later Blake Edwards offered him the lead role in the TV series of "10", which he was co-producing with. . . Warner Bros!) "They dropped the lawsuit—but I haven't heard a thing about the series since. It's a crazy business."

But it's the craziness of the business side of music which has inspired Alan to spend the past two years writing a musical which, he says, is ". . . guaranteed to play Broadway. Either the stage or the sidewalk."

Knowing Alan's determination and his penchant for doing things in the most dramatic way possible, I'm sure it won't be long before we see,

"ME!

an egocentric musical"

up in lights on a Broadway marquee.

This writer, for one, has seen his show and can highly recommend it as an event not to be missed.

—Alan's Mum.

235

p.s.

I haven't found it hard to remember all this so far. What is hard is to write a complete chapter on each of the guys. I've attempted it a couple of times but it just won't come out right. I've been honest and found it just too personal for this book.

Cop out? I don't think so. Who says what a biography should say, anyway? After all, "They Made a Monkee Out Of Me" is the name of this book. Let's just leave The Monkees the way we found them—smiling, running, joking—and the best of friends.

R605

R606

"Bum di Bum di Bum"

Milton Keynes UK
Ingram Content Group UK Ltd.
UKHW020100081024
2052UKWH00032B/78

9 781939 828088